Electric Utilities Moving Into the 21st Century: 18 Views of the Elephant

Edited by
Gregory B. Enholm and J. Robert Malko

1994
Public Utilities Reports, Inc.
Arlington, Virginia

First Printing, January 1994
Library of Congress Catalog Card No. 93-087624
ISBN 0-910325-49-9

Printed in the United States of America

Table of Contents

Preface

Electric Utilities Moving into the 21st Century

Gregory B. Enholm and J. Robert Malko

This book is intended to assist people who are concerned about the future of the U.S. electric utility industry. Electricity plays a key role in the U.S. economy, and changes in that industry will affect most Americans and American businesses. We have seen major upheaval in other regulated industries—trucking, airlines, telephone and natural gas—as competition was introduced. Our goal is to provide a forum for the perspectives held by various industry experts about where the industry is going and how it will change in the future. Our intent is to give those experts an opportunity to express their opinions, thoughts and forecasts.

Our hope is that those who read this book will have a better understanding of the factors driving change in the electric utility industry and a better appreciation of the different outlooks of the various affected groups. We believe that the industry's transformation over the next decade will be smoother for all concerned—and the results more satisfactory—if the participants carefully consider not just their own needs, but the desires of other affected groups. In that spirit, we sought out experts who could articulate their thoughts and opinions in a manner that would be understandable to persons who may not possess their expertise and perspective. We wanted to produce a book which would be useful to a broad audience who want to learn more about the industry and where it is going.

We have included contributions from as many different industry participants as possible, given availability and space constraints. Because the people who work in the industry itself have the greatest exposure to change and have much at stake in the outcome, we have five chapters written by utility executives and managers. We also have included chapters written by those who have regulated electric utilities, consultants who advise large power users, a consumer advocate, and an environmentalist. Additionally, two institutional investors, a securities analyst and an advisor to a major investment bank provide their perspectives on where the industry has been and where it is going. A public utilities professor places the industry in a broader, societal context. A survey of electric utility senior manager's attitudes, with commentary, is also included.

This book would not have been possible without the efforts of the authors who contributed 17 chapters. We express our sincere thanks for the work they have done. We also thank Susan M. Johnson of Public Utilities Reports, Inc. for her devotion to moving this project along for the past year. We would like thank the individuals who assisted Susan in making this book possible—most of whom we have not met. In preparing this book, we were inspired by the contributions to the industry made by the late Robert G. Uhler., His innovations while at the Federal Power Commission, the Electric Power Research Institute and National Economic Research Associates continue to shape both utilities and regulatory agencies. Finally, but most importantly, we would not be able to successfully undertake this kind of effort without the support, encouragement and understanding of our families, especially our wives, Crystal A. Enholm and Sandra S. Malko.

Gregory B. Enholm

J. Robert Malko

Chapter One

ASSESSING THE ELECTRIC UTILITY INDUSTRY'S FUTURE

Gregory B. Enholm and J. Robert Malko

The U.S. electric utility industry is undergoing a transformation. What is causing the changes? What will electric utility companies look like in the future? How will electric utility customers, personnel, regulatory staff, investors and others be affected by the changes? Can change be reasonably forecasted? Can the new structure for the industry be identified now?

We asked a wide variety of industry experts representing diverse interests to contribute their thoughts on where the U.S. electric utility industry is going. Our guiding principle for creating this book is based on the ancient story in the Tales of Dervishes regarding blind villagers and an elephant.[1] Six blind villagers approached an elephant. Each felt only one part of the animal. While each could provide an accurate description of the part touched, the listener who had never encountered an elephant before would be baffled by hearing separate descriptions of the trunk, tusks, ears, legs, body and tail. However, if the listener realized that each villager was describing just part of an elephant rather than giving conflicting accounts of what an elephant was, then an integration of these comments would provide a reasonable impression of an elephant.

We believe that story can be applied to the collection of views on the electric utility industry which follows. Seventeen chapters

Gregory B. Enholm is President of Electric Utility Research Inc and J. Robert Malko is Professor of Finance at Utah State University.

---

[1] This story can be found in *Tales of the Dervishes* by Idries Shah, The Octagon Press, London (1984) at pages 25-26.

were contributed by experts sharing their views. It is doubtful that any expert can foresee the future perfectly or comprehensively—so in that sense, much like the villagers in the tale, they suffer blindness. Thus, while each individual chapter may not provide the full insight to foresee the industry's future, all read together could.

We have developed a diagram to guide our exploration and forecast of the U.S. electric utility industry. It serves as an organizational chart for the institutional structures affecting the industry and shows how various groups interact to change the future of the industry. As in the diagram, we begin in Chapter 2 with an assessment of the factors causing change. A brief history of significant events is presented by Mark D. Luftig, Senior Vice President of Kemper Securities. Using the investors' view point as his guide, Luftig sees economics and technology as the key factors driving change in the industry. According to Luftig, regulators and legislators have been reactive, not proactive—a theme other authors endorse in their later chapters. In the 1980s, utilities continued to build large power plants even though the need for them was not clear. This over-building damaged many utilities financially; damage from which a few are still recovering. The higher electric rates that resulted from the inclusion of these plants in rate base forced regulators and utilities to rethink their basic assumptions. The stage was set for the changes now underway. Kenneth Nowotny is professor of economics at New Mexico State University. In Chapter 3, he takes a different, broader view of the industry. Nowotny emphasizes that customer expectations created by utilities and environmental and market ideology are the important factors driving change. The ultimate response to the industry's economic problems was that something was wrong with regulation—competition is a better regulator than government. This theme is developed in more detail in Chapter 8 by Illinois Commerce Commissioner Terrence Barnich, Philip O'Connor and Craig Clausen.

Major shifts in industry structure are envisioned by two electric utility chief executive officers who have been outspoken in their efforts to focus on the need for change. Erroll B. Davis, Jr. of WPL Holdings, Inc. (the holding company for Wisconsin Power & Light

Conceptual Framework for Understanding Change in the Electric Utility Industry

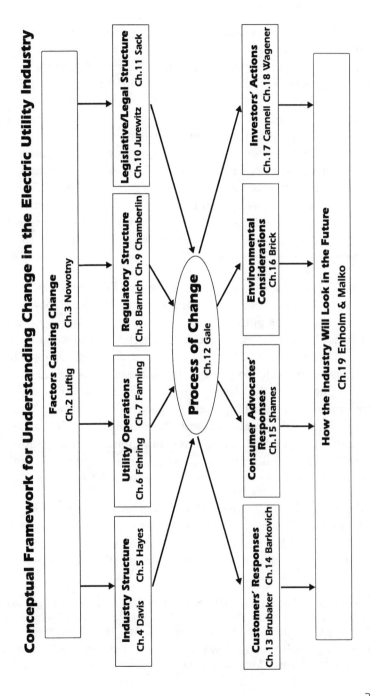

Factors Causing Change
Ch.2 Luftig   Ch.3 Nowotny

Industry Structure
Ch.4 Davis   Ch.5 Hayes

Utility Operations
Ch.6 Fehring   Ch.7 Fanning

Regulatory Structure
Ch.8 Barnich Ch.9 Chamberlin

Legislative/Legal Structure
Ch.10 Jurewitz   Ch.11 Sack

Process of Change
Ch.12 Gale

Customers' Responses
Ch.13 Brubaker Ch.14 Barkovich

Consumer Advocates' Responses
Ch.15 Shames

Environmental Considerations
Ch.16 Brick

Investors' Actions
Ch.17 Cannell Ch.18 Wagener

How the Industry Will Look in the Future
Ch.19 Enholm & Malko

Company) sees competition clearly emerging in the electric utility industry.[2] According to Davis, however, utility and regulatory resources are often diverted into pursuits that do not enhance anyone's well being. Utilities must learn how to become competitive business enterprises. Customers will benefit with more choices, better pricing and service. Rate base regulation rewards utilities that add assets regardless of whether those assets economically benefit their customers. As the industry changes, the traditional utility shareholder may find the risk and return profile unacceptable—creating the need to find new investors. (In Chapters 17 and 18, institutional investors offer their perspectives.) Davis believes that if everything utility and regulatory personnel did had to meet a value-added standard, a lot less would be done within both companies and government agencies.

John E. Hayes, Jr., chief executive of Western Resources, Inc. (formerly the Kansas Power and Light Company) draws insights from the transformation of the telecommunications and natural gas industries. He sees permanent change affecting regulated companies. That change is driven by customer demand, changes in economics and technology, competition, the need for critical mass and capital needs. Technology permits open transmission access; customers are demanding it; and the economics encourage it. According to Hayes, regulatory directives simply increase or decrease the speed of the inevitable. Customer and public involvement in utility planning and operations, he predicts, will become even more pervasive as we enter the 21st Century.

What do electric utility managers think about where their companies are going? Managers below the chief executive level offer their projections in Chapters 6 and 7.[3] These authors are in close contact with their company's immediate policies addressing change.

---

[2] For more on this topic, see *Competition in Electricity: New Markets and New Structures* edited by James L. Plummer and Susan Troppman, Public Utilities Reports, Inc. and QED Research, Inc. (March 1990).

[3] For background on the development of the industry, see *The Power Makers* by Richard Munson, Rodale Press (1985).

Thomas H. Fehring, Wisconsin Electric Power Company's Manager of System Engineering, outlines the issues causing electric utilities to change. While Fehring sees an end to "business as usual" operations, his outlook is more for evolution than revolution. Thomas A. Fanning, Vice President of Finance for Mississippi Power Co. (a subsidiary of The Southern Company), argues that dramatic change is ahead. Competitive pressures will create circumstances similar to a fist fight. Providing reliable service and developing a competitive employee culture will be two fundamental factors in the achievement of success. A utility must understand a customer's business in order to win and keep that customer. Electricity will be priced less on utility cost inputs and more on the cost inputs and product needs of the customer. As utility business risk profiles change, the utility shareholder base will evolve, especially as utilities secure earnings mechanisms that are significantly different from those of today. A sophisticated investor relations effort will be mandatory.

One current and one former state regulator, Terrence L. Barnich and Philip R. O'Connor, team up with a regulatory staff member, Craig M. Clausen, for Chapter 8. They propose a future path for regulation called "Progressive Choice", where the customer becomes the regulator. They see the current regulatory framework as being out of sync with competitive realities.[4] According to the trio, a fundamental overhaul that incorporates incremental change and entropic principles is needed. Under their proposal, customers would decide whether to accept core status (regulated) or be in the non-core (negotiated) market. Price and other terms of service would be set under market conditions in the non-core sector, especially through negotiations between utilities and customers. The authors emphasize one key concept: customers would be allowed to switch between the core and non-core sectors. This would en-

---

[4] Regulatory practices are discussed in *The Regulation of Public Utilities: Theory and Practice*, Third Edition, by Charles F. Phillips, Jr., Public Utilities Reports, Inc. (July 1993).

courage regulators to accept a reasonable balance of attractiveness between the two categories based on risk and other factors.

In Chapter 9, John Chamberlin of Barakat & Chamberlin, Inc., provides a forecast of the future of integrated resource planning (IRP). IRP, he emphasizes is not strategic planning. Competitive pressures, he predicts, will likely cause poor IRP results. IRP has evolved out of resource planning in only ten years but, according to Chamberlin, is now becoming obsolete. Intervenors, competitors for building generation, and the utility are pushing for their self-interests in commission proceedings. As a result, IRP can become so complicated, detailed, time-consuming and costly, that it ceases to be viable for decision-making. IRP, Chamberlin predicts, will be replaced by a strategic process sensitive to the market.

Many experts believe that the Energy Policy Act of 1992 could accelerate the transformation of the industry. In Chapter 10, John Jurewitz, Manager of Regulatory Policy for Southern California Edison Company, provides background on what led to passage of this legislation and what changes are underway. The key elements Jurewitz examines include: the potential for friction between the Federal Energy Regulatory Commission and state regulatory agencies; wholesale transmission access; transmission pricing; how states will handle retail wheeling; and the effect of the new "exempt wholesale generator" on the generation market.

An advisor to Morgan Stanley, Judith B. Sack has served as an electric utility common stock analyst and an industry consultant. In Chapter 11, she provides a perspective on what the Energy Policy Act of 1992 really means by looking beyond the laws to the underlying reality. For her, market forces always overpower regulations. Technology, economics and customer demand drive the electric utility industry. According to Sack, market forces have been set in motion and cannot be stopped.

The early chapters of this book examine the factors driving changes in industry structure, utility operations, regulatory structure and legislative/legal structures. A transitional process is clearly occurring in the industry. In Chapter 12, Roger W. Gale, president of the Washington International Energy Group, presents the results of a September 1992 survey of electric utility officials—primarily senior managers. The survey reveals that a shift has occurred to concern over bedrock business performance from an issues orientation. Of those responding to the survey, 66 percent report that their utility has down sized operations. Transmission they conclude, is was the most important issue facing the industry. Earnings, competition, cost-cutting measures and amendments to the Public Utility Holding Company Act of 1935 round out the list of top five concerns for these managers. Environmental issues received significantly less emphasis. The survey revealed an interesting divergence on the need for change: 79 percent of respondents said that utilities in general need to change priorities and management style, while only 54 percent report their utility required those changes. In his summary, Gale states that generation is no longer either a natural technical or economic monopoly. Broader transmission access, he claims, is inevitable. Drastic changes—including the demise of many of today's electric utility corporations—will occur. Some companies may not have a long term future. His observations are consistent with the points raised by Thomas Fanning in Chapter 7.

In terms of our diagram, we see a major shift in emphasis after the process of change. Now, instead of the focus being the utility and regulation, the emphasis is on the utility's customers and investors. Two consultants who are active in advising large power users—especially industrial customers—report on what they see as the desires of this important group. Maurice Brubaker of Drazen-Brubaker & Associates, Inc. (Chapter 13) sees large power users—especially those whose electricity bill is a high percentage of production costs—as the main source of competitive pressure on electric utilities. These users operate in competitive markets—they already deal daily with what electric utilities are just beginning to contemplate. These large customers are active in the regulatory and legislative arenas and they usually belong to one or more organizations focused on their power supply concerns. According to Brubaker, these users are increasingly disenchanted with the regulatory process. Utilities have not been required to

justify their costs. Regulators and utilities have avoided accountability when the large power user and others suffer. The issue of
subsidies of residential users is another major concern raised by
Brubaker. Large users want competition in the electricity market
as they now see in the natural gas market. To that end, electric
utility attitudes must change. Retail wheeling and alternatives
such as self-generation must be considered. In Chapter 14, Barbara Barkovich of Barkovich & Yap, Inc. and William Booth see
large power users shifting their emphasis from cost allocation issues to questioning utility revenue requirements and costs. They
note that regulation now is well suited to reducing utility risk and
permitting social experimentation by regulators. It does not,
however, provide choice for customers, nor does it provide efficiency incentives or competitive pressures for utilities. According
to Barkovich and Booth, procedural reform is needed with questioning of the value of adjustment mechanisms.

A consumer advocate, Michael Shames, executive director of Utility Consumers' Action Network in San Diego, argues in Chapter
15 that small electricity users will resist change. They will not necessarily welcome choice, especially when confronted by choice
without adequate information to select an option. According to
Shames, this ambivalence arises because small users are not now
demanding change in their electric service. He proposes five principles to guide electric utility reform. They are: change should be
fair for all customers; choice must be meaningful; captive customers must be protected; regulators should encourage greater utility
efficiency in areas without competition; and regulators should
promote meaningful choice.

Environmental concerns have become major factors to be considered by electric utilities. Stephen Brick of MSB Energy Associates
discusses in Chapter 16 how the attitudes of electric utility officials
toward environmental issues have evolved. He predicts that emphasis on environmental issues will continue to increase with new
regulations. New costs, Brick notes, are certain. The utility that attempts to minimize (or block) new regulations and then take only
the minimum steps will find that an unsatisfactory strategy in the

future. According to Brick, utilities have operated as if the most recent change was the terminal state. Anticipating new regulations, he explains, would be less costly. The trend toward market-based pollution trading systems will allow utilities to take credit for pollution reductions. Realistic assessment of future environmental regulation and risks should become standard procedure for utilities.

We end the consideration of the groups affected by the process of change with chapters by two institutional investors.[5] In Chapter 17, Julie Cannell, the portfolio manager with Lord, Abbett & Co. who manages America's Utility Fund, shares with the reader expectations that investors have regarding U.S. electric utilities. The investor mix for utilities is changing, she notes. Communication with utility management is essential for institutional investors. These investors must select stocks to outperform their own performance targets. According to Cannell, investors recognize change is underway in the industry and will accelerate. She has several recommendations for utilities. Utility companies must develop and follow an appropriate corporate strategy and convey that the right questions are being asked about their business. Managements must make the tough decisions to control the company's destiny. They must help investors understand the company and communicate candidly with those investors. Managements should reach out to the appropriate investors, but recognize there will be times when the company is out of favor. Finally, utility managements and directors must increase their stockholdings in their companies.

Gregory Wagener, an analyst with Brinson Partners, contributes his views in Chapter 18. He sees the length of the transition to competition and the final structure of the industry as key unknowns.Wagner discusses current methods used to value electric utility stocks but notes that these methods are increasingly less

---

[5] The investors' perspective on the industry as well as its historical development are presented in *America's Electric Utilities: Past, Present and Future*, Fourth Edition, by Leonard S. Hyman, Public Utilities Reports, Inc. (May 1992).

applicable as change occurs. It is common to have utilities described as "special situations," he states. Relative costs of power generation across companies are likely to become increasingly important in common stock valuation. Analysts will look to future free cash flow, Wagner predicts, and multi-stage discounted cash flow valuation models will be used.

To complete our exploration of the industry and consider the final step in our diagram, we return at the end of the book to attempt to forecast how the electric utility industry will look in the future. Drawing on the insights from industry experts, including these chapters, and our combined 35 years of involvement with the industry, we offer our projections. We hope, at least partially, to answer the question: What is really going on in the electric utility industry?

Chapter Two

FACTORS DRIVING CHANGE IN THE ELECTRIC UTILITY INDUSTRY

Mark D. Luftig

This chapter reviews the evolution of the electric utility industry over the past thirty-five years, highlighting the most important events from an investor's point-of-view. Two perspectives are taken: factors affecting electric utility stock prices and major trends. We consider key factors such as rising fuel prices, changing demand for electricity and pursuing generating capacity additions that, as they evolved, controlled stock prices. At the same time, we will explore economic, technological, legislative and regulatory trends. It should become apparent to the reader that it is economics and technology that have been, and are likely to continue to be, the real driving factors. For the most part, regulators and legislators have been reactive and not proactive.

The mid 1950s to the mid 1960s

The mid 1950s to the mid 1960s were truly the good old days for electric utilities. Technology was bringing down average costs. Newer, larger, more efficient plants were driving down the cost per kilowatthour (Kwh). On average, the industry had a double A bond rating. New long-term debt was issued at four to five percent and average dividend yields were in the two to three percent range. In 1961, for example, electric utility stocks were selling at twenty times trailing earnings and 2.5 times book value, with premiums on fast growing companies. Florida Power & Light Company was selling at 40 times earnings and was yielding only 1.5 percent. Between 1954 and 1968, the installed capacity of the investor-owned portion of the industry increased by about 175 percent, from about 80 gigawatts (Gw) to about 220 Gw.

Mark D. Luftig is Senior Vice President and Manger of the Electric Utility Group at Kemper Securities, Inc.

The typical chief financial officer had no formal financial training and earned his stripes as an engineer. Very often he (we do not recall any female financial officers in those days) was not an integral part of the construction planning process because he could deliver whatever capital was required on reasonable terms.

Rate cases were uncommon. Usually companies reduced rates voluntarily (sometimes with a little arm twisting from the regulators). From 1955 to 1965, the average electric utility rate to residential customers decreased by 15 percent, while the Consumer Price Index increased by 19 percent. The Hope Natural Gas case, decided by the Supreme Court in 1944, was the law of the land:

> "... the return to the equity investor should be commensurate with returns on investments in other enterprises having corresponding risks."

During most of this period, the case was interpreted to require a comparable earnings standard, i.e., the returns on book equity for a utility should be the same as the returns on book equity of enterprises of similar risk. In the relatively few rate cases that took place, the rate of return witness twirled his Phi Beta Kappa key (no female witnesses either) and pontificated a number. During this period the industry was earning 11 percent-12 percent on equity. The discounted cash flow (DCF) approach was introduced into utility proceedings toward the end of this period. In an informal review of AT&T's long distance rates in 1964, before the Federal Communications Commission, DCF was rejected because the Commission found the proof to be a "tautology." Legislation was not a significant factor throughout this period.

The late 1960s to the mid 1970s

This was an extremely turbulent period for the electric utility industry. New technology for fossil generation hit an impasse. Costs no longer could be reduced by building larger plants, but the industry continued construction at its previous pace. Between 1968 and 1975, installed capacity increased by about 80 percent to about

400 Gw from about 220 Gw. While nuclear power started to become a factor, it was not until 1976 that construction expenditures for nuclear plants exceeded those for fossil plants. The price of electricity to the consumer, as measured by the electricity portion of the Consumer Price Index increased by 66 percent but the average residential rate being charged by the utilities increased by only 51 percent, from 2.12 cents per Kwh in 1968 to 3.21 cents in 1975. Eighty-four percent of the increase occurred during the last two years, 1973 to 1975.

The big drivers during this period were economic ones. The Organization of Petroleum Exporting Countries (OPEC) drove up oil prices, which contributed to increasing inflationary pressures. In late 1973, following the Yom Kippur War, Arab oil producers imposed an embargo on shipments to the U.S. Oil prices doubled between 1973 and 1975. Yields on long-term, A-rated utility bonds soared from about 6.5 percent in 1968 to over ten percent in the 1974-1975 time period. In addition to the inflationary pressures, there was great concern about national security because of the country's heavy reliance on imported oil.

Electricity was a cheap commodity during most of this period, with significant price increases by the mid 1970s. However, even with higher price levels, electricity was still a bargain when compared with the price increases from other forms of energy.

Electric utility financial measures, however, plummeted. A comparison of key market indicators for the 100 largest electric utilities for 1968 and 1975 shows the following:

	1968	1975
Market/Book Value	185.0%	69.0%
Dividend Yield	4.6%	8.7%
Return on Avg. Equity	12.3%	11.8%
Payout ratio	69.0%	69.0%
P/E	15.1%	7.8%

Source: Kemper Securities, Inc.

Pretax interest coverage (earnings before interest and taxes divided by interest), the most significant measurement of the credit worthiness of a utility bond, dropped from 3.1 times in 1973 to 2.4 times in 1974. It began to increase after that because allowance for funds during construction (AFDC) started to become a significant part of non-cash earnings.

Because of escalating oil prices, Consolidated Edison Company eliminated its dividend for one quarter in April 1974. The dividend was reinstated the following quarter at a reduced rate. This dividend reduction action attracted the attention of utilities and regulators throughout the country. They quickly realized that if steps were not taken to offset increasing costs, other utilities would face the same fate. The number of rate increase filings, which had begun to accelerate in 1972-1973, grew dramatically.

Capital spending began to rise in the mid-to-late 1960s. For example, in 1966 the investor-owned industry raised $1.5 billion of additional capital to finance a $4 billion construction program. The balance came from internal sources. By 1970, the industry was raising almost $8 billion externally to support a construction program that exceeded $10 billion. Thus the percentage of outside financing increased from 38 percent to almost 80 percent of the construction programs' cost. Because construction was increasing, the absolute amount raised from outside sources increased by over 400 percent. By 1975, the amounts grew to $12 billion of new capital to support a $16 billion construction program. Thus, over a period of 10 years, construction quadrupled and new money requirements were eight times as high.

The increased capital expenditures were a result of several factors. In the 1960s Kwh sales were growing by 6 to 8 percent a year and most of the construction was to satisfy projected needs. In addition, a blackout in the northeast U.S. in 1965 caused utilities to reconsider reliability requirements. Finally, this period saw the beginnings of the environmental movement. Installation by utilities of non-revenue producing pollution control equipment escalated.

Congress began to talk about oil independence and utilities were encouraged to use less oil. Plans were made to reconvert plants originally built to burn coal, but later converted to oil, back to coal. New England Electric System was one of the industry leaders in that reconversion. And, of course, nuclear power, which was going to be too cheap to meter, was encouraged.

The mid 1970s to the mid 1980s

For electric utilities, the period of the mid 1970s through the mid 1980s was one driven by inflation and changes in capacity levels. For decades, electricity prices had been decreasing. Consumer response had been to increase usage. No one had experienced what would happen to usage as consumer bills increased. In 1974, for the first time since the 1946 transition from a war to a peace time economy, kilowatthour sales from the previous year dropped. Over this entire period, the industry consistently reduced its forecast of secular growth and each year it overestimated growth. Finally, by the mid 1980s forecasted growth had declined from 6 to 8 percent to around 2 percent. Many new generating plants that were on the drawing board were cancelled, as were a few under construction. No nuclear plants were ordered after 1973. The most notable cancellation during this period was the Marble Hill nuclear plant, cancelled in 1983. The plant, which was owned by Public Service Company of Indiana (now PSI Energy), also suffered from construction flaws. Its cancellation nearly bankrupted the company and caused the elimination of its common and preferred dividends. Public Service Company of Indiana had a reputation as a financially strong and stable company, but in a little more than two years, from November 1981 to January 1984, the company's first mortgage bonds were downgraded from double A to double B— below investment grade.

No one was sure what would happen if a nuclear plant, upon which hundreds of millions or even billions of dollars had been expended, was cancelled. Despite having problems in construction, utilities expected that a nuclear plant would be granted full— or nearly full—cost recovery if completed and operating satisfactorily. Until the Wolf Creek nuclear plant rate decision, that assumption was true. After the plant began operating in 1985, the Kansas commission concluded that costs would be recovered based on Wolf Creek as a coal plant—causing a large effective disallowance of investment. Kansas City Power and Light Company and Kansas Gas & Electric Company, which together owned 94 percent of Wolf Creek, litigated the disallowance to the Supreme Court on the ground that construction of the plant was prudent when undertaken and the regulators were unlawfully judging them with the benefit of hindsight. A settlement was reached that resulted in the appeal being withdrawn, but both companies were forced to reduce their dividends.

The cost of nuclear construction skyrocketed for three reasons: First, as a result of the accident at the Three Mile Island nuclear plant in 1979, the Nuclear Regulatory Commission ordered extensive modifications to plants under construction. Second, because of inflationary pressures in the economy, costs of capital increased. The rate on new long-term A-rated utility bonds, which had declined from double digit levels in 1974-1975 to 8 percent to 9 percent in 1978-1979, rose to 19 percent in 1981. They remained in the double digit range until 1986. Third, because of decreased load growth and the high cost of capital, some utilities slowed nuclear plant construction schedules.

A rate spiral ensued. Even with regulatory constraint, the higher costs led inevitably to higher rates. Electric utilities were allowed about $2 billion of rate increases in 1975, $3 billion in 1977, over $5 billion in 1980 and over $8 billion in 1981. The higher the rates were increased, the greater the reduction in usage as a result of price elasticity.

The result was higher reserve margins (unused capacity during peak divided by peak usage). To provide reliability, the industry was historically engineered to have a reserve margin of 15 percent-20 percent. This level was maintained through 1973. By 1982, the reserve margin reached 41 percent. In fact, the margin became so embarrassingly large that the industry referred to the capacity margin (unused capacity at peak divided by capacity) in order to be able to quote a lower figure. A 41 percent reserve margin became a 29 percent capacity margin.

With excess capacity, construction of new generation all but ceased. Utilities that were not ensconced in nuclear construction programs began to generate cash for the first time in decades. For those companies there were three obvious choices: shrink the size of the company, increase dividends, or use the cash to start nonregulated or less regulated businesses. The choice was an easy one.

Utility managements owned relatively few shares and were self-perpetuating entities. It was not in their best interests to shrink the size of their companies. In addition, they felt so frustrated from regulation that they believed they could easily earn superior returns in a competitive environment. History has proven that decision to be a poor one. There were colossal failures when some utilities tried to move outside of the electric business they understood into insurance, banking and investments. For example, FPL Group and Pinnacle West Capital Corporation each lost more than $500 million when they entered the insurance and savings and loan businesses. The companies that did relatively well were those that formed nonregulated generating companies.

Regulators reacted to high costs and excess capacity. For a decade they had been told that utilities needed fair rates of return to raise capital in order to build plant necessary to meet their requirements. If excess capacity existed, there was no need to raise capital for building plants. Hence, it was not as important to allow a fair rate of return. Utility officers claimed that regulators had broken the regulatory compact. More probably, the officers misunderstood the regulatory compact. Regulators operate as substitutes for competition. When they perceive that a market price for electricity would exceed cost of production, the regulators set utility rates equal to cost. But, during the 1930s, for example, the regulators set rates equal to perceived market price which, because of the depressed economy, was less than full cost including a fair return on invested capital. For the next 40 years, through advances in technology, cost was lower than market price and utilities were regulated on the basis of cost. When market price became lower than cost again, regulators kept rate increases in check through such devices as prudence and used-and-useful disallowances.

Another major phenomenon that occurred as a result of the large construction programs was the effect on earnings of allowance for funds during construction (AFDC). AFDC is a non-cash, accounting entry by which the capital carrying charges of projects under construction are capitalized and added to the cost of labor and materials. When the project is completed the company receives a return on the full amount. Using ADFC smoothes a utility's reported earnings. Without AFDC, earnings would decline during a construction period and then surge after the asset began producing cash revenues. AFDC is also used to avoid charging current ratepayers for assets which have not been placed into service yet. Once providing service, the AFDC is collected over the life of the asset from future ratepayers who are benefiting from the services. Unfortunately, the use of AFDC makes the earnings of a weak company with a large construction program look satisfactory. Many investors were shocked to discover that, if regulators did not allow full cost recovery, reported earnings would plunge after a rate decision. This often led to a dividend reduction from what appeared to be a healthy company earning a high return on its equity. Because AFDC is a non-cash item and rises as a construction program becomes costlier, the utility is deprived of cash revenues when the need is greatest. When AFDC is used, the utility receives the cash after the plant is complete through higher depreciation and rate recovery rather than while the utility is building.

Quality of earnings became an important concern. AFDC, which accounted for about 4 percent of income available to common stock in the 1960s, rose to 49 percent in 1980. For some companies this non-cash accounting item exceeded reported earnings by significant percentages. Thus utilities could have what appeared to be reasonable returns on equity, but actually have poor cash flow. These measures returned to more reasonable levels as construction projects were completed.

Electric utility stock prices continued to react to changes in long-term interest rates. As interest rates declined, utility stock prices moved back to book value and achieved parity in 1977. Interest rates spiked as inflation increased and, by October 1981, utility stocks were again selling at a 25 percent discount to book value. During 1984, seven large electric utilities reduced or eliminated their dividends, six as a result of nuclear-related construction. By year end 1984, however, the stocks were again selling at book value. Long-term interest rates had declined by about seven percentage points from their peaks but they were still well into double digit levels. The earned return on average equity, however, was about 15 percent.

Key financial indicators at year end 1985, relative to 1975, were as follows:

	1975	1985
Market/Book Value	69.0%	110.0%
Yield	.7%	8.8%
Return on Avg. Equity	11.8%	14.5%
Payout ratio	9.0%	69.0%
P/E	.8%	7.9%

Source: Kemper Securities, Inc.

Over this period, the industry's bond rating dropped from double A to single A. In 1975, a majority of the companies still had senior debt rated double A or triple A. That percentage dropped to about 40 percent in the 1980-1985 time period. It would decline to about 25 percent by 1990.

Congress reacted. First, it encouraged utility investment through more liberalized tax depreciation. In 1978, Congress passed the Public Utility Regulatory Policies Act (PURPA) and the Fuel Use Act. These statutes were designed to deal with perceived oil and gas shortages. PURPA was designed to promote small cogeneration and hydroelectric projects. Few suspected that it would give rise to a major independent power industry. The Fuel Use Act prohibited the use of gas as a boiler fuel for new utility projects because of a perceived shortage of gas. Soon after passage of the legislation gas prices increased and the nation quickly went from a gas shortage to a gas bubble. The restrictions were repealed formally in 1987, by which time exemptions to the restrictions had become routine.

The mid 1980s to 1993

The mid 1980s began another transition period for electric utilities. The PURPA legislation, which was passed in 1978, was affirmed by the United States Supreme Court in 1982 in *FERC v. State of Mississippi*. Utilities continued to experience massive disallowances of new plant construction. No nuclear plant went into service after 1985 without a significant disallowance. It was no wonder that utility managers were unwilling to consider building new plants of any kind. Also, they were relatively unconcerned at that time with the provisions in PURPA that required utilities to purchase power from "qualifying facilities" at "avoided cost". It was thought that cogeneration or hydro facilities would be small and insignificant. In any event, sufficient base load capacity existed in most places, so that it was not a problem.

Two events occurred in the latter half of the 1980s that would make a major difference: The 1986 Chernobyl nuclear plant disaster provided additional impetus to the environmental movement; and the development of a more efficient medium sized combined cycle gas turbine made it economic for relatively small independent power producers to compete with utilities. The Chernobyl accident also sealed the fate of new nuclear generation, at least through the remainder of the century. In August 1993, Texas Utilities Electric Company's Comanche Peak unit 2 went into commercial operation and probably became the last investor-owned nuclear plant to go into operation this century. (There are other plants that still have not been officially abandoned, but they are not likely to be completed.)

The decade of the 1990s is likely to be remembered as the decade of the environment. Environmentalists are concerned especially with acid rain and global warming. Electromagnetic fields (EMF) drew considerable attention in the early 1990s but interest waned temporarily, awaiting further scientific proof. EMF is likely to be a subject again in the mid 1990s.

Partially in reaction to the increased attention to the environment, Congress passed the Clean Air Act Amendments in 1990. For the first time, it provided an economically based method for reducing pollution. Standards were set and emissions allowances were issued. Generators could choose to comply with the standards or purchase allowances from others who could over comply. The economics of environmental externalities is relatively new and is likely to expand many fold throughout the decade of the 1990s.

Aided by a lack of enthusiasm on the part of utilities to construct new plant, independent power producers, (IPPs) flourished. Forward looking utilities began forming IPP affiliates and subsidiaries in the mid 1980s and today about thirty utilities have IPP affiliates. The largest is SCEcorp's Mission Group of subsidiaries with about $3 billion invested in energy-related assets.

The growth of IPPs was also aided by regulators. State regulatory commissions liked the idea of having an independent benchmark against which they believed they could measure utility performance. Furthermore, they reasoned that if a utility could purchase power from IPPs for less than the utility's cost of production, rates would be lower. Purchased power costs generally were passed through to consumers without any compensation to the utility for the additional risk incurred as a result of long-term purchase commitments. This position which is currently being reviewed in several jurisdictions.

Some regulators became over enthusiastic. For example, rates in California and Oklahoma are substantially higher than they probably would have been without IPPs because utilities were required to offer generous take-and-pay contracts to IPPs. At times, utilities reduced generating output at their own, less expensive plants to meet their purchase power contractual commitments. There was a similar pattern in New York as a result of legislation that arbitrarily fixed avoided costs at 6 cents a kilowatthour, when the actual avoided cost was 3.5 to 4 cents. The New York legislation was re-pealed in 1992 and a revised standard offer contract was intro-duced in California in 1993.

Competition for wholesale customers also increased among regu-lated utilities. Utilities with unused capacity were anxious to sell power to municipals and to cooperatives even if those customers were located in what would have been considered another utility's service territory.

By 1990, IPPs were responsible for half of all new generating ca-pacity. Today, they account for about 6 percent of the electric en-ergy being produced in the U.S.

As IPPs became stronger and competition increased, the need to have access to the utilities' transmission systems became greater. Most utilities resisted the effort, claiming that unfettered access to the system would disrupt it. Electric systems, they argued, need to be in continual balance. Electricity flows in paths dictated by the laws of physics and not by the provisions of contracts. This is simi-lar to the argument by the Bell System that attachment of non-standard telephone equipment to the telecommunications system would cause interference. That argument was rejected by the Fed-eral Communications Commission. Other utilities, particularly those with large amounts of cheap power for sale, were more than willing to open their transmission systems.

Among other things, the Energy Policy Act of 1992 also provided for mandatory transmission access and wholesale wheeling of power (wheeling to utilities). It did not provide for mandatory re-tail wheeling (wheeling to ultimate customers). Mandatory retail wheeling has already begun in Georgia, where there are few, if any, IPPs. Retail wheeling will spread on a state-by-state basis in the next one to three years and be prevalent well before the turn of the century. The Energy Policy Act also provided for the creation of exempt wholesale generators (EWG). This was a way of allowing utilities into the IPP business without subjecting them to the pro-visions of the Public Utility Holding Company Act.

Going forward it will become necessary for utilities and IPPs to become very cost conscious, not just with respect to overall costs but with respect to marginal costs for each segment of their businesses. Electric rates are likely to be unbundled, just as gas and telephone rates were unbundled. Competition will ensue in various segments of the business. To be competitive, rates for each of these segments will have to be based on costs.

As competition in the generation business has increased, utilities and IPPs have begun looking abroad. There, on an unregulated basis, they have the potential of earning the high rates of return that had been available in the IPP business in the U.S. in the 1980s. One question that history will answer is whether the additional political and currency risks of dealing in such places as Latin America and eastern Europe will be rewarded.

Utility stock prices skyrocketed from the mid 1980s to 1993, principally as a result of plummeting long-term interest rates. For example the rate on new, long-term A-rated utility bonds dropped from 11.75 percent at the end of 1985 to 7 percent in September 1993. At the same time, utility stock prices moved from 110 percent of book value in 1985 to 170 percent in 1993, while the average yield decreased from 8.8 percent to 5.3 percent.

	1985	1993*
Market/Book Value	110.0%	170.0%
Yield	8.8%	5.3%
Return on Avg. Equity	14.5%	11.6%
Payout ratio	69.0%	80.0%
P/E	7.9%	15.2%

*September 30, 1993

Source: Kemper Securities, Inc.

Conclusion

Thus, economic events such as changing interest rates, fuel shortages, and supply-demand imbalances and technological changes such as nuclear power and efficient gas-fired combined cycle generating plants have been the driving factors behind changes in utility stock prices. For the most part, legislators and regulators reacted to changes in the market place. This is a healthy situation and one that is likely to continue into the future.

Technological changes that will take place over the next few years could make a dramatic difference in the path the industry takes. For example, more efficient transmission systems could reduce the need for new generation and slow the growth of the IPP industry. On the other hand, smaller, more efficient generating units would enable location of them closer to the customer's premises, would make transmission access less important, and would likely cause early retirement of older, fossil plants, particularly those will emissions problems. Increased competition should accelerate utility merger activity and the move toward partial deregulation of generating assets.

Chapter Three

EXPECTATIONS AND IDEOLOGY DEFINE ELECTRIC UTILITIES

Kenneth Nowotny

The electric utility industry has been the recipient of a diverse array of shocks over the last twenty-plus years, much as has been the rest of the U.S. economy. But the environment in which the electric utility industry developed its responses is unique, being more comprehensively regulated than all but a few other industries. The electric utility industry's response to those shocks has been conditioned by that environment, and changes in that environment.

Therefore, my analysis of the electric utility industry focuses on the ways in which electric utility responses have been or would be *different* from other, less regulated, industries. For the electric utility industry the factors driving change today may be listed as follows: environmental ideology, market ideology and the industry's own history. The discussion will follow in the reverse order of the assertions.

Brief History

From the start up of Thomas Edison's first central station until about 1972, the electric utility industry experienced an era of almost constant growth. During almost this entire period the price of electricity fell, usually in nominal, but always, at least, in real terms. This price decline was a result of economies of scale and scope, economies of density and diversity, vertical integration and technological change.

Then, in the 1970s, along came oil embargoes and oil price increases, troubles with nuclear generation, environmentalists, consumer

Kenneth Nowotny is Professor of Economics, and Associate Director, Center for Public Utilities, New Mexico State University advocates, inflation, unprecedented interest rates, qualifying facilities, and dramatically slowing load growth. Utility executives, in response, made some mistakes. But regulators made some mistakes as well, as did environmentalists, consumer advocates, Presidents, senators, congress people and consumers.

The special problem of electric utilities was *not* the rising real price of electricity. The real price of energy inputs affected all production processes and contributed greatly to the underlying inflation of the 1970s. The unique problem confronting the electric utility industry was the discrepancy between society's expectations and experience. Generations of Americans had grown up experiencing an ever expanding horizon of opportunities, in large part, hooked to the end of an electric wire. Suddenly, it all got very expensive. The sticker shock for keeping one's home warm in winter or cool in the summer became a shattering experience.

"Nothing that awful can just happen;" we thought, "it has to be someone's fault." Utility executives had blundered and regulators had allowed them to do so, and now we were all going to have to pay for the mess. "There just has to be a better way to do this."

Market Ideology

Webster's New Collegiate Dictionary[1] defines ideology as "a systematic body of concepts esp. about human life or culture, . . ., the integrated assertions, theories, and aims that constitute a sociopolitical program." This is what is meant here by the term ideology. It is not intended that the term "ideology" be construed in a pejorative fashion, in and of itself. For my purposes, ideologies are not a problem; they may be an essential part of human communication. Ideologies only lose their approbation when they lose touch with reality. The first ideology discussed here is the one about free markets and competition.

---

[1] *Webster's New Collegiate Dictionary.* 9th ed., s.v. "ideology."

The Carter Administration deregulated the airlines, the motor carriers, the thrifts, natural gas producers and reduced regulation on the railroads. The Reagan Administration eliminated regulation of the oil companies, cable television, and with little else left to do, the interstate buses. Reagan appointees on the Federal Energy Regulatory Commission (FERC) began the struggle to, in effect, deregulate the interstate pipelines.[2]

The notion was/is simple and powerful: competition is a better regulator than government. The competitive marketplace, the assumption goes, does a better job of measuring consumer wants and producer costs than the hired help. The marketplace gives producers all the incentive necessary to make efficient (i.e., least cost) choices[3]: the threat of bankruptcy, the promise of profit. Competition will keep profits down to something called "normál" in the long-run, and in the meantime, "excess" profits will be invested wisely and efficiently according to market incentives.

On the other hand, regulation provides a myriad of perverse incentives. Regulated utilities, the argument goes, have the incentive to gold plate their investments[4], and/or place an excessive number of personnel on the payroll[5], and/or cross-subsidize among customer classes[6], and/or subsidize unregulated aspects of the business to the diminution of competition[7]. Moreover, tax-

---

2 I say "struggle" because federal judges had the persnickety notion that since Congress had regulated the pipelines, only Congress could deregulate them. To date, Congress has chosen not to do so.

3 "Least cost" within the parameter of consumer wants and the given distribution of wellbeing.

4 The so-called Averch-Johnson-Wellisz-Takayama-Etc. effect. See Averch, Harvey and Leleand L. Johnson, "Behavior of the Firm Under Regulatory Constraint," *American Economic Review* 52:5 (December 1962):1052-69.

5 So-called X-inefficiency. See Leibenstein, Harvey. "Allocative Efficiency vs. 'X-Efficiency," *American Economic Review* 56:3 (June 1966): 392-415.

6 See Posner, Richard A."Taxation by Regulation," *Bell Journal of Economics and Management Science,* 2:1 (Spring 1971):22-49, on how bad all this might be, or not, if it actually occurs.

payers have to foot the bill for the regulatory staff that is oversee-ing all of this inefficiency.

The only question remaining was, will competition work in the electric utility industry?

Way back during the "energy crisis" in 1978, the Congress had cre-ated a class of electric generators that were not electric utilities: quali-fying facilities (QFs). These QFs were supposed to use otherwise wasted heat to generate electricity, which, in turn, could be sold to the electric utility at the utility's avoided cost. Whether or not a lot of energy was, in fact, saved, is beside the point: nonutility generators began to pop up all around the landscape like dandelions.

Moreover, as a result of all of their problems utilities were becom-ing somewhat nervous about building new generating stations, es-pecially base load stations. On to the scene came a new class of entrepreneur, the independent power producer (IPP), who would, for a fee, build a generating station and sell power to the utility. That some of the biggest players in this game were subsidiaries of electric utilities or gas pipelines[8] was not something that con-cerned those selling the market ideology.

The QF and the IPP were evidence of the potential for competitive entry into the electric generation business; all the evidence, it seemed, that was necessary. Competition would work in the elec-tric utility industry.[9]

---

[7] A non-myopic reading of the original Averch-Johnson article would lead one to believe that this is what they were really concerned about. For example, in a 16 page article, only 5 pages are devoted to worrying about the single market A-J effect.

[8] (looking for a market for gas)

[9] For a full discussion, challenging the notion that the market will work for electric utilities, see Gegax, Douglas and Kenneth Nowotny, "Competition and the Electric Utility Industry: An Evaluation," *Yale Journal on Regulation* 10:1 (Winter 1993): 63-87.

The market folks were also not concerned about the ominous events in the airline industry, as one by one, airline firms disappeared, creating an oligopoly tighter than the one deregulated in 1978.[10] They were not concerned by the savings and loan debacle. They were not concerned by the some $30 billion in take-or-pay obligations[11] that had been inherited by the interstate pipelines. They were not concerned at the evidence of huge profits in the cable television industry, which ultimately became reregulated in 1993.

They were not concerned by the small towns all across the U.S. that had been abandoned by the railroads, the airlines and bus lines. They were not concerned that the U.S. had only one interstate busline left and it was in bankruptcy court. They had a "sociopolitical program" to advance and were not about to be turned aside by petty details.

There was only one problem left to be dealt with, the bottleneck. In the electric utility industry the bottleneck for generators is the transmission grid owned and operated by the utility. That the transmission grid was built for and paid for by the native load customer was another thing that did not concern those pushing the marketplace agenda[12]. On a case-by-case basis the Reagan/Bush FERC began to open up transmission grids to nondiscriminatory access. The loop (so to speak) was finally closed by the Energy Policy Act of 1992 which gave the FERC power to order *wheeling for the purpose of a wholesale power exchange.*[13]

---

[10] For a discussion of the implications, see Cudahy, Richard D, "The Coming Demise of Deregulation," *Yale Journal on Regulation* 10:1 (Winter 1993):1-15.

[11] read, "stranded investment."

[12] For example, in the *Northeast Utilities* case, the majority thought it would be just fine, thank you, if the native load customers lost their top priority status. "Generally, when system constraints occur, firm transmission service should be accorded priority over non-firm service, even if the latter would otherwise benefit native load customers." 66 FERC ¶ 61.296 at 61.356. See also, Commissioner Trabandt's spirited (as usual) dissent.

[13] For details, see Chapter 10, this book.

Now, all of the problems in the electric utility industry would be solved by wholesale power competition. We could now be certain that all electricity would be produced at the lowest possible cost. There would be no rate base padding, no x-inefficiency, no cross-subsidies because competition would compel everyone to exert every last ounce of effort in the quest for profit or simply survival.

Environmental Ideology

Another powerful ideology, however, was driving the electric utility industry at the same time: the environmental ideology. In fact, this second force was older and has had a greater impact on electric utilities, to date, than the marketplace ideology. In many ways, environmentalism is a rejection of marketplace ideology. Environmentalism observes that the production of goods, and often, services, also produces pollution: what economists call an externality. The electric utility industry is just like producers of other goods, and its processes can and do pollute the air and water.

But unlike other kinds of producers, electric utilities are regulated as to prices, profits, and major investments. State public utility commissions (PUCs) may have a requirement to certify investments as to their environmental benignness. Thus, because utilities are regulated, those pushing the environmental ideology have an automatic entry into decisions made about production processes, unlike, say, at General Motors Corporation. What you do is you get your governor, now sensitized to such issues by a recent election scare, to appoint to the PUC, people possessed of the environmental ideology. These new PUC commissioners can then, fairly quickly, sensitize utility executives: carrot and stick.

In effect, the environmental ideology was able to piggy back this "sociopolitical program" on contemporaneous efforts concerning the alleged efficiency problems of the industry. Some state PUCs had begun to implement "least cost planning" efforts.

Least cost planning quickly evolved, with the help of the environmentalists, into integrated resource planning (IRP).[14] Given some projected demand, say, for electricity, and some shortfall in existing capacity, the question is asked, "What is the *socially* least cost method of achieving the desired result?" In arriving at the answer, such things as air and water pollution, and endangered species are assigned values. Thus, one method may be "better" in the context of producing less pollution, or endangering fewer species, even though the out-of-pocket cost may be higher.

In this context, one of the most benign methods for meeting future electricity needs is "not consuming" electricity. A kilowathour not produced is sulphur and nitrogen oxides and other gunk not spilled into the atmosphere. Keeping down the growth of electricity demand, particularly during peak periods, is called demand side management (DSM)[15].

The uninitiated usually react to DSM by asking why an electric utility would get involved in *not* selling electricity. The answer is simple: because the regulators have given them financial incentives to do so. In effect, utility managers are being bribed to bribe the public not to consume so much electricity.

The economist in me is somewhat repelled by the notion. If the product were priced properly, then the decision about what and when to consume ought probably be left to consumers, and consumers left to their own devices. It strikes me that researching and producing and lending money for the installation of DSM hardware are activities not likely to be of a natural monopoly character. But Southern California Edison Company(SCE) has a state-of-the-art research and demonstration facility for precisely these purposes.

---

[14] You can usually tell the permanence of an institution in the regulatory area by whether or not it has acquired an acronym.

[15] *Public Utilities Fortnightly* recently published a set of articles on the up and downside of DSM. See Bartsch, Charles and Diane De Vaul. "A Bright Idea for Industry" and Houston, Douglas, "A Losing Proposition for Consumers," *Public Utilities Fortnightly* 131:9 (1 May 1993):16.

Where are the entrepreneurs? If DSM hardware is so sexy, why do consumers have to be bribed to install it ?[16] In any event, if utility managers were too incompetent to produce electricity efficiently back in the 1980s, how is it we can now rely on them to pick the right equipment for *not* producing electricity ? I'm sorry, the critics can't have it both ways.

Now, of course, none of this is new. Thomas Edison did invent the light bulb, then strung wires up and down Manhattan Island so that he could sell the things. Ronald Reagan used to try to sell all-electric homes on television, and most electric and gas companies used to (and some still do) sell kitchen ranges and home heating equipment out of the front office. The DSM thing is just a reprise with a minus sign in front of it.

In any event, the presence or lack of logic or consistency is not an essential matter when you are pushing a "sociopolitical program." Here the lack of consistency is perhaps the most unfortunate thing for the electric utilities. Each state has its own environmental program, and each state regulatory body to one degree or another assists in implementing that program. Then of course, there is the federal set of standards and regulations. In California both the Public Utilities Commission and the California Energy Commission have veto power over certificates of convenience and public necessity for new large utility investments.

The Balkanization of environmental efforts is hurting not only the electrics, but also the environmental effort. Smaller utilities, with shallower pockets will not be able to spread the risk, horizontally, of various environmental programs. Such utilities will become financially weaker and customers will pay relatively more for electricity than would be the case with larger, horizontally integrated utilities. Such utilities are likely to become prime

---

[16] See a recent article to this effect. Kahn, Alfred, "An Economically Rational Approach to Least-Cost Planning," *The Electricity Journal* 4:5 (June 1991):11-20.

targets for takeover by larger utilities, reducing the likelihood of success of the market ideology.

The nascent but growing concern about "greenhouse gases" is an example of ideology ignoring facts. The fact is that geophysical researchers of all stripes have yet to come to any kind of consensus on the "greenhouse effect". But this seems not to be of any importance to those pushing the environmental ideology.[17] Said geophysical researchers can't even agree on whether or not global warming would be a bad thing in the event it occurred.[18]

John Henry Faulk used to tell the story about when he was six or seven running with a buddy in south Austin. His Mom had asked the boys to get a chicken snake out of the hen house. When confronted with said snake at about half an arm's length, the boys tried to get through the hen house door simultaneously and presented themselves to Faulk's mother scratched and bruised. She pointed out that they knew well enough that a chicken snake could not hurt them. Faulk's buddy, Boots Cooper, said "Yes, Ma'am, but there's some things'll scare you so bad, you'll hurt yourself."[19] I have a profound hope that carbon dioxide is not one of those things.

I am certainly *not* saying that environmental effects should be ignored, *nor* that the 1968 Environmental Policy Act, or any of its amendments should be repealed. I am suggesting that the electric utility industry should be treated like any other potentially polluting industry, that its product be priced correctly and that unsubsidized consumers be left to make their own choices. The PUCs need to formulate some strategy for environmental treatment

---

[17] See "Conspiracy, Consensus or Correlation ?" *World Climate Review* 1:2 (Winter 1993):7-11.

[18] I have, elsewhere, undertaken to estimate the cost of sufficiently reducing U.S. carbon dioxide emissions. The result is a very large number, something equivalent to the existing U.S. national debt. Nowotny, Kenneth, "The Greenhouse Effect and U.S. Energy Policy," *The Journal of Economic Issues* 23:4 (December 1989): 1075-84.

[19] Paraphrased from Molly Ivins' column "View from Texas", reprinted in the *Las Cruces Sun-News*, 113:5, Monday, 5 April 1993.

across jurisdictions so that all consumers of electricity are receiving the same environmental signals. If electric service companies (ESCOs) appear, so be it, but we should watch that utilities do not leverage their market power into a market which should be inherently competitive. By and large, these suggestions have been universally ignored.

Brief Summary

Electric utilities left a period of relative well being ending in 1970 and entered an era of turmoil and difficulty. Some of the difficulties confronted by the utilities can be blamed on the utilities, some cannot. The response to all of this was to conclude that something was wrong with regulation. Various solutions for what was wrong with regulation were proposed, among them, introducing competition into whatever segments of the industry possible, reducing to an irreducible minimum that which had to be regulated. Faith in free markets permeated the debates about the utility "problem."

The result is that, for the immediate future, one can anticipate increasing movement in the direction of nondiscriminatory access to utility transmission grids by unaffiliated third parties to provide wholesale power to neighboring utilities. In all likelihood, this last circumstance will evolve into retail wheeling, irrespective of the potential for massive financial harm to the wheeling utility and its native load customers.[20]

The other fix for the utility "problem" was closer scrutiny by regulatory commissions of the production mix adopted by the utility. IRP has evolved into a tool to press forward the environmental agenda, which, among other things, involves reduced output (and, of course, reduced consumption) of electricity. Like competition, the environmental course of action is being imposed in a setting where it otherwise would not likely evolve, as for example in the refining, manufacturing, printing or sandwich making industries.

---

[20] Cudahy, Op. cit., for a discussion of the advisability of all of this.

Both of these "fixes" for the utility "problem" have had and will have significant implications for utility costs and revenues. These results, in turn, have implications for strategies that utilities may adopt in order to keep balance sheets more in the gray to black rather than pink.

Stratagems

In observing the electric utility industry over the last couple of years, I have identified five strategies that individual utilities seem to be adopting. None of these are pure, in the sense that they are the *only* effort being made by the utility. Some may be adopted in combination with another. But clearly, utilities have begun to respond to the pressures the marketplace and the environmental groups are placing upon them.

■ The "Roll Over and Play Dead" Maneuver

One approach that may commend itself to a utility, depending on the jurisdiction, is simply responding in the most positive and cooperative way possible to each and every initiative presented by the regulators or legislators. The positive potential *for the company* of such a maneuver is to cater favor with the regulators. If regulators and other intervenors view the company in a highly favorable light, they may be more willing to accept the company's position on revenue and rate requests.

The downside is that: 1) all of this stuff is expensive; 2) there is no guarantee that regulators will be forthcoming with rate increases; 3) a new regulator may not remember the promises of the old; or 4) the pace of change may be too rapid for even regular rate increases to keep up. Up until now, however, the two or three utilities adopting this posture have done fairly well and seem to be keeping up, financially.

■ The "Tell Them to Go to Hell" Maneuver

This strategy can, of course, be viewed as the direct opposite of the first. Likewise, the upside and downside of this strategy are the reverse of the first. Regulators must drag such a utility kicking and screaming into whatever is the most recent and trendy thing for electrics to do. An example might be Southern California Edison Company's (SCE) response to the majority in the *Sun Peak* decision. In effect the company said "No, we won't open up our transmission grid, and no, we don't need to build a generating station in Nevada so badly that we would be willing to do so."

Fortunately for SCE, they did not have so much at stake as say, PacifiCorp, or Northeast Utilities. This strategy is also not recommended to smaller utilities with less leverage in any instance than the very large.

■ The "Position the Company" Maneuver

In this strategy, the company analyzes its strengths and weakness with respect to the diversity of its market, the relative size of large customers, transmission dependent municipal utilities (TDU), etc., and the aggressiveness or relative timidity of neighboring utilities. The company also looks at its generating mix, including age and scheduled retirements. The company is looking for points at which it may be attacked, both currently and through time.

Are electric rates competitive? Is there any threat of self-generation? Are any of the TDUs unhappy with us? will we need new base load in the next ten years? Is our stock undervalued? Is a neighbor's stock undervalued? Do we need to acquire a large number of sulphur dioxide emission credits? It may be time to acquire a neighbor with recently ratebased base load and excess capacity.

The upside of this strategy is that utility management becomes prepared to respond to potential threats from regulators, customers and neighbors. The company may discover a highly lucrative opportunity. The downside is that management may spend so much time thinking strategically that they forget to keep in touch with the basics of a reasonably priced and efficiently produced service.

■ The "Abandon the Dead Wood" Maneuver

One response to the economic tribulations confronting utilities during the late 1970s and early 1980s was diversification. With a tiny number of exceptions, the diversification efforts were utter failures and contributed, often substantially, to the failing fortunes of several utilities.

Even in instances where subsidiaries are not actually losing money, it may be time to concentrate on the business of being an electric utility: it is what customers expect, and I believe, what stockholders expect. Many, if not most, utilities that acquired land development companies, banks, hotels, and heaven knows what else, are actively trying to divest themselves of these nonutility holdings.

The upside of this strategy is that managers can concentrate on their responses to the new regulatory environment. The downside is that the utility subsidiary will often have to recognize a capital loss and this could affect utility bond ratings. For the long term, however, this maneuver may be essential.

■ The "Spin Like a Top" Maneuver

It may very well be that the utility would be advised to go one step further in divestiture. One strategy for confronting competitive entry (such as it is likely to be) and mandated wheeling of power could be to set up separate generation, transmission and distribution utility subsidiaries. Under revisions to Public Utility Holding Company Act (PUHCA), it may be entirely possible for the generating subsidiary (depending on the rolled-in costs) to actively compete for the markets entrants are seeking.

Indeed, a utility with excess transmission capacity may find that it can make a good deal of money wheeling electricity, depending on rules promulgated by state commissions and the Federal Energy Regulatory Commission (FERC). On the other hand, don't count on it. When the FERC in Order No. 636 compelled the unbundling of interstate pipeline services, it established a capacity releasing mechanism. The pipeline capacity that one customer wished to released could be put up for sale to the highest bidder. Well, not really. The capacity could be had for no more than the rolled-in cost-of-service cap established by the FERC. FERC wants markets to clear, except for the market for transmission capacity. The asymmetry in all this apparently escapes the marketeers at the FERC.

In any event, Public Service Company of New Mexico proposed this strategy back in the mid 1980s, but the New Mexico regulators, for good reasons of their own, turned it down. Others, however, in the current regulatory environment appear to be moving in this direction.

The strategies, as noted, can be adopted in combination. For example, getting rid of the deadwood, and spinning off subsidiaries could both be part a plan to better position the company in the market. On the other hand, one might ought to avoid telling regulators to go to hell if you are planning any major acquisitions for which you need their approval.

The Future Failure of the Competitive Ideology

I have previously cited the article by Federal Judge Cudahy entitled "The Coming Demise of Deregulation."[21] Judge Cudahy makes the case that when the economy is growing and there is plenty of money floating around, deregulation and the market ideology may seem like it make a good deal of sense. I would amend that by saying that when the economy seems strong, one can get away with doing silly things that you would not even think about in the middle of a recession. You might find it curious then, that the Energy Policy Act was passed in 1992,[22] if not in the middle of a recession, certainly not in the midst of boom times.

My response is that the conventional wisdom will exert extraordinary influence on the thinking of the faithful, irrespective of

[21] Cudahy, Op. cit.

[22] Pub. L. No. 102-486, 106 Stat. 2776 (1992)

incontrovertible evidence to the contrary, at least for some substantial period of time.[23]

In any event, Judge Cudahy uses the airline industry as an example of an industry headed for some form of reregulation. The reason is that in anything but absolute boom times the airline industry will be subject to destructive competition, predatory behavior, increasing concentration, customer dissatisfaction, and decreasing quality of service.

The restricted availability of gates in and airspace over today's urban airports ensures the existence of a bottleneck. This bottleneck will come under the control of any hub-and-spoke airline which enters quickly and operates with sufficient ruthlessness. Such predatory behavior guarantees increasingly destructive competition. The hub-and-spoke technique, together with the market power to force passengers onto ever more crowded planes guarantees the discomfiture of said passengers.

For reasons I have put forth elsewhere, I believe that what has happened in the airline industry will also be true of the electric utility industry.[24] At some point in time, stockholders and consumers alike will go to the Congress and say, "Enough is enough!" Some IPPs and ESCOs will undoubtedly survive the debacle, but in the long-run I suspect that they will be swept up into a series of consolidations.

Many utilities, weakened by the loss of large customers and stranded investment will operate under Chapter 11 of the Bankruptcy Code and cut rates to gain back customers and utilize capacity, putting many IPP projects out of business and making it tough for even financially strong utilities to make a profit. Eventually, the weaker utilities will be bought up by the neighboring

---

[23] "The real world constantly astonishes the adept economist." Lekachman, Robert, *Economists at Bay* New York: McGraw-Hill Book Co.: 185.

[24] See Gegax and Nowotny, Op. cit.

large utilities at fire sale prices. At the lower stock prices the newly merged utility will be able to produce a normal rate of return, even in the now diminished circumstances. Electricity rates will begin to rise again, incurring the wrath of the average consumer. Stockholders and consumers will make common cause and the industry will be reregulated. For the electric industry the market ideology will be dead, at least until the next spin of the wheel.

All of this should probably happen within a decade of the first state retail wheeling law. Certainly, there will be large self-generators that will not return to the fold. Indeed, it is such recalcitrant former consumers that will ensure that weak utilities remain weak enough to acquire.

It is possible, even likely, that solar photovoltaics and other technologies will lead to personal generation facilities for homes and other small consumers. Likewise, the need for utilities to broaden their service area to re-achieve economies of diversity will therefore hasten the demise of utility competition.

Following the shakeout, the U.S. landscape will be served by rather fewer and rather larger electric utilities than we presently find. Reintegration of generation, transmission and distribution will occur in the primary ways in which vertical integration has always occurred: acquisition or long-term contracts.

The Horizontal Impact of Environmental Regulation

One element of environmental regulation that is under-investigated is the incentive such regulation gives to horizontal integration. For example, Southwestern Public Service Company (SPS) in Amarillo, Texas primarily uses coal base load plants. SPS's neighbor to the west is El Paso Electric Company (EPE), which has considerable capacity at Palo Verde Nuclear Generating Station (PVNGS). In the event of a clamp down on fossil fuel generating stations, SPS would have considerable incentive to merge with a neighboring nuclear based utility.

Likewise, a fossil based utility might have reason to acquire a neighboring utility with considerable access to hydroelectric power. A coal based utility would have incentive to merge with a natural gas based utility.

All of these scenarios are only reinforced by the circumstance of two neighboring utilities which may also peak at different times of the day or year. The combination of environmental regulation and peak supply shaving might prove irresistible.

While we might well encourage closer coordination of peak supply advantages through tight power pools, increased mutual ownership can offer monopoly leveraging problems we might want to avoid.[25] In any event, one can expect the environmental ideology to continue to be a significant presence for electric utilities long after the market ideology has been laid to rest. The continued existence of the one and the death of the other presage an increasingly concentrated electric utility market.

Other Factors

Other important factors that are likely to affect electric utilities have to do with changes in other markets and developments in electric generation, primarily the potential for nuclear fusion.

With respect to other markets, I am here concerned particularly with the telecommunications industry. Williams Energy has made significant entry into the long-distance telephone business by stringing fiber optic cable through its gas pipelines. The moral of the story is that given a sufficient market, a firm that has cheap access to right-of-way can enter the telecommunications business.

---

[25] For a useful discussion of pooling, see Gegax, Douglas and John Tschirhart, "An Analysis of Interfirm Cooperation: Theory and Evidence from Electric Power Pools," *Southern Economic Journal* 50:1077.

Moreover, the state-of-the-art electric company will, very soon, purchase meter reading services from the local telephone or cable company, or provide the service itself. But telecommunications facilities are possessed of enormous economies of scope. If a company can read its own electric meters, it can also provide telephone service, cable television, data communications, etc.

It is only a matter of time before electric companies will be entering this new market, probably encouraged to do so by regulators anxious to spawn telecommunications competition. Doubtless there will be institutional hang-ups and rule making procedures before the above scenario takes place, but I would suggest that it will not be 2010 before the day arrives.

Finally, for the long-run, there is the matter of nuclear fusion: limitless, virtually pollution free energy, having a minute marginal cost. Others know better than I whether fusion will be commercialized by 2025 or 2050. Fortunately for those in the prediction business, we won't live long enough to be confronted with our errors in this instance.

But, because fusion is likely to have inordinate fixed costs and small to nonexistent incremental costs, like the interstate highways, I would think that fusion will lead, ultimately, to the nationalization of the electric grid.

If only because taxpayers will have paid for most fusion research, there will be some justice in having taxpayers reap most of the reward for fusion generation. But, in order to pay for fusion reactors, they will have to be fully utilized. It is quite likely that the full utilization of fusion as a resource will require the abandonnement of unamortized existing generating facilities. The socialization of these utility losses may require the nationalization of the industry.

Conclusion

The electric utility industry is in what one might call a state of dynamic disequilibrium. The causes of this status have very little to do with that which is inherent in the technological and financial condition of the industry. For many, if not most, consumers, the real price of electricity is falling once again. The balance sheets of most electric utilities are apparently healthy and market-to-book ratios are and have been mostly in excess of unity.

Rather, forces external to the firm are driving the electrics into this dynamic disequilibrium, to wit: the marketplace and environmental ideologies. The response of individual firms in the current ecology of regulation will dictate how a firm fairs in the shake-out that must inevitably come.

Whether or not the cost of all of this is worth the benefit to be derived from reducing whatever perverse incentives may (or may not) be provided by regulation should be a question in the mind of legislators and regulators alike. It is interesting that at just the point in time regulators had gained invaluable information about how regulation, as practiced, worked in a time of stress (the 1970s and 1980s), and how it might be improved, others have decided to attempt the untested and the untried without very good reasons for doing so.

Chapter Four

ELECTRIC UTILITIES LEARNING TO COMPETE

Erroll B. Davis, Jr.

Not since the Public Utility Holding Company Act of 1935 has there been such a watershed event, in the utility industry, as the passage of the Energy Policy Act of 1992. This piece of legislation would seem to erase any doubt that utility deregulation is coming. Open wholesale transmission access is now the law. Retail wheeling experiments are either beginning or are under consideration in Georgia, Michigan and New Mexico; retail wheeling legislation is being considered in at least eight states at this writing, and the number is growing daily. Legislation has already been put in place in Nevada.

It is not legislation, however, that is driving the changes in the electric utility industry, but the emergence of competition. Today, many utilities are still large, ponderous, bureaucratic organizations that have lost track of why they are here. Regulators, calling for more and more studies, and more and more experiments have aided and abetted in this trend. Far too many utility resources are taken up in elaborate, sophisticated, intellectual dances among utilities, regulators and "professional" intervenors, that have no meaning for the average person and fail to focus on how to enhance the quality of life for customers.

Under the current system of utility regulation, there exists as much as a 375 percent cost differential for a residential kilowatthour. No unregulated commodity market would or could tolerate such a disparity of price! Deregulation is poised to change all of that. Finally, utilities will be forced to learn how to do business like everyone else. Competition, not regulation, will ensure utilities allocate

---

Erroll B. Davis, Jr. is President and CEO of WPl Holdings, Inc. and Wisconsin Power and Light Company, and Chairman of the Board of Heartland Development Corporation.

their resources to best meet the needs of customers at the lowest cost. Under that framework, history has shown us that customers will not only benefit, but also they will have a far greater voice in defining the terms and conditions of service.

At one time, it was undeniably true that the "natural monopolies" created in the early days of utility systems needed close regulation. Today, however, competition among utilities is not only possible, but in fact exists. Additionally, independent power producers and cogenerators are already in competition to supply future generating capacity. To the extent that regulation is artificially keeping competitive forces from working for the benefit of the customer, it is inevitable that such regulation of the utility industry must diminish over time. Economic and political efficiency will demand it.

Although some industry organizations are publicly vowing to fight legislation to reduce regulation's role and enhance competition, such an effort is futile. Competition in its many forms will be relentless. I suggest we would do well to stop wasting our time arguing the fine points of legislative and regulatory privilege and refocus our resources toward how, not if, we are going to compete.

At this time, the electric utility industry really does not know what customers will expect or want in a competitive environment. The extent to which individual utilities or unregulated affiliates of separate firms are able to identify customer needs, and meet them first, will determine their future viability, assuming market forces are allowed to work.

There is not much likelihood that regulators will simply stay out of the competitive arena and let competition take its course, however. We can, therefore, anticipate a time of jurisdictional chaos, as federal and state regulators wrestle to balance state vs federal interests. Utilities and their customers will certainly be caught in the middle.

Open Access And Retail Wheeling

Open access transmission is setting the stage for the competitive environment we will face when retail wheeling becomes a reality. There will certainly be winners and losers among the competitors, but, on balance, customers should benefit. Wisconsin Power and Light (WP&L) began preparing for open access some time ago. In 1987, we filed an open access transmission tariff that FERC has characterized as a model in simplicity. The company's interconnections with many companies in two regional power pools place WP&L in an ideal situation to wheel as well as purchase and sell power.

To take advantage of bulk power opportunities that exist outside of WP&L's system, an energy brokering unit was recently formed under another part of our holding company, WPL Holdings, Inc. That unit will provide new options to bulk power purchasers in this emerging market.

Currently, WP&L's retail and wholesale rates are the lowest in our region in almost all rates classes. As part of our last rate case we requested a three and one-half year retail rate freeze to further ensure our competitive price advantage. If price remains a basis of competition, we clearly hope to be among the winners. However, I recognize that neighboring utilities feel equally confident about their futures. Until we have a better understanding of how regulators will intervene into the competitive process, it is difficult to anticipate the timing of many outcomes, but the future should treat utilities very differently. Competitive marketplaces reward the strong and penalize the weak and inefficient. Public service commissions have often operated in the exact opposite manner in the past. They have allowed higher rates of return to weaker utilities and decreased rates of return for the stronger. In a truly competitive environment, market forces will be allowed to work and the results should be quite different as customers select their electricity supplier on the basis of price and service rather than because they are captive ratepayers.

Regional Regulation

For the future, I would support regional transmission regulation only if the regulation is not incremental. States need to give up some of their jurisdictional authority—something they are not likely to want to do—if regional regulation is to work. Constitutionally, there is no basis for regional regulation and I see jurisdictional nightmares while the battle for authority over regional transmissions systems wages on.

Vertical Disintegration

When one discusses competition, the issue of vertical disintegration inevitably arises. I see no inherent reason why competition should automatically lead to vertical disintegration, although there may well be good reasons in the future to organize differently internally. If a utility can provide all of the services its customers needs in a cost effective manner, there is certainly a competitive advantage in doing so. What will be important will be to unbundle service lines and costs and allocate them appropriately so that utilities can determine if they are providing the various aspects of their bundled utility service—generation, transmission, distribution, sales/marketing services—in a cost-effective and competitive manner. If a segment of the business cannot be run cost competitively, then it should be sold or stopped, not subsidized by more profitable areas, as may have occurred in the past.

I would anticipate that most utilities would not automatically vertically disintegrate in a deregulated environment. Most have achieved a level of competence in operating the various parts of their business and will want to continue to provide as full an array of services for customers as possible. Individual functions may become more self-contained and some centralized services may need to be shared or charged back according to the degree of support they provide to each business segment. For most utilities this means more accurate record keeping and better information systems in place to track, measure and allocate costs.

The Regulatory Environment

In the near term, the success of resource allocations based upon customer demands will be challenged by state regulation, but always, of course, in the names of "fairness", and "equity". I anticipate an interim period between today's regulation and "near" deregulation where jurisdictional chaos will dominate the regulatory environment. We are already seeing this in the "candid" dialogue between FERC and the National Association of Regulatory Utility Commissioners (NARUC) over some jurisdictional authority. FERC's position may be strengthened if more interstate transmission systems develop, but it is clear that states will fight for the authority to regulate these systems, as well. Also, states will give up control at different paces, leaving the industry disorganized, disadvantaged, and discordant until the issues are finally resolved. Unfortunately, historically strong commissions, because of their past regulatory successes, will be the least inclined to give up control, thereby working the hardest against natural market forces.

Customers with choices do not need commissions to "protect" them. In nonregulated business environments, customer satisfaction is not an issue, because dissatisfied customers change to suppliers who satisfy them. Admittedly, regulation exists to prevent fraud and abuse, but the purpose of this type of regulation is to mitigate the downsides of competition, not to frustrate it. The bottom line is that customers with options do not stay dissatisfied long.

I would welcome the opportunity to prove this hypothesis to regulators by way of a three-year experiment, where several utilities would be allowed to operate in a totally unregulated manner. At the end of three years, let's compare the cost and quality of service to customers with the cost and service trends of regulated utilities over this same period. My sense is that this experiment might shed some light on the cost/benefit trade offs of regulation. I would even go so far as to suggest that you would see even better planning and certainly more aggressive pursuit of all *cost-effective* demand side management measures, since we would no longer be rewarded for merely throwing assets at customers, as we are today.

Preparing For The Future

Although I believe retail wheeling and other truly competitive issues may come slowly to Wisconsin, WP&L is doing many things to be ready for that day. Perhaps most significantly, we have undertaken the task of changing the culture to embrace—not scorn—the competitive marketplace. The company has put an emphasis on quality initiatives and reengineering our internal processes. We have enhanced our strategic planning efforts, and begun to unbundle our services in order to better understand our costs and shed nonprofitable activities. We have also aggressively pursued synergies with nonregulated activities, but these efforts are by no means unique. In fact, we know that our competitors are doing the same things to be ready as well. Rates have already become an issue, as the major Wisconsin utilities have all announced rate targets which will require reducing costs over the next few years. Surprisingly, we even anticipate difficulty with regulators over the issue of reducing our costs. Fears have already surfaced that cutting cost means poor service to customers. If the Japanese have shown us anything, however, it is that low-cost does not automatically mean low quality.

Another thing we must learn to do better is to move quickly to respond to opportunities. A series of summer storms left many areas of our service territory hit hard by flooding. Within a week of the floods, I received a personal letter from AMOCO concerning payments on my credit card. While I am on the board of directors of AMOCO, this was a letter sent to all customers in the region. It offered to arrange special payment terms for those who had suffered flood damage and expressed a sincere concern for the well-being of AMOCO's credit card customers. Two weeks after I received this personalized offer from AMOCO, WP&L was still sorting out the details, getting approvals from the management group and trying to put a similar program together for its customers.

This behavior is typical of electric utilities. We have not yet learned when and how to move swiftly in response to customer needs. Gas industry deregulation has shown us that those who move the quickest, restructure the quickest, and respond the quickest—will be successful. Enron Gas Services is but one excellent example of this.

Unresolved Issues

There are clearly unresolved issues that make the future of utility competition somewhat murky. It is important however that we see these as just issues—there to be resolved—and not barriers. The barrier posture is one that is often used by both regulators and utilities alike.

Utilities cannot ask to operate in a competitive environment without assuming some of the risk. In a competitive environment, utilities cannot expect to be held harmless for stranded investment, for example. This is held out as a barrier by many utilities. Private industry routinely builds plant and capacity that is at risk. If a company's product isn't purchased, the capacity goes unused or they convert it to another use. That is the business risk all industries face.

Utilities have also frequently used the "obligation to serve" argument to suggest that we need to be protected. There are few customers in any market that go unwanted by *everyone* in the market. Someone will find a way to serve them. There are always options—higher price, subsidies, substitutions. Using "obligation to serve" to block competition is a bogus argument. We have chosen this business to be in, and our customers will tell us how they need to be served.

Future And Competitive Markets

One of the greatest challenges utilities will face in the new competitive environment is a lack of certainty about what the markets will be. I personally believe niche markets will emerge and we will need to select a few of them in which to excel. In preparation for that, WPL Holdings is using a holding company format to find out more about utility customers and their needs. By diversifying into energy management, housing and environmental services, we intend to be able to add value to customer relationships in numerous ways. Looking to a time when all customers may be at risk, learning about their specific needs will be a strong competitive advantage for any company. In my personal vision of the future of WPL Holdings, I see one company with both regulated and unregulated services, meeting the needs of various customer groups. Exactly how that will evolve, especially in our state regulatory climate, is less clear.

Using the airline model, there are "cargo only" airlines, feeder airlines, and short haul lines. Players have selected one or two niches to fill successfully. At this point, we cannot anticipate on what basis we will similarly distinguish ourselves. Price will certainly play a role, especially in the bulk power commodity market. In a regulated environment, however, price is the only variable. In a non-regulated environment, the options are limitless—whatever creative tailored service that interests customers becomes a niche opportunity for the company.

Changing Regulatory Climate

As my comments suggest, I am generally not supportive of the current utility regulatory framework within this country. This objection, which is not a personal issue, is one motivated solely by a quest for economic efficiency. Perhaps I should take a moment, however, to mention that I do not foresee a time when utilities will ever be totally unregulated, and I am not against regulators themselves. As I suggested earlier, customers should be protected against fraud and abuse—but not, however, from making the choices *they* want to make.

In practice, regulators have taken on an in-loco-parentis role. They often look at worst case scenarios, assume utilities would do that and proceed to make policy on that basis. There seems to be this pervasive view that utilities do not have the desire to serve their customers well. Regulation has seemingly assumed the philosophical point of view that mankind is inherently evil. We all still seem to be paying sixty years later for the sins—real or imaginary—of Samuel Insull whose financial machinations led to the creation of the Public Utility Holding Company Act. The utility industry has been relatively scandal free and relatively well managed, given its operating conditions, since then. My sense is that this is more a result of ethical people taking their responsibilities seriously than it is a reflection of the effectiveness of regulation.

From a financial perspective, I am particularly opposed to rate-based regulation. This system rewards utilities for penalizing customers! Utilities can earn a return on an asset simply by putting it in place and charging for its use. There is no reward for choosing the right asset or operating it efficiently. This system has created the most asset intensive industry in the world, but it is by no means the most cost-effective one.

If given a choice, I would select market-based regulation. But, I would even prefer incentive regulation over rate-based regulation. Incentive regulation, were it to be implemented, should be symmetrical—an equal opportunity for risk and reward—to be effective, and it should also allow utilities, regulators, and the public to reach agreement for the first time on just what things are important and what should be incented. If the public truly participated in that process, I would suggest that we might be focused on a few different priorities today.

If I were allowed to modify just one ideology of our regulatory climate, it would be to dispel the notion that it is sinful for companies to be profitable. Regulation should ensure that customers are getting cost-effective products and services. Beyond that, profitability should be a function of management skill, not regulatory largess.

Other Challenges

As utilities change to address niche markets and compete, we can expect that customers and shareowners will also change. Share-owners will not see utilities as low-cost bond substitutes in the future. There will be a wider difference in financial quality and stock market performance of utility stocks. Utility investors will become more astute, and utilities and analysts will have to do a better job of talking to them about individual companies—not just the industry. Some of our traditional shareowners will sell their holdings and we will need to attract new ones. Finding the right investors for an industry that has traditionally not focused on discussing risk profiles may not be an easy task. I would hope that we will get some help from our professional organizations in bringing the changing nature of utility investment to the public's attention.

Our customers will change also. They will welcome choices, but they will certainly have concerns about our ability to serve them. Deregulated industries have not universally done well for customers, at least not right away. Few people would say airline service is uniformly better today than it was before deregulation—but telecommunications services seem to be better and cheaper. Generally, the world model is toward more privatization and more deregulation. Canada, Australia, New Zealand—all are looking to privatize their utilities; Great Britain, Spain and Argentina already have. Bureaucracies had grown to intolerable sizes and had lost their effectiveness in many of those countries. Yet, many of those same trends continue to occur in the United States as regulators continue to push the view that better service comes through more, not less regulation. Large scale bureaucratic planning processes collapsed under their own weight in Eastern Europe and they will collapse here as well. History is replete with this lesson. Customers have every reason to believe that they will ultimately be better served in a competitive environment, but competition will provide some risk as well. Customers will need to be smarter— understand their options and make good choices. As in any business situation, those who select good suppliers of cost-effective services will have a competitive advantage over those who do not.

The Utility Of The Future

In my personal vision, the utility of the future will not be a utility at all. It will be something more—an energy service company; a heating and air-conditioning company; a comfort shoppe; an environmentally-friendly power operation; an uninterrupted power source. One aspect of competition, however, will be the same—get there first with an acceptable level of quality at an appropriate price. In an unregulated environment, what is important is time, the product delivered, the product's quality, and what customer needs are being met.

Regulation makes all of us—regulators and utility personnel—engage in a great deal of non-value added work. The overriding question should be whether a task adds value to the customer. If everything we both did had to meet a value-added standard, there would be a lot less done within our companies and within regulatory agencies as well. Costs to the consumer would be reduced and resources would be channeled toward what is most important to the customer—the services they purchase. No utility executive in the United States, including me, has had the courage to put regulatory costs on the table and demand that they be justified. What is the cost to consumers? What have we lost in global competitiveness with our balkanized system of state regulation? Ask an industrialist on the northern Illinois border if they value Illinois regulation enough to justify the 40 to 80 percent premiums they pay compared with costs a stone's throw but jurisdictionally a million miles away in Wisconsin.

I refer to the twentieth century Austrian economist Joseph A. Shumpeter, who described competition as "the process of creative destruction." Instead of trying to thwart the forces of competition, government should instead seek to mitigate its negative face. Instead of protecting markets, government should facilitate retraining and relocation of workers and capital. Those in government that come to understand this will serve the public interest better than those who insist on resisting competition until it is ultimately forced upon them at a pace they can not possibly cope with—to those who don't believe this, I would refer them to all those who used to be at the now non-existent Civil Aeronautics Board.

Chapter Five

MANAGING THE TRANSITION TO COMPETITION OR THERE'S A PONY IN THERE SOMEWHERE

John E. Hayes, Jr.

The Nature of Change in Regulated Industries

Every industry and company has a belief system, a sense of mission, or a defined purpose to which management and other employees look for guidance. Change always forces an industry or company to re-examine its beliefs and culture. Often, such a re-examination shows beliefs and the resulting business practices to have lost relevance.

The electric industry is a product of the Industrial Age that began over a century ago. The purpose of electric utilities until recent years was essentially the same as it was in the 1930s: to provide safe, adequate and reliable service to all comers. The federal and state rules that were written to guide these utilities also were products of this industrial era. Many state laws regulating utilities date back to the early 20th century. The laws were primarily designed to prevent "ruinous competition" through costly duplication of utility facilities, and, in turn, to protect customers against exploitation by a monopoly.

For a variety of reasons, however, America's industrial era economy, once geared to providing a few essential needs, gradually has shifted to an economy concerned with supplying endlessly diverse products to discriminating and demanding consumers. As affluence increased after World War II, the range of wants widened. Consumers emerged and they insisted on goods and services tailored to individual tastes. Old approaches to the market were

John E. Hayes, Jr. is Chairman of the Board, President, and Chief Executive Officer, Western Resources, Inc.

designed to standardize. They were replaced by new ones that made customizing possible and affordable. As a result markets began to segment.

Coincidentally, the electric industry became a mature industry. During the period of growth, technological innovations in power generation, transmission, and distribution produced more efficient equipment. Economies of scale, technological advances, and fast growth led to steadily declining unit costs. But eventually growth slowed and economies of scale were largely exhausted. At the same time, capital and operating costs began to grow at unprecedented rates. Incremental technological advances alone, therefore, were not sufficient to maintain a declining cost curve. The result was a sharply increasing unit cost curve and an impetus for change that has driven customer demand and turned technological development away from large centrally operated facilities.

Change in the electric industry and within individual utilities now seems inevitable based on the increasing competition in the marketplace. Similarly driven changes have already occurred in the telecommunications and natural gas industries. Those changes provide a "road map" for electric utilities.

Lessons from Other Regulated Industries

In the telecommunications industry, a key market segment was large-volume users who increasingly demanded better communications systems as a central part of their operation. For these customers, basic voice-to-voice service, no matter how efficient, was not good enough. In hindsight, telephone companies seemed not to recognize that the needs of large-volume customers were widening. For example, in the early 1970s customers requested call-restriction equipment on their Bell-owned PBX switchboards. These customers wanted to prevent long-distance calls being made from certain work locations. Bell resisted such inquiries because it did not want to sell anything that would interfere with people making long-distance calls. By doing this, however, Bell ignored the early signals of a changing market.

As customer demands went unmet, competitors arose to satisfy ignored market niches. One of the products they were successful in selling was call-restriction equipment! Bell had not taken advantage of the opportunity to sell value-added products that could be transformed into a marketing advantage simply by satisfying the customers' perceived needs. Instead, they reacted to maintain the "status quo," and in the process, lost market share, image, and to a certain extent, research and development leadership.

Eventually, the former Bell System companies learned how to capitalize on change and became very strong customer-oriented competitors in the marketplace. They learned to give customers control of the market and choice in the market. An important lesson was learned: even if most customers prefer vanilla, they still want to choose from 30 other flavors.

The natural gas industry learned similar lessons through a series of market upheavals: acute shortages in the mid 1970s, a violent price fly-up between 1978 and 1982, and then an unnatural combination of an acute supply surplus and rising prices. Despite all the subsequent regulatory tinkering, the force that prevailed throughout these crises was customer demand for market control. Customers "seized" control by turning down the thermostat, switching to alternative fuels, and forcing the local natural gas distribution company to transport gas purchased from others.

The experiences of the telecommunications and natural gas industries teach the simple lesson that if customers demand change, it will occur. The key, then, for the electric utility industry is to *anticipate* change and take advantage of the resulting opportunities.

Change: From Monopolistic to Competitive Markets

I believe permanent change in regulated industries is driven by five factors as regulated companies move from a monopolistic to competitive enterprises. Labeled the five "Cs," these factors, and the ability and willingness of a utility's management and its regulators to take them into account, will determine the structure of an individual company and the entire industry. The five Cs are:

■ Customer Demands

Change in regulated industries begins before regulatory decree. It begins when customers perceive a need for new choices or control, usually manifested as interest in a new service or product. The threshold question is: Who will meet the market demand, the traditional supplier or someone else?

Customers want choices—product choices, service choices, and price choices. Companies must offer those choices or risk losing market share. Lest that seem a hollow threat, consider that as a regulated monopoly a utility already enjoys close to a 100 percent market share. So, unless the customer receives the choices he or she demands, the utility's market share can only go down. The challenge to the electric utility executive is two-fold: minimize loss of market share and enlarge the market.

■ Changes in Economics and Technology

Changes in economics are inevitable, and the successful utility in the 1990s will adapt rather than resist. While resistance may be successful in the short run, over time it almost always results in a misallocation of resources. Technological changes come about in large part because of new customer demands. One of the principal effects of new technologies is to knock down or at least weaken artificial barriers to entry (e.g., to generation or transmission systems).

For an environment in which marginal costs are less than average embedded costs, the local utility must become more price and service competitive to retain not only the large user, but ultimately all users, from potential alternative suppliers. The local utility has no other option. Competition always forces prices toward marginal costs; subsidization of customer classes—while politically desirable—becomes economically impossible; customer classes demand additional price and service options.

■ Competition

The emergence of competitors within regulated industries has some unique implications. Potentially radical results occur in an industry in which members have previously held a monopoly position and, due to changes in demand, technology, or economics, must suddenly confront competition.

Generally, the former monopoly faces the dual situation of one part of its market base remaining noncompetitive, while the second part becomes heavily competitive. The combination of regulation and competition creates both opportunities and market distortions that all too often are feared, ignored, or misunderstood by industry and regulatory decision-makers.

Competition forces companies to divide the available revenue pie among more players. If the pie does not grow larger, a smaller share will be available to existing companies as new competitors seize their share.

■ Critical Mass

A promising approach to competitive viability is to achieve "critical mass." This is the process by which companies adjust their size to attain a new, larger "mass" that allows them to absorb previously unexperienced losses of revenues. Critical mass, however, does not suggest that size alone will permit a company to survive.

The key aspect of critical mass is that it provides an opportunity to reduce unit cost of service through operating and financial synergies, thereby allowing a company to compete.

The achievement of critical mass usually can be accomplished in one of two ways: capturing a dominant market share in a rapidly expanding market or merging with one or more other companies. However, as already noted, in a monopoly environment a utility has 100 percent market share. Introducing competition simply gives it the opportunity to lose market share, never increase it.

The utility industry's history is replete with mergers. The prospect of further consolidations is not radical, but reflects the results of continually evolving economic, technological, and customer-based realities. Under this critical mass scenario, small companies become medium-sized and medium-sized companies become large. The largest companies become the strategic providers in the industry with the smaller ones becoming niche providers. The smaller companies also may be relegated to serving the less accessible or smaller market share areas.

■ Capital Needs

The electric industry is capital-intensive with relatively high levels of fixed charges. With plant investment tailored to load demands, even the loss of a few industrial customers can severely damage net income and necessitate the re-spreading of fixed charges over a remaining slow growth or no growth customer base. That attempt to re-spread costs meets with customer, and therefore regulatory and political, resistance. That resistance, in turn, results in negative financial consequences. The ability to compete for the remaining large customer business is impaired, causing the entire business-loss-and-consequence cycle to be not only repeated, but also accelerated.

If capital is not deployed efficiently, the capital markets will take that into account in the pricing and marketability of the company's securities. Achieving critical mass enables a company to spread risk and achieve financial objectives more efficiently thereby safeguarding the company's standing in the capital markets.

Contemporary Issues in the Electric Industry

Given these factors of change, how does an electric utility thrive in this era of open access transmission, competition, accelerating technological change, integrated resource planning, demand side management, increasing price and service options, and shareholder restlessness?

First, it should be recognized that while each of these issues is important, each is simply a point along a continuum of issues, all of which will be resolved. Others are not yet clearly identified, but will become prominent issues in the future.

Second, and most importantly, as each specific issue rises to be resolved, it surely sprang from one or more of the factors previously examined: 1) customer demands, 2) technological changes, and 3) the economics which facilitate the rise of competitors to the traditional energy supplier.

■ Open Access

Open access is not new. It is simply a restatement of customer demands for improved service at lower cost at a time when the technology exists to satisfy the demand. The question is whether the customer's traditional energy supplier will meet the service and price demand or whether a competitor will.

The electric industry traditionally rationalizes monopoly status with talk about duplicate facilities and huge sunken investments in generation and transmission systems. In many cases, those investments have been perpetuated because of our "natural monopoly" status. Competition, in the form of wheeling, can promote the sharing of existing facilities, thus avoiding building additional ones. In fact, greater transmission system access means fewer base load generating facilities will be needed if generation can be better matched with market demand.

The key issues are protecting one's ability to provide excellent, reliable service to all existing customers, have a "level playing field" in which we can compete for existing and potential customers, and having incremental costs covered if construction is necessary to enable transportation services to be provided.

Technology permits open access, customers demand it, and the economics encourage it. Regulatory directives simply increase or decrease the speed of the inevitable.

■ Integrated Resource Planning

As a general rule, improvements in planning help companies to better understand their customers' needs and how to meet those needs.

There is a significant risk in integrated resource planning, however, that prescriptive rules, and attempts to comply with them will dominate the planning process. The industry should be extremely careful about having implemented a command and control approach to utility planning which may be circumvented in the future by competitive forces which cannot be controlled.

As an example, a few states' IRP rules require evaluation of resource options using an all encompassing Societal Cost Test. This requires regulated utilities to charge customers for so-called "externality" costs, while private generators of electricity and other manufacturers are not required to pay such costs. This requirement may drive large industrial customers from the regulated utility system and cause them to generate their own electricity with a potentially greater negative impact on the environment.

Their departure would also leave utilities with fewer customers from whom to recover their tangible fixed costs.

■ Public Involvement

Regulatory directives attempting to incorporate everything from environmental and quality of life concerns to social engineering, have moved discussions on resource additions such as transmission lines from the board room to the political/social arena. No longer are utilities able to site generating and transmission structures in the most cost efficient locations. Customer concerns about electric and magnetic fields and aesthetics are but the precursors to additional demands and concerns.

Integrated resource planning, customer quality circles, and other venues to elicit public support for the electric utilities' decision-making have been anathema to many utility industry managements. Customer/public involvement in utility planning, operations, and management will become more pervasive as we enter the 21st century.

■ Pricing

Competition for customers means that it is no longer feasible for some classes of customers to subsidize other classes of customers if the traditional utility is to compete with other suppliers entering the market. As the natural gas industry has done, so too the electric utility will unbundle rates and competitively market generation, transmission, distribution, and such customer services as dispatch and billing.

It is true that the "traditional" electric utility must be concerned about independent generators and others securing a significant market share when the latter are unburdened by the construction and maintenance of transmission and distribution systems necessary to ensure universal service. But unbundling services and the clear delineation of prices for each class or type of service permit the utility to maintain or achieve competitiveness.

It is only a small step from cooperatively developing, owning, and operating generating facilities, having transmission line interconnects, and cooperating in regional power pools, to sharing other parts of the electric transmission and distribution systems. Just as the telecommunications, natural gas, trucking, and railroad industries use other industry members' facilities at agreed upon prices, so too the electric industry will reach the same modus operandi.

Achieving Success in the Competitive Marketplace

Since we cannot turn back the clock to a protected marketplace, what should we learn from the experiences of those other industries? We should learn that competition to meet customer demands is won or lost on only a few factors: supplier willingness to meet customer demands, technical ability to meet those demands, and appropriate pricing of products and services.

It is important to remember that electric utilities provide not only a product, electricity, but also a service, especially in the forms of reliability and responsiveness. Educating customers that price, though very important, should not be the sole criteria for choosing an energy supplier is important if the traditional utility is to successfully balance the commitment to provide universal service and retain its large industrial and commercial customers who have energy provider options. The "real" costs associated with alternative energy suppliers must be communicated in terms of "value" parameters that the customer understands—service reliability, power quality, technical support, and emergency service availability.

Given the pace at which the electric industry, and hence each company, must confront change, how does a utility survive? We have identified six "guides" which strategically and practically address a utility's ability to adapt to changing business conditions. The six "survival" guides are:

■ Concentrate on Customer Service

A competitive environment demands more concentration on what customers want than a monopoly environment requires. Thus, customer service must be among the highest priorities. This is true of all customer classes and requires not only the attention of the company's management, but also that of regulators. Programs and options demanded by the largest customers will be echoed by other customer classes. The most successful path to success is for all employees to focus on achieving customer satisfaction with the company's products and services.

■ Assign Strategic Planning a Much Higher Priority Than It Probably Holds Currently

A competitive environment places a much larger premium on strategic planning than does a noncompetitive one. It is not sufficient merely to meet existing customer demands. One must anticipate these demands as well. Ideally, the company introduces the customer to new service options rather than the customer introducing the company to them.

■ Align Goals with Those of the Regulators

That does not mean the "watch dog" nature of the regulatory agency will cease; it does mean that the long-term best interests of all customer classes must be mutually recognized. It also means that planning horizons for both utility executives and regulators need to be synchronized.

Prudence reviews and least-cost planning are fine for minimizing rates of return in the short-term, but may be inadequate to address both long-term customer needs and potentially larger long-term costs to society, such as an inadequate and/or unreliable power supply.

■ Achieve Critical Mass or Identify a Unique Market Niche and Fill It

If a company does not achieve critical mass or find a market niche, it will not be able to adapt to marketplace changes, and will be vulnerable to loss of market share and ultimately to failure. Critical mass will largely determine whether each company is the acquirer or the acquiree, and will affect the necessity for, access to, and cost of attracting capital.

■ Eliminate Cross-Subsidization of Specific Customer Classes

In the evolving competitive marketplace, social engineering is a luxury which the energy company simply cannot afford. Prices for all customers' services must be based on what it costs to provide those services. Remember, competition drives prices toward marginal cost.

■ Embrace Competition

Competition is the foundation of our economic system, and the sooner a utility recognizes that the natural monopoly marketplace is dying and embraces the world of competition, the sooner that utility will be positioned to be successful. Learn from others' mistakes—resisting inevitable forces only results first in the faster loss of market share, and ultimately the failure of the business.

Other Options

Having discussed the "shrinking" of a company's potential market share from 100 percent under monopoly conditions to something less than that due to the influx of competition, we should address a few steps electric energy company managers can take to "expand the size of the revenue pie."

■ Diversification

Although many utility companies diversified during the 1970s and 1980s in attempts to increase revenues, many of the experiences failed. Few companies during that early period were able to increase shareholder benefits through their diversification strategies.

Diversification can provide successful new revenue streams if the firm is equipped on the front end with senior management expertise—I mean real expertise—in the target enterprise.

The key to success is in integrating the diversification efforts into the total corporate planning, marketing, and financial strategic plans. Corporate management should understand the operations, finances, and relationship between the diversified holdings and the corporate mission.

Otherwise, diversification should probably be little more than passive investments or joint ventures with partners who have proven expertise and financial strength.

Conclusion

As competition for market share evolves, industry leaders must continue to motivate employees, identify and meet evolving customer demands, recognize and adopt technological capabilities, and further develop internal resources.

We are not guaranteed success, only the opportunity to pit our minds and efforts against our competitors.

The customer has little concern for how an electric transmission grid works or what load growth means to service reliability and investment requirements. What we must continually remember is that the customer demands access to lower price opportunities and new technologies and will seek both from our competitors—including other utilities—if necessary. As the local energy company, we must provide those choices *and* emphasize and deliver customer service which begets customer satisfaction.

Change is inevitable and it is fruitless to resist marketplace forces. We are all managers of change. Our task is to manage that change for the benefit of our customers, shareholders, and employees.

Chapter Six

EVOLUTION, NOT REVOLUTION, FOR ELECTRIC UTILITIES?

Thomas H. Fehring

Where are you going, my little one, little one?
Where are you going, my baby my own?
Turn around and you're two,
Turn around and you're four,
Turn around and you're a young girl going out of the door.

Alan Greene and Melvina Reynolds [1]

My oldest daughter just turned 20 and is fast becoming an energetic young adult. As I think back on her growth, the passage from infant to toddler to adolescent to teenager to adult was so gradual that the changes were almost imperceptible. It is only by reflecting back upon the years that I become amazed at how quickly she has grown up.

So it is as an insider in an electric utility. I may be too close to notice the transition that is occurring. Change, when experienced as a continuum, is less evident than it is for others who are watching the industry from the outside. Yet, when I compare the electric power industry today to what it was 10 years ago, it is apparent that it is undergoing transformation. I think it is likely that the next 10 years will bring about a radical restructuring of the industry.

The forces that are placing the most significant pressure upon electric utilities are the burgeoning competition for generation, the

Thomas H. Fehring is Manager of System Engineering for Wisconsin Electric Power Company

---

[1] Song by Alan Greene and Melvina Reynolds as sung by Harry Belafonte, recorded 1958, Copyright by Radio Corporation of America.

movement favoring the opening up of access to the transmission grid, competition in other forms, and the changing regulatory environment. I would like to reflect on these changes, and try to provide some insight as to what may be in store for the future of the industry.

Competition for the Generation Business

Simply put, the business of electric utilities is the production and sale of electricity. In many areas of the country, however, electric utilities are moving out, or being moved out, of the production side of the business. In 1990 for the first time in recent history, nonutility developers placed more electric generating capacity in service than did traditional electric utilities. Nonutility developers appear ready, willing and able to step in to build and operate power plants. They have become increasingly sophisticated and aggressive.

Generation was long considered a natural monopoly[2] largely because of barriers to entry. One of the most significant hurdles was that "economies of scale" dictated that economic electric power was almost exclusively produced by large and costly power plants. If everything else is equal, units that are 100 megawatts (MW) in size cost less per installed kilowatt than units, 10 MW in size. And units over 500 MW in size generally are more economic than units of only 100 MW capacity.

From the perspective of the utility planner, the clear direction during the last several decades was to push the design envelope to permit increasingly larger unit construction. With units reaching 1,300 MW in size (enough to power 13 million 100-watt light bulbs), construction costs often climbed into the billions of dollars.

---

[2] It is interesting to note that this has not always been the case. In the early days of the industry, it was common for competing companies to construct power plants in competition for the same markets. These companies also competed against customer-owned generating units.

Only the large electric utilities had the financial ability to build such units.

As new units became enormous, however, so did the task of their construction. Lead times for new construction usually approached and often exceeded a decade, even when everything went well. The complexity and size of these projects usually resulted in something not going well. Construction delays became the norm in the industry. As interest rates soared in the late 1970s, many of these new units became uneconomic. Yet with the majority of their costs "sunk," most utilities proceeded to move these units toward completion.

Imagine how utility leaders must have felt when they were able to finally bring these large units on line only to discover that the impact upon utility bills was so dramatic that the loads these units were once forecast to meet did not materialize. Many utilities were left with high rates and excess generating capacity. It could not have happened at a worse time for the industry. While many utilities pressed on with conventional plants, the economic environment was changing.

In large part because of the natural gas shortage in the late 1970s, the Carter administration had proposed legislation to encourage the cogeneration of electricity and thermal energy. Cogeneration had been around as long as the electric power industry has existed. While there were exceptions, however, its application was largely limited to large industrial firms that installed units to meet both their own electrical generation requirements and supply steam for process and heating loads.

Recognizing the potential of cogeneration as an energy saving measure, Congress passed the Public Utility Regulatory Policies Act (PURPA) of 1978. The Act encouraged companies to install cogeneration plants and required utilities to purchase any power offered. The Act also entitled the cogeneration plant developers to charge the utilities for the power at the rate the utility would otherwise incur if the cogeneration power was not available.

In the years following passage of PURPA, several factors came together that caught many utilities unprepared:

➡ Natural gas, the use of which was severely restricted[3] in the late 1970s and early 1980s, became abundant and relatively inexpensive as bottlenecks in the supply and transportation of natural gas were cleared. What was called the "natural gas bubble" is now referred to as a "sausage," as natural gas continues to be in ready supply.

As a surplus of natural gas became available in the mid 1980s it has become possible to contract for natural gas for lengthy periods—either at fixed rates, or at rates tied to escalation factors.

➡ Development of combustion turbines, for which progress had slowed during the hiatus when natural gas and fuel oil usage was restricted, restarted in earnest when the market began to open up. Technological progress has led to higher firing temperatures, with resulting increases in efficiency and capacity. When combustion turbines are coupled to heat recovery boilers to capture the exhaust heat, steam can be generated. The steam can be used for process use (an effective form of cogeneration), and at the same time excess steam can be used in a steam turbine to produce additional electricity.

➡ Regulatory commissions began reviews of the "prudence" of the utility's decisions to proceed with the construction of new plant. These reviews resulted in billions of construction dollars being disallowed from being recovered from utility ratepayers. Many utilities became reluctant to expose their shareholders to the risk of expensive new plant construction programs.

---

[3] The use of natural gas for electric generation was all but prohibited by the Fuel Use Act of 1978, except units that were licensed for operation only during a limited number of years to meet system peak loads or for use in cogeneration units.

➡ The high rates for electricity charged by many utilities allowed developers to easily meet the avoided costs of those utilities, and obtain contracts to sell power. Armed with these contracts, the nonutility developers have been able to establish attractive financial arrangements—arrangements that have often enabled the developers to obtain essentially 100 percent debt, project-based, financing.

Independent developers have been quick to seize upon the opportunities that these events have provided. In many areas of the country, cogeneration projects owned by nonutilities are predominating the market for new generation.

The track record of many of the contracts signed with nonutility developers has not been exemplary. What often appeared to be a reasonable contract—based upon forecasts of future avoided costs —became outrageous when fuel costs dropped in the late 1980s. Even before many of these plants became operational it was apparent that they were no longer economic in comparison with other alternatives. Yet the utilities were locked into paying excessively high costs without any contractual ability to reopen the contracts. In some cases, utilities have bought their way out of contracts—paying high penalties—to avoid even higher penalties for future power purchase costs.

The response of the industry to nonutility generation has been not been uniform. Some utilities have decided—often prompted by their regulators—to seek competitive bids for all of their future generating capacity requirements. Among these utilities, some have set up their own nonutility affiliates and are trying to compete directly with the nonutility developers. Other utilities are striving to build plant in the conventional fashion, and to maintain their monopoly over generating plant ownership in their service territories. The industry has been referring to the choices as the "build vs. buy" decision. This dichotomy of response will likely continue, because there is not a single correct answer to the "build vs. buy" question that is appropriate for all utilities. What are the implications of a movement toward the "buy" strategy for the industry?

Utilities that decide to purchase their future generating requirements may, by doing so, be able to reduce overall capital expenditures, and thus avoid associated incremental increase in their electric rates. They may also be able to limit their potential exposure to construction risk and the inability to collect the full cost of construction in utility rates. If these utilities select the "right" projects and are careful in establishing contractual provisions to provide some protection against future movements of fuel prices, etc., they may achieve these ends.

However, I think it probable that some of these utilities will see their contracts with independent developers declared imprudent —with certain costs becoming uncollectable from their customers. Regulators are likely to use the same type of hindsight in reviewing long-term purchased power contracts as they have used in reviewing major plant construction programs.

Utilities that adopt the "buy" strategy will limit their earnings growth potential—as long as conventional regulation continues [4]— unless they undertake other enterprises to offset this effect. It is not clear that a lower earnings growth rate by itself is undesirable, since most financial experts would agree that the return on the common equity invested in a company is more important than growth in earnings.[5]However, many in the utility industry see this as a disincentive toward the adoption of the "buy" strategy.

---

[4] This occurs because the earnings to shareholders that are authorized in the rates that utilities charge for electricity are based upon the equity investment of shareholders in capital expenditures. For most utilities, investment in generating plant outweighs all other investment. Some utilities are establishing nonutility subsidiaries to compete for future generating capacity outside of their service territory. If these enterprises are successful, this can offset the impact of not building utility generating plant.

[5] An increase in earnings growth might be caused solely by increased equity investment.

One of the significant concerns within the industry about purchasing future power requirements from others is the risk associated with signing long-term power contracts. Indeed, most nonutility generating developers attempt to deal all elements of project risk to other parties in order to obtain financing and maximize the debt leverage. Substantial risks are assumed by the utility in the process, usually including the risk that future fuel price swings may ultimately make the energy from the facility uneconomic. Considering that most nonutility projects use natural gas as their principal fuel, this risk is real.

It may be arguably less risky to contract for the power from a plant than to build that plant, but a utility that builds a generating plant hopes to earn a return for its shareholders to compensate for that risk. While in the case of purchased power contracts, there are no potential compensating earnings (at least in the current regulatory environment).

Several utilities have had their debt ratings reduced as a result of purchased power contracts. As a result, utilities have begun to request a return on purchased power contracts. To date, no public utility commission has allowed a utility to earn an equity return on purchase power contracts. I suspect that they will continue to refuse such requests, because it could lead to a substantial departure from past regulatory policies. If utilities are not authorized a return on purchased power contracts to compensate for the risk, over time utilities will be forced to increase the percentage of equity in their capital structures. Otherwise they will be unable to avoid undesirable weakening of their financial strength. This represents a largely hidden cost that should be considered when making the "buy vs. build" decision.

As stated earlier, the majority of the capacity developed by independent developers has been fueled with natural gas. One of the most difficult risks to deal with is the potential run-up in natural gas prices when shortages in supply or deliverability again occur. Developers have offset this risk by either passing it on to the utilities, or by obtaining long-term fuel contracts at fixed rates or with escalation factors tied to other commodities that may be less volatile. Even if the latter strategy is adopted, I question whether these contractual provisions will provide protection if the difference between the contract price and the market price becomes enormous.

Even though the majority of nonutility generating capacity developed in this country has been fueled with natural gas, I see nothing that will preclude the future construction of large, coal-fired generating units by independent developers—especially as utilities move toward "all source" bidding.[6] It is interesting to speculate whether the development of the future generation of fail-safe, nuclear power plants might be undertaken by nonutility project developers. They are already developing clean coal technology at several plants.

In spite of these concerns, I believe that an increasingly large percentage of capacity will be purchased from nonutility developers in the future since political and regulatory bodies will continue to view increased competition as favorable.

Many utilities accept this as a foregone conclusion and have adopted "all source" bidding for their future generation requirements. These utilities have typically been offered many times the capacity that they have solicited in their requests for proposals. It is evident that the planning process will become increasingly complex as the options available to a utility expand significantly. The utilities that will do well in this changing environment will be those that do exceptional jobs of screening and selecting projects, and in establishing effective contractual safeguards for itself and its customers.

---

[6] Under "all source" bidding, utilities generally seek bids for capacity from all potential suppliers, not only from facilities that qualify under PURPA as cogeneration facilities.

Transmission Access

Another barrier to entry that has prevented significant competition in the production of electric power has been that access to the electric transmission grid has been restricted. The market for power from independently owned power generating facilities is obviously limited if the developer can only sell to the utility in whose service territory the plant is located. These barriers are falling. The Energy Policy Act of 1992 has opened the grid for the sale of electricity to wholesale customers. As a result, nonutility generating plants will be enabled to sell to whatever utility they can cut the best deal with.

While this appears significant to the industry on the surface, I believe that the importance of this change is being overemphasized. The capability of the transmission grid is not infinite, and existing transactions between utilities use up much of the capability of the transmission interfaces. Furthermore, in order to prevent wide area blackouts[7], it is essential that a portion of the interface capability between utilities be reserved for reliability.

The Act provides for construction of additional transmission to meet the demands of the various interested parties. However, construction of new transmission facilities in an era of concerns for the health effects of electric and magnetic fields (EMF) from transmission lines, and the environmental impacts that are commonly attributed to new transmission, will limit the ability to construct new lines, or to reinforce existing lines.

---

[7] The construction of the interconnected transmission system was largely justified by electric system reliability requirements. By interconnecting systems, it was possible to greatly reduce the amount of generating reserve capacity that needed to be maintained to provide adequate reliability. The consequences of wide area blackouts, which would greatly increase in likelihood if the required transmission reserve levels are not maintained, are clearly undesirable to society.

Finally, charges for transmission services limit the economic transmission of power over long distances. The electric utilities charge rates (usually referred to as "wheeling rates") for transmission services, to account for the cost of the transmission system and the electrical losses. If an entity is transmitting power across several systems, each system generally will receive a tariff. As a practical matter, this limits the distance over which an entity can economically transmit power.

I believe the true significance of the requirement to provide wholesale access will be measured by whether it will be a prelude to retail access. In passing the Energy Policy Act of 1992, Congress left the question of retail access in the hands of state regulators. This debate is underway in a number of states. It is clear that significant battles will be fought over this issue in the near future—the outcome of which will shape the industry.

Many experts—including utility officers—believe that it is a foregone conclusion that retail access will be mandated in the future—that the only question is "how soon?" In support of this position, they point out that significant differences between electricity rates can no longer continue to exist across state lines (or within borders between utilities). Indeed, an increasingly intensive lobbying effort is underway by some of the largest industrial firms in the country to open up competition for the retail electricity market.

Perhaps it is only wishful thinking on my part, but I do not consider it a foregone conclusion that retail access will be a reality in the near future. I base this belief, in large part, upon the fact that the individual state commissions will oppose arrangements that may harm captive customers. And to some extent, I would expect the regulators to be careful not to cause significant financial harm to the utilities that they regulate. Much of the debate about retail wheeling will continue to evolve around "cream skimming" and "stranded investment."

Cream skimming refers to the likely tendency, under retail wheeling, for the most lucrative customer loads to be "skimmed" away from a utility, either by other utilities or by nonutility suppliers. It is generally expected that customers with the most lucrative loads (generally industrial and big commercial firms that have large loads with high capacity factors and in good financial condition) will be most likely to leave the native utility system for cheaper rates from other suppliers. Other customers (generally residential and smaller commercial customers) will probably continue to be supplied by their local utilities.

It has been questioned whether such skimming will really matter to the utility industry. The utility that no longer generates power to its customers will presumably receive fees for transmitting and distributing the power to these customers. A similar transition has occurred in the natural gas industry, and the local natural gas distribution companies have generally done quite well. The electric utility industry, however, is quite different from the natural gas utility business. The investment by electric utilities in distribution systems is generally swamped by their investment in generating capacity and transmission.

A utility that loses a substantial part of its load to others due to retail wheeling will generally have excess generating capacity, unless it can find other customers for that capacity. Of course, in such an environment the utilities with the most economic generating plants will always be able to find a market for their power. Utilities with uneconomic power plant capacity, however, are in a different situation. Many of these utilities already have excess generating margin. As they lose customers to others, their generating reserves will become so high that greater portions will be declared surplus for conventional ratemaking purposes. These plants will not be able to sell into the competitive market at rates that will recover the full investment—leading to stranded investment. Will utility regulatory commissions be willing to let this occur? They have in the past demonstrated a willingness to disallow uneconomic investment in generating plant in the past. I think the potential environment for retail wheeling is different because the regulators will work to protect the captive customers.

First, commissioners are going to try to protect the residential and small commercial customers who may be forced to pay excessive costs under retail wheeling.

Second, public utility commissions will not permit economic power plant capacity to be transferred to serve other markets. These plants will be retained in rate base to serve the utility's native load. Only uneconomic, excess plant is likely to be allowed to be transferred to serve other customers. And these plants are unlikely to be able to compete in these markets.

Third, as explained in the section below, retail wheeling will run counter to efforts by state commissions toward integrated resource planning.

Fourth, states with low-cost power are likely to resist efforts of the utilities within that state to sell outside their native markets, if the result will be to increase in-state electric costs. Rather than retail wheeling, what I see evolving is a drive by each utility to become competitive. The more the "retail wheeling" threat is pushed, and the greater the risk that it may come about, the stronger will the incentive be for utilities to get their rates in line with those charged by their neighbors. This movement toward competitive electricity rates will occur whether or not retail wheeling occurs. The industrial firms clamoring for retail wheeling will benefit either way.

In the long run, it should not really matter to the large industrial customers that are pushing for retail wheeling whether they get it or not. They will achieve their real aim, which is not retail wheeling or increased competition; it is paying lower rates for electricity.

In the new environment, utilities that have high electric rates compared to other utilities in their region must lower their rates. Utilities that are currently low-cost producers in their regions will face pressure to maintain their competitive advantage.

One can speculate that the large industrial customers might be better off if the electricity markets are *not* opened to retail wheeling. I can envision a future in which large customers leave their native utilities to receive power from nonutility generators, only to see their electricity costs increase substantially if, for example, natural gas becomes increasingly expensive. Indeed, I have heard that companies in England are wondering why, if retail wheeling is so good, their rates have gone up so much.

Competition On Other Fronts

While the battles mentioned above are generating a lot of publicity, utilities are also fighting it out on other fronts. These battles, which might be characterized as border skirmishes, have changed the relationships among utilities.

Utilities have recognized for a long time now that they are often in competition with every other utility in the region when it comes to attracting, and sometimes retaining, large customers. When the economy was strong in the 1980s, however, utilities did not experience the competitive pressures that they now do. The tie between electricity costs for industrial and large commercial customers and the economic health of a utility's service territory is strong. As a result, utilities are fighting it out for new customers by working to reduce their rates.

These same competitive pressures are being felt over municipal customers. Many municipal communities have historically purchased their generation from the local investor-owned utility. However, with the markets for transmission opening up, these communities are often free to purchase their power from other utilities.

In addition, municipal utilities have occasionally been competing for load by annexing a portion of the local investor-owned utility's service territory containing industrial and large commercial customers. With the right of annexation, and the advantage of lower cost financing[8], investor-owned utilities are often at a disadvantage at the borders of these communities.

---

[8] The bonds of municipal electric companies are exempt from federal taxation. Furthermore, they do not pay federal, state or local taxes.

The Changing Regulatory Environment

The regulatory environment that electric utilities face today is changing dramatically as a result of integrated resource planning, the imposition of the cost of various "externalities" in selecting future resource additions, and in a move toward different ways of regulating utility rates.

■ Integrated Resource Planning

As this is being written, thirty-five states[9] are engaged in some sort of integrated resource planning. One of the major goals of integrated resource planning is to plan the future of the system such that the *net* cost to the customers is minimized. If it is less costly for the customers to install more efficient lighting, as an example, rather than for the utility to build and operate a new power plant, than the utility should provide incentives to encourage its customers to do so. The cost of the incentives are added to its rates.

This leads to some rather interesting phenomena. The customers that participate in the programs see their net bills go down and benefit from the incentives to offset their costs. The programs are typically designed to ensure that the participants are clearly benefited. But what about the non-participants? They may see their electric bills increase above that which it would have if the utility had proceeded with plans to install generating capacity instead.

In a noncompetitive environment, this does not work out too badly. A utility's customers are provided price signals to encourage them to participate in various conservation or load management programs. If they elect to participate in those programs their net costs will be lower, even though their electric rates may be higher. If they elected not to participate, the choice was theirs.

---

[9] According to Ashley Brown, former Commissioner, Public Utilities of Ohio

However, in a competitive environment, problems clearly develop with such programs. A company selling a commodity like electricity must be able to compete on price. The electricity sold by one company is largely indistinguishable from the electricity sold by another. If the first company's rates are higher because of its programs to encourage conservation, it will be less competitive.

This phenomenon has caused some to speculate that competition and integrated resource planning cannot effectively co-exist. After one company invests substantial resources to make its customers more efficient, its rates will likely be higher as a consequence. Another entity can then come along and sell power more cheaply to the same customers that received the conservation incentives from the utility they used to receive their power from. If this situation evolves, utilities will clearly have a disincentive to invest in conservation measures.

While there are mixed results and continue to be concerns for the value of demand side programs, the feedback on the initial programs is beginning to validate their use. Planning techniques and regulatory involvement will continue to evolve in many states—leading to greater than ever regulatory oversight of future plans. As competition within the industry intensifies, this will lead toward inevitable conflicts with the regulators as utilities attempt to reduce costs so they can compete effectively in the marketplace.

■ Externalities

To plan effectively, utilities must have some idea of what to optimize plans toward. In the past, utilities established plans to minimize the future revenues that they would be required to collect from their customers—in other words, they established plans that would tend to hold down electric rates. Regulators are taking integrated resource planning another step. If the goal of IRP is to reduce the total cost of the customers of energy decisions, in theory it makes sense to include costs to society of all of the impacts of electric generation, not just the cost of producing the power.

Utilities are being told to impute the cost of environmental impacts of various generating strategies, in developing their integrated resource plans. For example, the Public Service Commission of Wisconsin recently ordered the Wisconsin utilities to include the cost of so called "greenhouse gases" in establishing their resource plans. Preliminary results indicate that at the monetized levels ordered by the commission, the impacts upon the marginal cost of generation will be substantial. The utilities are likely to be ordered to use these marginal costs to justify conservation and demand side management programs that would otherwise be clearly uneconomic. In addition, the resource plan for future generating plants will likely be substantially more expensive as a result of the externalities.

The conflict between planning for externalities and the burgeoning competitive market for electricity appears obvious. Utilities that are ordered to include the cost of externalities in their planning will ultimately see their rates increase in relation with utilities in other states.

■ Loss of the Regulatory Compact?

The regulatory compact is viewed as dead in some areas of the country. The large disallowances of plant expenditures experienced by some utilities over the last decade, and the concerns for flexibility in response to an increasingly competitive environment, are causing many in the industry to look for other, non-traditional, methods to establish the rates charged for electricity. A number of utilities are asking for incentives to comply with various actions that the regulators are requesting. Examples of this include incentives for adopting demand side programs and incentives to purchase power from nonutility generators.

Under incentive ratemaking schemes, rather than rates being fixed at a level that will recover a utility's costs for such programs, utilities are provided with an incentive to do better than some target level. In the case of conservation and load management programs, the state commissions have provided a number of incentives.

Nearly two dozen states already authorize utilities to capitalize such expenditures. Capitalization provides the utility shareholders a return for such investments in essentially the same way that new generating plant is handled. Several states also adjust utility earnings to reflect loss of revenues due to demand side incentives. In this way, if a utility does better than projected in attaining conservation goals it is allowed to earn as much as projected without the reduction in load level that comes about as a result of its successful conservation program.

Utilities have also proposed incentives to target the core business. Earnings would be allowed to increase if, for example, cost-reduction goals are exceeded. A variation of this is price-cap regulation, in which utilities effectively propose to hold their rates flat—employing increased productivity in order to offset inflationary and other cost increases. As I will explain below, the movement to incentive and price-cap pricing structures could significantly impact the industry.

■ Mergers

Five years ago I stood in front of a group of utility analysts and portfolio managers and discussed my view of utility mergers. At the time, utility analysts from Shearson Lehman were predicting that there would be a massive shake-up of the industry. To illustrate the point, they began using the theme "50 Electrics in 5 Years". Our message to the analysts was that there has been a historical trend toward consolidation in the industry—a trend that will continue—but that significant impediments will continue to limit mergers. And to make the point, we presented the audience with T-shirts that said "5 Electrics in 50 Years".

We now know that the prediction by analysts from Shearson Lehman was not accurate. I suspect that my prediction will not be particularly accurate either—but then I will probably not live long enough to find out.

The reality is that there currently are substantial impediments that make it very difficult for one utility to acquire another. The principal obstacle is conventional utility rate base regulation. When utility regulation was established decades ago, rates were based on a system designed to cover utility operating costs as well as provide a return of and on utility investment. This treatment, largely unchanged to this day, results in utility earnings being tied to the cost of its investment in utility plant.[10] If another entity wishes to acquire a utility, it generally has to offer significantly more for that utility than the equity that is currently supporting its rate base. In today's markets, where most utility stock is selling for well above "book," most utilities attempting to acquire another utility will experience significant dilution.

In other industries, the acquiring firm can potentially overcome dilutionary affects by savings associated with various synergies or cost reductions. In the case of the electric utility industry, however, most savings are generally passed on to the customers.

In considering mergers and acquisitions, this flowing of savings to customers is a strong impediment. This observation is not to imply that utility acquisitions will not occur. There are circumstances under which a utility acquisition will make sense. However, in most cases, the underlying economics will limit utility combinations to friendly mergers.

It has been speculated[11] that electric utility mergers will be more likely as competition spreads, as utilities strive to form strategic

---

[10] Utility plant is largely made up of power plants, transmission lines, and distribution equipment, as well as office buildings, etc. The depreciated sum of capital expenditures for this equipment is called a utility's "rate base." A utility's rates are set to cover the utility's investment in its rate base, meaning that rates are high enough to cost of the associated debt and equity investment. In addition, a utility's rates also cover the depreciation of those assets.

[11] As an example, Charles Studness stated in an article that appeared in the February 15, 1993 *Public Utilities Fortnightly* that the proposed merger between Cincinnati Gas & Electric Company and PSI Resources, Inc. could indicate a merger trend is starting, and that utilities that

alliances to strengthen their competitive positions. While this sounds good in principle, in practice it may not make sense for most situations. In part, it seems to rely upon the theory that combining smaller utilities to form larger corporate entities will result in stronger, more competitive, utilities. The problem with this is that it might not be true. Many small electric utilities today seem more competitive than the giants of the industry.

In addition, it is generally accepted (as explained below) that the future is going to require that utilities get closer to their customers—to form strategic alliances with them to most economically meet their overall energy needs. I am not sure that bigness is an advantage to customer service.

It is my belief that electric utility consolidation will continue at its historical pace, as opportunities present themselves, unless something changes conventional rate base regulation. On the other hand, if rate base regulation is replaced by an incentive rate making mechanism of some sort, or if we actually move toward market-based electricity pricing, than we are likely to see a merger frenzy.

Future Technological Developments and Customer Bypass

A number of utilities are already experiencing the threat of "customer bypass"—of customers leaving the electric grid and meeting their own electric needs. Even without retail wheeling, if an electric utility's rates are high enough, large electric users are able to construct and operate their own power plants at a cost less than buying from the local utility. Utilities have come to realize that, to survive in an era of customer choice, they must price their product competitively—but for many utilities this task is formidable.

---

merge early are likely to be in a more competitive position than those that merge later.

The bypass risk will likely increase as technological developments reduce the cost of customer-owned generation. As developments in combustion turbines allow higher firing temperatures, their efficiencies should increase and their installed costs should decrease. However, there are other technologies that may provide even more difficult challenges to utilities.

Progress on at least one of these technologies has the potential to shake the foundation of the electric power industry. Research on advanced fuel cells is showing encouraging promise. It is conceivable that over the next decade highly efficient fuel cells will be perfected that could be economically installed in individual residences and businesses. Fuel cells are silent, and for the most part pollution free. These devices could not only satisfy the owner's electrical requirements, but the heat generated from the fuel cells could provide energy for space heating, hot water, and (coupled with an absorption unit) provide air conditioning. While a customer with such a device might still desire to be connected to the local utility for back-up power, high saturation of customer-owned fuel cells would largely bypass the electric utility.

Fuel cells still have a long way to go in order to provide reliable and economic power as envisioned above. It is not clear that they will ever be able to achieve the cost thresholds necessary to make them viable. Perhaps the greatest impediment to their development might be the lack of a readily available, low-cost fuel source. Natural gas has been in plentiful supply over the last decade; and at an attractive cost. If the availability of natural gas begins to tighten later this decade, however, its cost is sure to rise.

There are several other technologies that also could have ramifications for the industry. In particular, recent solar and wind developments have shown promise. The costs are coming down and reliability is improving. Both wind power and solar energy are currently finding their niches, but their economic development for most markets also requires low cost devices for electricity storage. When storage costs are coupled with power production costs from wind and solar cells, it appears that their role will be to supplement electricity from other sources—but it is unlikely that they will provide an economic means to bypass electric utilities.

Re-Electrification of the Utility Industry

In light of the changing environment, how will the electric power industry evolve? The industry is facing competitive pressures it has not seen for over 85 years. I believe the response will be to "re-electrify" the industry. A number of utilities are already in the process of doing this—restructuring into strategic or functional business units to improve responsiveness, to become more flexible to meet the challenges of the changing environment, and to reduce costs significantly.

It is generally accepted that in order to succeed in the emerging competitive environment a utility must be a low-cost producer in its region. To achieve or maintain that status companies are shedding layers of management, incorporating processes of continuous improvement, comparing operations to the best performances inside and outside the industry in a systematic manner (usually called "benchmarking").

Utilities have also come to recognize the importance of a high level of customer satisfaction. In response, they are striving to improve the value to their customers of the services delivered. Load will no longer be viewed as just a burden on the system, but a result of customer needs.

In meeting those needs, electric utilities will sell more than just electricity in the future. The goal will become "find out what your customer needs and provide it." Electric services will be unbundled for many customers, with utilities providing energy, and various levels of reliability of capacity and power quality. More importantly, electric utilities will provide equipment and facilities; not just those directly related to the delivery of electricity, but also for other energy needs.

The future will be no place for "business as usual."

More utilities will likely establish generating subsidiaries to compete with nonutility companies. And the competition for meeting future generating needs will be intense. I believe this will eventually lead toward the consolidation of many of these subsidiaries. Ultimately these generation companies will become large—licensing, building, and operating power plants globally—with assets in the many billions of dollars. I think it will ultimately be these companies that build the next generation of nuclear units.

Unlike other industries, I believe the transition in the electric utility industry will be somewhat more gradual—although I am certain that we will look back 10 years from now and marvel at the dramatic changes that have taken place.

Chapter Seven

CHANGING HOW ELECTRIC UTILITIES DO BUSINESS

Thomas Fanning

The years of the 1980s and the early 1990s have seen tremendous changes occurring within industrial America. Many industries with a long history of being highly regulated, with highly structured markets and minimal competition, were changed profoundly. The power of free-market forces and government deregulation has fundamentally transformed the markets in which these industries compete and, therefore, altered the combination of skills, talents, and philosophies necessary to compete successfully.

The electric utility industry is on the verge of just such a fundamental change. The Public Utility Regulatory Policies Act of 1978 provided the first forum for the emergence of a reregulated, more competitive utility industry. The passage of the Energy Policy Act of 1992 was the first step in what will probably be widespread re-regulation and perhaps the virtual elimination of franchise markets within the electric utility industry.

One of the major tenets of the Energy Policy Act of 1992 is to permit transmission access—that is, permit competing utilities to make available their transmission systems to wholesale transactions from one utility to another. Specifically prohibited from the Act were retail access transactions—that is, one utility selling across another utility's lines to the ultimate purchaser of energy, such as a large industrial consumer. While this legislation specifically prohibited retail access transactions, both the market and individual states have already started to accelerate the pace of

Thomas Fanning is Chief Financial Officer for Mississippi Power Company change, which will ultimately result in widespread retail access by probably the mid to late 1990s.

As a result, the model for success in the electric utility industry must change dramatically. With highly structured markets and regulated environment, the focus of the utility was to generate electricity in the most reliable manner possible and to build up the capacity of the industry in order to meet forecasted market demand. In the future, those skills will still be valued and, in fact, required in order to compete successfully. But the new model of success will place increasing importance on the skills of finance and marketing.

Utilities will be forced to recognize that their product is a commodity, and the most fearsome competitors in commodity industries are low-cost producers. Utilities will be rewarded for differentiating their product by pricing it to meet the needs of segmented markets and surrounding it with value-added services offered to an increasingly demanding customer base. Finally, throughout its organization a utility must inculcate the talent of finance—achieving an optimal balance of risk and return, in order to provide maximum value to the utility's owners.

The competitive pressures brought to bear on the industry will create a tremendous battle in the marketplace. A fistfight is a useful analogy to illustrate the stages of change which utilities will have to undergo in order to succeed in this new environment. In a fistfight, events generally happen quickly and unexpectedly, both competitors get battered, and there are winners and losers, but the definitions will only be relative to the combatants involved. Nobody really wants to get into a fistfight, but if you must, there are three factors you would like to be able to control or influence to maximize your chances of success.

First, *get ready*—pick the time and the place for the fight. Prepare for the fight so that when the fight breaks out you will be in peak physical condition. At the same time, try to time the fight so that the opponent is at his weakest—preferably, just as he was coming out of surgery! For example, in the electric utility industry this means implementing internal strategies such as cost control programs before you are forced to, and investing in external strategies such as an improved competitive intelligence capability.

The second key to success is *swing first and make it count.* Swinging first and making it count is at best a risky proposition. You don't want to swing too early in the fight because you may not be at your competitive best, but you certainly don't want to wait until your opponent has realized all the signals of the fight and has prepared himself to his utmost to win. In the electric utility business, swinging first is giving tremendous attention to developing and implementing quick-strike marketing attacks on the prime customers in the region.

The third fight tactic is to *sustain your competitive advantage.* If steps one and two have been accomplished effectively, your opponent should have been damaged, and you must move quickly to consolidate your advantage. In the electric utility industry, this will mean solidifying a gain in market share by continuing a focus on cost competitiveness and encouraging long-term retail power purchase agreements between the utility and its best customers. Further, business strategies must be put in place to demoralize your recently-defeated competitor and to discourage other potential competitors from coming into your markets.

As a winner you maximize the chances that other potential competitors will focus on other competitors and other markets which they feel may be an easier conquest. In addition, successful utilities will invite the proactive alliances offered by competitors who would rather be part of your team than to fight against you. Each of these three strategies—getting ready, striking first and sustaining your competitive advantage—form the basis for enhancing a utility's success in the new competitive environment. As the environment evolves, the transition from one strategy to another will dictate how a utility should orient its business planning and execution.

Measuring Success

Utilities must focus on a few critical internal factors, shown in Figure 1, which can be used as benchmarks for measuring success in the business.

Figure 1

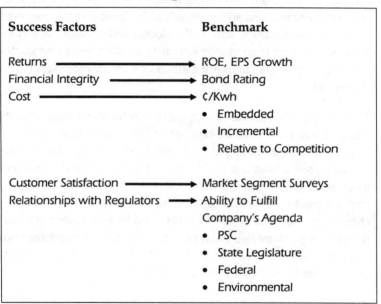

Success Factors	Benchmark
Returns ⟶	ROE, EPS Growth
Financial Integrity ⟶	Bond Rating
Cost ⟶	¢/Kwh
	• Embedded
	• Incremental
	• Relative to Competition
Customer Satisfaction ⟶	Market Segment Surveys
Relationships with Regulators ⟶	Ability to Fulfill
	Company's Agenda
	• PSC
	• State Legislature
	• Federal
	• Environmental

The first two factors, return and financial integrity, should be evaluated together as measures of risk and return. Optimizing the balance between risk and return will maximize the total returns afforded the firm's shareholders. For internal performance management, however, this concept of shareholder value may be measured by combining the positive aspects of achieving maximum return, as measured by return on equity, and maximizing financial integrity, which may be measured by using senior debt ratings. Utilities' emphasis on maximizing return on equity (ROE) is commonplace in the industry. Improved ROE over time leads to greater sustained growth in earnings per share, and therefore to regular, predictable and sustainable increases in dividends per share. Equally as important and often overlooked is financial integrity—the financial strength which a company draws on to permit it to withstand times of duress such as eroding economic conditions and increasing industry competition, and afford the company the flexibility to meet changing business conditions.

As suggested earlier, both combatants in a fistfight are likely to be battered. High levels of financial integrity going into the fight will help assure maximizing success coming out of the fight. The measures of risk and return must work in tandem. Companies should establish minimum requirements, not only on a corporate level, but also for divisions within the firm which have profit responsibility. As the risk evaluation of a company or division or market increases, so should its return requirement.

Further, absolute thresholds must be established. That is, a maximum level of risk tolerance (irrespective of returns) must be established as well as minimum levels of returns requirements (irrespective of risk). Figure 2 shows the conceptual relationship utilities should use in managing risk and returns in its business.

The third factor for benchmarking a utility's success is cost. Clearly an important, long-run indicator of the utility's ability to compete is its fully-loaded, embedded cost structure. However in a retail access environment, for periods of time, the major focus will be on incremental or marginal pricing. Therefore, attention must be given to minimizing the fixed and variable costs that are required to produce electricity. Further, it will be more important to focus not only on the cost characteristics internal to the utility, but also to understand those of your competitors. A critical success factor then will be assessing the value of energy to a utility's customers. Utilities will need to cut costs to a level where they can price to beat the competition, but within acceptable levels for its customers. A final important comment about cost is that, in the long run, every cost is variable.

The fourth benchmark that utilities should use to measure their competitive performance is customer satisfaction. Enhancing customer satisfaction will accomplish two things for utilities. First, es-

97

Figure 2

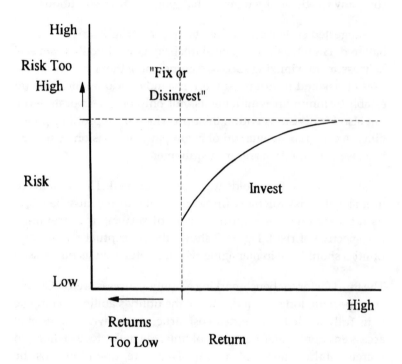

pecially for the franchise customers, primarily residential and small commercial classes, a broad base of political support is created which will be crucial in gaining support for the regulatory and legislative initiatives utilities will need to undertake as the competitive market emerges. Second, for a utility's most attractive customers, the large commercial and industrial classes, excellent customer satisfaction may allow a utility to price its product at margins equaling or even slightly exceeding its competitors and still keep the customer. Pursuing high levels of customer satisfaction will be manifested in many different strategies including:

highly segmented customer-focused energy consulting services, power quality enhancements, flexible pricing schemes, etc., that will be designed to create symbiotic relationships between the utility as a marketing entity and its customers.

The fifth internal benchmark of a utility's success is the quality of its relationships with its regulators. Even in a deregulated environment, utilities will more likely become reregulated, rather than unregulated. Therefore, there must be specific strategies with the state public service commissions, state legislatures, and federal regulators at FERC and the Securities and Exchange Commission. Federal legislative strategies must also be developed. Even potential regional regulation must be taken into account in developing a cohesive regulatory and legislative strategy that will ultimately support the company's strategic business objectives. Finally, in conjunction with enhancing relationships with our regulators, a utility must continue to pay attention to its corporate citizenship, with a special emphasis towards enhancing its environmental stewardship.

Two Other Success Factors

Left unsaid so far in evaluating a company's likelihood for competitive success are two fundamental issues.

Number one, a utility must continue to provide reliable service. However, the focus on the production side of the business should be the ability of the business to produce efficiently from a cost-effective market driven perspective. Clearly, if you are not able to produce the electricity in a cost-efficient manner so that you can sell it at a profit, the generation capability becomes a liability rather than an asset.

The second fundamental issue is likely the most important—developing a competitive employee culture for the future which emphasizes entrepreneurship and empowerment and which responds to a clearly communicated vision. Even more important than the vision, though, is building and believing in a tight core of immutable principles. At the most fundamental level, these principles provide the common basis upon which employees can act both internally and with customers. Only if this is achieved will utilities be able to respond effectively to a competitive, ever-changing marketplace. Corporate culture will underpin every other competitive strategy that the utility must undertake. Employees will drive the results.

Specific Strategies For Specific Stakeholders

A utility may be thought of as having four major stakeholders—customers, employees, shareholders, and external publics. The following is a summary of specific strategies for running an electric utility in the 21st century.

■ Customer Focus

"Seeking Value Through the Purchase of Energy,
Capacity, and Value-Added Services"

Utilities of the future will organize the company around its customer base, with the marketing organization emerging as the focal point of the company. In fact, as retail access erodes the historical concept of franchise customers, so will the geographic oriented organizations of utilities diminish. Overall, the strategy for the marketing and sales organization is one that will be designed to provide a reasonable return on and significant market share of potential customers in a variety of classes. Such an organization will also be able to purchase its electricity to serve these customers from the most economic source available—not necessarily its sister generating company.

Those segments still retaining some semblance of a franchise, primarily residential and small commercial customers, will be served differently than large commercial, industrial and wholesale customers. These markets will still be served through geographically distributed district offices. However, because of the renewed focus on the need to be a low-cost producer, there is likely to be significant pressure brought to bear on reducing the local town presence commonly found today in electric utilities. To be competitive, distribution services will reside in the marketing arm of the franchise market for electric utilities.

In rate strategy, the predominant effort will be to price electricity to these markets so that the utility is able to earn a reasonable return. In most regulatory jurisdictions today, commercial and industrial customers subsidize relatively lower rates to the residential class. The importance of retaining large industrial and commercial loads will necessitate a reallocation of cost to the residential class. If such reallocations are not politically possible, then the utility will be forced into significant cost cutting strategies in order to preserve attractive returns for its stockholders.

In the long-term, it may be that the residential and small commercial markets lose many of their franchise-like qualities. For example, municipalization could occur whereby neighborhoods or large groups of residential markets combine to form a single purchasing entity. For example, a small town which has a single dominating industrial facility may seek municipalization. Further, the fragmented buying power of individual residential customers may become much more powerful by creating alliances between themselves and a large industrial customer who has great market power.

Because there is a relative limit of rate increases that these customers are willing to bear, the most likely rate structure to evolve for residential and small commercial customers will be some form of a modified rate cap mechanism. In effect, term contracts at specified rates will become common between these customers and the utility.

Large commercial and industrial customers will prove to be the single largest battlefield in a retail access environment. In fact, unlike today's markets, the geographically oriented nature of these markets will evolve into account-based markets. For example, a utility will seek to enter into a contract with Wal Mart to serve its stores in a large region rather than a franchise territory at a fixed or indexed price for all of the customer's locations. The same logic may apply to large industrial customers who have facilities located in a different geographic areas. Price pressure to these most desirable customers will be fierce, and in the intermediate term, electricity will be priced at levels approaching the utility's variable cost structure. As a recurring theme, the resulting revenue reductions to the utilities will be so great that in order to maintain financial integrity and to provide sufficient growth, dividends, and earnings per share, significant cost cutting must be undertaken. Some pressure on cost cutting may be alleviated by passing on rate increases to other customers, but the likelihood of any significant relief will be minimal.

Term structures of contracts will become increasingly common and will resemble the purchased power agreements commonly found in the cogeneration and independent power markets. In fact, among all the classes, residential and small and large commercial, industrial, and wholesale, term structures of contracts will become a principal area of focus in matching capacity supply with the capacity requirements of the market. From the seller's standpoint, the utility, in order to lock up long-term load, will probably have to offer some price discounts. In short-term markets, utilities may be able to charge higher prices, because the permanence of that load becomes increasingly volatile as time increases.

Suppliers should expect a negatively sloped capacity yield curve, with short-term capacity sales being priced higher than long-term capacity sales. In fact, from a supplier's point-of-view, there is an interesting portfolio allocation problem. There will be a certain term structure and cost to the supply of its capacity, and on the marketing side, a certain portfolio allocation to the types of returns and term structures that it is able to create in the market. In the future, capacity and market portfolio management will prove to be an emerging sophisticated practice undertaken by successful utilities.

As a final issue, while low cost may prove to be the ultimate competitive advantage of utility companies, in certain instances utilities may be willing to pay a short-term premium in return for long-term cost flexibility. That is, they will value being able to create flexible cost structures that can move in unison with volatile markets and, therefore, stabilize and help preserve a floor to returns.

Market Segmentation And Customer Intelligence

In the future, because franchises will evaporate and customers are no longer geographically defined, understanding a customer's business will be key to winning, and keeping that customer while creating the maximum profit for the utility. Because there will be a much more competitive environment in which to seek out and retain these most attractive customers, competitive intelligence will expand to include customer intelligence and will play an increasingly important role in running utilities. Detailed information must be obtained for the customers' energy supply requirements, what kinds of term obligations they have on their products, and how energy fits into their production processes. The utility will be able to design its commodity product more efficiently and, hopefully, will find more uses for its application by displacing other less efficient sources of energy such as natural gas. Industrial marketing representatives must be able to help differentiate their commodity energy product by offering a full range of value-added services that will encourage the customer to contract for long-term capacity and energy.

Domestic And International Industrial Development

In the early days of the electric utility industry, the purpose of industrial development was to foster economic growth in geographic regions. While that is still an admirable objective, a second function will arise out of industrial development activities. Utilities must foster long-term, wide-spread relationships with valuable industrial and large commercial customers so that, even if the company does not succeed in attracting the plant location into its immediate geographic area, it may at least win the power sales contract to supply energy and capacity to those customers both domestically and world-wide.

Just such potential has been created with recent legislation enacted by Congress. With the Energy Policy Act of 1992, a new class of competitor has been formed called an exempt wholesale generator (EWG). This classification of supplier, when extended into an environment of retail access, may become potentially a very powerful competitor for energy supply markets. The EWG classification allows utilities to compete anywhere in the United States, as well as internationally. This ability, combined with alliances between equipment suppliers and large consumers of electricity, could create an international playing field for currently unrelated entities. For example, in return for using a certain type of equipment in building new generating capacity, a utility may enter into a reciprocal agreement to sell capacity and energy to an industrial facility in Ohio for ten years. Further, the utility may procure transformers from an international equipment supplier in return for that equipment supplier investing with the utility in Asia in certain energy ventures. The net result could be the development of currently unforeseen alliances between equipment suppliers, large industrial consumers of electricity, and large electricity suppliers.

Rates

In general, rates will evolve from being totally cost based to being primarily market driven. As suggested earlier, the evolution of cost-based rates for franchise customer markets such as residential and small commercial could result in a modified rate cap structure. This structure would assure a utility a base of revenue, and allow pricing for large commercial and industrial customers with great flexibility and varying term structure commitments. This structure will also protect the franchise customer markets from increasingly higher allocations of cost and insulate them from the volatility of the highly competitive large commercial and industrial markets.

An interesting evolution will be the widespread use of commodity derivatives. Such derivatives could include indexing, commodity swaps, and rate structures having structural elements commonly found in financial securities such as caps, collars, call options and varying combinations of floating and fixed rate components. An example of this could be a utility selling to an aluminum smelter. The output of the aluminum smelter will rise and fall based on the market for aluminum. The utility may enter into a long-term rate contract, the capacity price of which is indexed to the market for finished aluminum product. The utility would, on its own account, enter into a commodity swap agreement, that essentially would swap the cost inputs involved in making electricity with the commodity price for aluminum. The utility would provide to the customer an indexed obligation that allows the customer a better linkage between the streams of revenue and expense and which helps insulate the utility from wide variations in the floating capacity rate.

Consider another example. Certain customers may be willing to pay for their energy by relying on spot markets. For example, a consumer may have a certain view as to the future spot prices of coal. The utility could price the energy portion of the tariff to mimic 100 percent spot coal purchases. The utility would then be free to purchase a greater than normal percent of coal in the spot market by allocating its greater cost exposure to that customer through a 100 percent spot cost to their contract. Further, if the customer is particularly sensitive to natural gas prices, for example, the company may sell electricity that is generated by coal but which is indexed to natural gas. The utility would in turn hedge itself in derivative markets to natural gas or may pass that risk on to the coal supplier. Essentially the utility would buy coal from the coal supplier using natural gas price indexing, forcing the coal supplier to undertake the hedge. In general, the implication is that utilities will move further and further away from pricing based strictly on its cost inputs and price more closely with the cost inputs or product outputs of its customers.

From a rate structure standpoint, capacity purchases will have characteristics more like bonds in the nation's financial market. For example, there will likely be a term and a rate. Some of that rate may be fixed, some may be variable. There will be certain conditions under which the power purchaser may buy out of the contract (a "put" option), and there may be certain instances when the utility may itself be able to cancel the contract (a "call" option).

In fact, as suggested earlier, the marketing organization of the utility will be able to construct a portfolio optimization of cost inputs. This optimization would include purchases of capacity for resale and revenue inputs. Revenue inputs will be portfolios of franchise and term contracts to retail and wholesale customers.

Other features that are commonly seen in the financial markets will also apply not only to the rate structures of utilities but also to their major cost inputs, especially fuel. For example, in a variable rate capacity purchase agreement between a utility and an industrial, there may exist a cap, a floor or a collar. Some of the risks in managing these price structures may be passed along to the major cost inputs or they may be undertaken willingly by a utility in order to gain market share.

In summary, utilities of the future will need the flexibility to construct rates and put them in place quickly and efficiently on behalf of large commercial and wholesale customers without tremendous regulatory intervention on either a state or federal level. As change occurs, the ratemaking process will more closely resemble price setting in a competitive market with a reduced need for regulatory oversight. This issue will be addressed later in this chapter.

Value-added Services

In a retail access environment, in cases where utilities lose native load to an outside competitor, a utility has the worst of all worlds. The utility still retains the obligation to serve; to keep transmission lines maintained; and to maintain the distribution lines in good working order. So, it still has all the burdens of reliability and yet has a markedly reduced benefit from the margin earned from the sale of electricity. In order for utilities to make the best of this situation, they must be able to understand all of the costs and all of the value of transmission, distribution and other value-added services, including power quality and a variety of demand side options.

Information resource technologies will probably play a tremendous role in enhancing a utility's ability to deliver value-added services. For example, certain technologies exist today through which the utility may be able to tie into the information resources of a large industrial customer and receive real-time, on-line information about the industrial process. This connection would allow a utility to react instantly to changes in load or variations in power quality critical to the success of the industrial customer.

This interaction will also hold true for residential customers. Through technology, a utility will be able to deliver all of the services it currently provides, as well as energy efficient "smart houses," security systems, cable television, or even provide the highway for telecommunications. All of these services may be offered by utilities in combination for a lower price than through separate third-party arrangements. In retaining customers, it will be critical to display the importance of these value-added services—important first, to have them and second, to understand what they are worth to the customer and how most effectively to price them.

The first manifestation of how emerging technologies will change the way utilities interact with customers may arise in the customer accounting area. Customer billing systems, as we know them today, will be replaced by comprehensive customer information services. Not only will a utility track how much a customer consumes and bill appropriately, the operations area will troubleshoot more quickly and efficiently, and the marketing organization will be able to gain valuable customer service intelligence, as well as better understand customer usage patterns.

The Importance Of Customer Satisfaction

Customer satisfaction will be critical to the success of electric utilities in the future. However, the drivers of customer satisfaction will be different for different types of customers. It will be a part of customer intelligence efforts to understand what provides value to which customer and how best to package the firm's services to meet their needs optimally.

Critical to designing successful customer satisfaction strategies is determining exactly what a utility receives from having highly satisfied customers. First, in an area of retail access where power sales to large commercial and industrial customers are widespread and tremendously volatile, having high customer satisfaction may permit a utility to be able to negotiate or, at worst, bid for customer load. Having a dissatisfied customer may cause the customer to turn away from a utility to a competitor before the utility is even able to compete. Second, customer satisfaction may allow a utility to price its product equal to or marginally higher than a competitor because a customer perceives tremendous value in retaining and fostering the long-term relationship. Therefore, there may be a real competitive advantage that has tangible financial benefit to encouraging customer satisfaction through marginal pricing strategies. Finally, another major benefit of customer satisfaction is that it may provide the utility with a broad base of political support, especially from its franchise customers, which will help the utility in carrying out its regulatory and legislative agenda.

■ Employees

"Fewer, More Flexible, Better Compensated, Working in Flatter Organizations"

Staffing Levels

In response to cost cutting strategies, the utility industry over the next ten years will undergo significant reductions in staffing levels, perhaps as high as 20 percent to 25 percent. That's the easy part. A key measure of a utility's chances of success in a competitive environment will be, however, not only its ability to reduce staffing but its ability to attract and retain a truly competitive workforce that will have the skills and culture necessary to compete successfully. For example, even though a utility may target a manpower reduction of 20 percent, in order to achieve the optimal mix of talent at the lowest reasonable cost, the utility may need to reduce its current staff by 23 percent and then rehire back from outside the company, or even outside the industry for certain key individuals.

All staff reductions are gut-wrenching for a company. But a lot of hard, cathartic changes that companies have had to go through in order to achieve these right levels could be avoided if careful planning, coupled with assessments of skills and needs and effective retraining had occurred several years in advance. A crucial aspect of planning involves reengineering work processes and eliminating work that is not necessary to enhancing a company's ability to words, companies undergoing downsizing must also cut the work, not just the staff. A company should always remember that it is most practical and humane to be staffed at the absolute minimum. The most inhumane outcome is to terminate employees because of poor business planning.

There are clear lessons to be learned from people that have consolidated staffing—how they were able to enter the process, go through it, and then exit the process in the best manner possible. Companies should communicate with employees in a reasonable manner as often as significant events warrant, starting with outlining the changes that are currently impacting the industry. Throughout the change process, there must be a fine balance struck between overburdening employees with information and not telling them enough, which could let the grapevine and rumors destroy production throughout the workplace.

First, there needs to be a consistent message that is sent to employees, in a consistent format, so that the same message gets out to all functional areas of the organization in a timely manner. Second, a lot of advance planning needs to be done in order to minimize the absolute number of displaced employees as the reduced staffing targets are achieved. One clear way to do this is to start implementing staff reduction programs early, through early retirement and attrition, and filling vacant positions by adding back staff in the form of temporary or contract labor. Then, as significant displacements begin to occur, specific job training can be undertaken for long-term employees so that the displaced employees have a greater chance of transferring into an area which will have more permanent job requirements.

In summary, a company has certain obligations to employees with respect to staffing. First, as a part of its ongoing business planning process, companies must plan staffing levels carefully and initiate programs as early as possible to minimize job dislocations. Second, companies must communicate with employees early and then continue to do so throughout the change process. Companies should then commit to retraining and the use of temporary labor should then commit to retraining and the use of temporary labor and do as much as it can to find positions for long term employees. Finally, for displaced employees, companies must put in place humane outplacement and severance programs.

Organizational Issues

Utilities' organizational structures will become flatter, more flexible and their functional lines of responsibility will become more blurred. Along with these changes, the management of the company must become more streamlined with responsibility and decision-making pushed down to the lowest possible levels. Spans-of-control should become significantly broader, so that each subordinate in the corporate hierarchy acts independently or as a part of a self-directed work unit exercising a great amount of latitude in carrying out job responsibilities. This transfer of authority will result in management focusing more time on strategic planning, competitive intelligence, and a great deal of time communicating relentlessly with employees the vision and strategy of the organization.

Utilities need to be streamlined at the highest levels, as well. The idea of large management councils comprised of multiple executives trying to participate in regular meetings and running the company will be a thing of the past. Committees are excellent for input, but poor for decision making. Utility management should adopt the philosophy that their role is to lead and that many of the best decisions will be those that are delegated downward.

The most successful utilities of the future will have organizations built around hard profit center business lines. For example, a major organization may be a generating company which has profit responsibility not just cost responsibility. Another major organization will be built around those that market electricity. The third organization should be as small as it can be and contain all of the other corporate overhead and service functions. This organization, a generating company, a marketing company, and a small service company is designed around products and customers rather than functions.

The product of the generating company is the production of electric capacity and energy, the majority of which may be sold at a profit, at least in the near term, to the marketing organization under term contract structures. However, the generating organization may also sell outside of that framework in the spot market or through other long-term contracts if greater profit opportunities present themselves. The marketing organization would be free to purchase capacity and energy from anywhere in the region, including its own generating company. From a geographic standpoint, the generating company could be structured around already existing plants. With the Energy Policy Act of 1992, and the creation of the EWG class of competitor, however, the generating company could have capacity located anywhere in the domestic United States—even internationally.

At the highest levels, the marketing organization should be structured around customers. The marketing organization might contain the only remaining geographic characteristics, which would be designed around franchise customers and could contain all of the distribution functions of the local utility. This area would also contain the responsibility for state regulatory transactions, including managing the rate base of the utility. The non-geographic lines of the organization would be dedicated to the large commercial and industrial customers of the utility.

The third organization within the utility of the future, the service company, would probably be headed by the chief financial officer. The coupling of financial skills and business judgment, along with the marketing and production organizations, will be critical to ensure success. The optional alignment of production capacity and marketing is designed to maximize shareholder value.

Compensation Issues

Utility organizations of the future will have direct, hard profit responsibility, and the decision-making for compensating employees will be driven more by value in their job contribution than by some formula for job worth. There will be much more widespread deemphasis of base salaries and much greater use of incentive pay, profit sharing and gain sharing. In determining incentive pay opportunities, the success factors will be driven by relatively simple and clear standards of performance—for example, market share and profitability. A key aspect of simplifying and broadening compensation programs will be that they will be much more easily understood by employees throughout the ranks. Therefore, employee actions will be better aligned to contribute to the achievement of these goals. Finally, stock options and stock awards will play an increasingly important role in properly incentivizing employees. Greater ownership of the company by employees, particularly management, will encourage better alignment of key corporate strategies with value building results.

If the goal programs instituted by the utility are structured properly, there will be a reduced need for management to direct the activities of employees. In effect, many of the functions of employees in performing their jobs will become self-directed. As a result, a by-product of successful compensation programs is a reduction in the management required in the organization.

With the advent of certain accounting rules and with changing demographics of the work force, issues such as post-retirement benefit obligations by the company for medical and life insurance present tremendous future financial burdens for the company. In effect, companies will find that they may no longer be able to make that promise and at the same time ensure their long-term viability. Some of these pressures will be reduced by lower staffing levels, and federal health care initiatives may clearly impact the future. But it is likely that companies will be driven quickly towards defined contribution programs as opposed to defined benefit plans for post-retirement obligations.

Utility employees of the future will also see a heavier emphasis on cash compensation displacing current benefit programs currently offered. Other forms of soft compensation such as perks will continue to erode. Perks such as large offices, company cars, corporate aircraft, and higher grade office furniture arise in an environment where cash compensation is rather limited. Therefore, soft compensation becomes more and more important in achieving status and stature within the organization. The utilities of the future will see these perks of the past disappear and emphasize instead cash compensation in return for running the business just as well as it can be run, achieving maximum market share and profitability.

Another area of change for utilities is that they will become less inbred. In order to compete effectively in the marketplace, employees leaving one company for another will become more common, and the companies themselves will be leading head-hunting raids for other companies' best talents. This change will result in more attention being paid to retaining the top achievers of an organization.

In summary, even though there will be fewer employees working in flatter organizations, it is very likely that these employees will be better paid, especially those employees that are attractive in the marketplace and could move to another utility.

Implications For Unions

The major issue facing labor unions in the utility industry in the future will be the need to reduce or eliminate the distinction between covered and non-covered employees in terms of their roles in the company. The lines of communication that currently exist will, as in all other areas of the company, be streamlined significantly. Company management will deal more directly with staff level union employees. Union employees will undergo training not only to become better students of the business and understand the competitive environment facing the utility, but also to achieve a common culture emphasizing an entrepreneurial, flexible work force that can respond more quickly and effectively to changing business conditions. As a practical matter, important developments in the work environment facing union members will be the need to acquire multiple skills and a trend toward participation in compensation programs that are weighted significantly towards incentive-based compensation programs.

In order to be successful, the utility of the future must have its union employees look and act more like non-union employees, and the utility must be willing to treat them in the same manner. The real challenge will be in working through this evolving relationship with union leadership and determining what their role should be in the future. The ultimate trends will be towards incentive-based compensation in flat organizations that have significant union membership interaction with non-union management. In order to carry out those activities, union employees must be educated, not only to become students of the business to better understand the environment of the utility, but also to be molded into a common company culture.

Future Demographics and Work Force Diversity

Utilities in the future will continue to evolve such that their work force continues to reflect more and more the general population demographics of their service area. Simply put, women and minorities will make up a larger percentage of the utility workforce at all levels—entry, management and executive ranks.

A real key for utilities in competing in the future is that in order to compete effectively, they must attract the best and the brightest talent available. Utilities can no longer seek to grow all of their middle and executive management talent from within. Therefore, there will be a market premium for women and minorities at senior and executive management ranks. Further, no longer will the searches for such talent be geographically oriented. Utilities will pursue talent all over the United States.

Some utilities have embarked on international activities. Therefore, people having knowledge and experience with cultural diversity, both domestically and internationally, will be at a premium. Increasingly, premium skills for the future will include: multi-lingual skills, combined with marketing, production and financial expertise. The trend of emerging work force diversity and the need for a truly competitive employee group will force utilities away from a paternalistic, local, and regional orientation to a truly diverse work force across staff, management, and executive levels, with a decidedly national and international flavor.

Developing the Culture of the Future

Reorienting the work force of the utilities of the future will be a difficult task. As mentioned previously, as utilities determine the appropriate future staffing levels, there may be a temporary downsizing below targeted levels in order to refill back to targeted levels with certain key individuals from outside the company or outside the electric utility industry. As a result, there will be a tremendous need to restore the compact between the employees of the company and management. Further, for the company to assimilate a much broader diversity of an employee mix into a common company culture, the company must emphasize more and different training. The training will likely occur in two phases. For technical job-specific training, it will be an orientation away from national seminars, with a greater focus made on internal person-to-person training programs within the technical areas of the company. A large emphasis, however, will be spent on companies trying to achieve a common culture that creates an environment encouraging empowerment and entrepreneurship to flourish. Much of the training will be to assure adherence to this company culture, assimilating a common set of operating principles that will serve as guidelines for employee behavior in doing the business of the future. This culture and assimilation of philosophies will replace the bureaucratic policies, procedures and rules which exist today.

A manifestation of this emphasis on culture will be the emergence of company colleges. This permanent facility will bring together diverse cross-functional areas of the company, with an emphasis on broad based education—becoming better students of the utility's business—for union, professional and non-professional staff. There will also be emerging courses at electric utilities which currently probably are not commonly found. For example, they may include foreign language skills, international currency management, and international cultural understanding. There will probably also be course work designed to better integrate the business of the company with the personal and family interests of the employees. In short, the employees of the company must become members of a team, as opposed to players in a bureaucracy. In return, the company must show concern and respect for the personal and familial issues facing employees.

■ Shareholders

"A Renewed Emphasis On Creating Value"

Evaluating Risk and Return

The old belief held by electric utilities was generally that risk was bad. Plants were overbuilt and operating procedures were set in place to minimize risks. Future management will increasingly recognize that risk, adequately compensated, is good so long as the absolute risk tolerance of the firm is not exceeded.

Future electric utility employees will gain increasing recognition that every piece of the business has elements of risk and return. In order to foster profit responsibility in organizations, there has to be a growing recognition of the fact that each employee impacts the company's ability to earn a return. How the employee structures business activities has implications for the degree of risk borne by the company.

Ultimately, the focus of the businesses of electric utilities will be much more oriented towards increasing shareholder value, enhancing cash flow, and managing risk. For example, in financial analysis there will be different hurdle rates for different types of projects having different risk characteristics. There may emerge in place of levelized discount rates, a discounting scheme that reflects the variability of risk over time, as shown in Figure 3. This evolution will reflect the risk differences of projects having different cash flow characteristics over different time frames.

Every area of the business—production, marketing and others—will have employees skilled in financial and risk analysis. While there will be core groups of areas for financial support, it will be an evolving requirement for all employees to understand the financial business of the firm. Technical functional job specialists will become less desirable. General business talent that is technically competent will be the most sought after talent for utilities in the future.

Figure 3

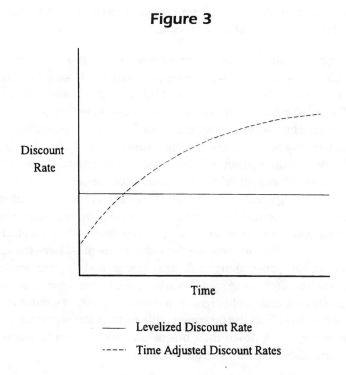

Discount
Rate

Time

―――― Levelized Discount Rate

‑‑‑‑ Time Adjusted Discount Rates

Management Information and Reporting Systems

Management information and reporting systems will be critical to a utility's success. Greater burdens will be placed upon employees to understand and respond to the needs of the marketplace, of customers and competitors' actions. Better planning must exist in order to anticipate future needs and threats.

There will be a period of time as utilities transition from their current state to the future and significant investments must be made in management information tools such as sophisticated customer information systems and management information and reporting systems. For example, the old electric utility customer billing systems will evolve into the future electric utility customer information system, whereby the utility will be able not only to determine what the customer's bill is but also to determine what his optimal load flows are; to determine certain demographic information about that customer, to perform real-time analysis; and to direct distribution and power quality work.

Management information reporting systems must also improve. In order for an empowered, entrepreneurial work force to make good decisions, the employees must have the information at hand that permits them to make good business decisions. They must be able to take into account the fully loaded cost and return implications, not only across functional lines but also over future time periods. Such information will be critically important, especially given an environment where the market for the capacity and energy of the utility will be much more volatile and streams of future revenue can no longer be assured. Decisions to add large amounts of fixed costs will have to be scrutinized much more carefully. Therefore, the frontline employees of the future must have the appropriate decision-making tools to aid them, and the intelligence must be built into these systems which sends consistent and appropriate cost and profit signals to employees. The executives of the future must likewise be armed with information reporting systems which break down their businesses, not only on functional lines, but also on customer-directed lines.

As in other organizations, the generation company and the marketing company must have hard profit responsibility. The generation business must be empowered with an ability to make a profit and create a transfer price for capacity and energy between the generating company and the marketing company. Corporate services must also undertake market-based pricing for their services, which will permit other company profit centers to elect to choose their service or to go outside for support. The internal corporate support systems that are truly efficient from a market standpoint will continue to exist within the company. Those general and administrative support systems that are cost-inefficient will be priced out of existence. Otherwise, the support systems within the company will never have to stand up to the true test of market cost, and they may balloon into the bureaucracies, a condition which afflicts many utilities today.

Competitive Cost Strategies and Resource Allocation

As mentioned previously, utilities will compete for market share primarily on the basis of price. As price becomes the dominant factor, the lower a utility's cost, the more able it will be to compete successfully and generate reasonable profits. As a result, in order to enhance their chances for success, utilities of the future will have to implement efficient allocation processes for capital and operations and maintenance projects.

The budgeting process of the future utility will work differently than current practice. First, utilities must have in place a firm corporate strategic plan that has as its guts hard tactical strategies which will translate the corporate strategy into real business results. In order to achieve the desired business results, a financial plan must be derived which balances business objectives with the financial objectives and constraints of the company. The ultimate financial objective of the financial plan will be value creation through stock price maximization. The financial planning process will target sustainable levels of spending for capital and operations and maintenance projects. The capital allocation process will occur at levels in the organization that are close to the actual areas of spending in each functional organization. All of the spending initiatives of capital and operations and maintenance (O&M) expenses of the company should be identified in a line-item format and presented to this cross-functional group. The group, in a very tedious process, will identify, within minimum thresholds, capital and O&M projects that will form a core group of spending strategies. There will then arise a list of contingent capital and O&M expense initiatives that will be ranked according to their strategic priority for the firm.

All of these projects will be considered discretionary. Within this list of projects, there will be two types of budgets for these spending initiatives—one that will be approved and funded, and a second that will be approved but unfunded. This list of discretionary projects will then be managed on an ongoing basis by this cross-functional group of employees who will add, delete and reprioritize projects as circumstances change. Top level management will interact with this group to establish the strategic priorities of the company and to approve the financial constraints, the risk and return guidelines, that the company is willing to undertake.

Reregulated Earnings Mechanisms
In order to be successful in the future environment, utilities must secure earnings mechanisms that are significantly different from what exists today. The trend will be towards market-based regulation which provides price protection to the political constituents of the public service commission and which also allows utilities to meet the market for the largest, most attractive loads in their service area. For example, utilities may pursue a modified price cap or performance-based rate setting mechanism for residential and small commercial customers which caps or ameliorates rate increases over time. Certain protection must be afforded utilities to account for natural disasters, such as hurricanes, and for mandated federal legislative initiatives, such as significant tax increases. By the same token, commissions would then, having protected their constituents, allow utilities to price their electricity and other services in whatever manner they choose to pursue large commercial and industrial customers. As a practical matter, state regulatory bodies will allow the market to regulate electricity prices for the largest customers.

In periods when regions have excess capacity, the pricing pressures brought to bear on utilities in order to retain market share will be extreme. The actions undertaken by utilities, given rate cap protection in certain areas of its business, will be to send the correct signals to the utility. That is, allow the utility to keep its market share by dropping prices to attractive customers, but not allow captive or franchise customers to be overwhelmed with the resulting need for rate increases. Utilities themselves will have incentives to undertake comprehensive, cost-cutting programs that will allow them to meet the market and still protect customers that have minimal market power.

In the capacity expansion process, electric utilities are already facing the future. That is, multi-source capacity additions from independent power producers, term power sales contracts from other utilities, as well as the emergence of demand side options now compete with a utility's own generation expansion alternatives. It is clear that demand side options will continue to be an area of increasing focus, especially considering an emerging interest in the cost of environmental externalities and the heightened environmental awareness in America today.

As a result, utilities will be forced to undergo comprehensive integrated resource planning hearings with their state commissions. In addition, regional regulation will become increasingly important as utilities become less and less geographically constrained and protected. On the federal level, with the advent of retail access, the market will more and more be the ultimate arbiter in setting prices, and ultimately profits, for utilities who are responding to cost signals in a competitive marketplace. Wholesale transactions regulated currently on a federal level will become almost exclusively market priced, and the need for federal rate regulation will diminish.

Corporate Financial Issues—Capital Structure

A common misunderstanding in the utility industry today is that in order to compete with independent power producers, utilities will have to leverage their own capital structures to obtain overall costs of capital approaching those found in highly leveraged IPP projects. A major reason for the difference in capitalization lies in the fundamentally different approaches to structuring risk taken by the two industries. In fact, IPPs are able to use significant amounts of leverage only because they have significant credit support inherent in a power purchase agreement from a utility. They therefore rely largely on the utility's balance sheet for credit support.

Utilities do not have the same long-term credit worthy contracts as their revenue sources. First, they rely on a franchise granted with an obligation to serve residential and commercial customers and only sporadically enter into long-term contracts with certain industrial customers. In addition, independent power producers shift significant amounts of risks through fuel procurement con-

121

tracts, turnkey engineering procurement and construction contracts, and operations and maintenance contracts with third parties with performance guarantees. Utilities, on the other hand, generally enter into cost plus contracts with construction firms, and generally operate the plants themselves on a similar basis.

The form of capital used by independent power producers, thin layers of equity and significant amounts of project finance debt, are more expensive than a utility's components of capital. The internal rate of return on after-tax cash requirements of independent power producers is more expensive than the returns required under a traditional equity investor's capital structure for a public utility. The reason, of course, is that the thin equity capitalization structure in an IPP project is inherently riskier to equity investors.

As a final note, the risk of the project finance debt is significantly greater than what is typically seen in traditional utility financings. Independent power producers typically rely upon debt having a term between 15-18 years and average lives in the 11-12 year range. Utilities rely predominantly on 30-year bullet maturity debt, having a single principal payment in the final year of maturity, resulting in a significantly extended average life. Moreover, the terms and conditions underlying project finance debt are significantly more onerous than those typically found in the utility's bond indenture. For all of these reasons, until there is major, widespread industry restructuring, electric utilities will probably tend towards retaining many of the same capitalization characteristics that are currently in existence today. In fact, if there is an emerging trend, it will be that utilities will become more focused on increasing equity in their capitalization structures. Because of tremendously increasing business risks and, as a result, more volatile earnings, utilities will be forced by investor demands to decrease the amount of leverage and increase the amount of equity in their capital structures. While the name of the game in an environment of retail access is cost control, introducing more risks internally to the company will only serve to compound the risk that it faces externally in the market and therefore impair the value enhancing balance of risk and return for the company.

Electric utilities should target their financial integrity measures so that they achieve credit quality statistics to achieve bond ratings ranging from A+ to AA-. With those financial structure statistics set as a target, the company should then modify its internal cost characteristics in order to achieve the optimal cost competitive position.

Dividend Policy — Because utilities will be facing increasing volatility in business risks, dividend policy is likely to change. It is likely two distinct groups will emerge with respect to dividend policy in the future. First, some utilities, that elect to stay in the core electric utility business and derive all of their earnings out of production and sale of electricity in the traditional sense, may find that earnings growth is harder and harder to achieve because of the price and resultant profit pressures being seen in the marketplace. As a result, dividend payout ratios for these companies will likely rise and remain in the 85-95 percent range.

The second group of utilities will come to the conclusion that, in order to achieve maximum growth, they will build business lines outside of generating and marketing power in the traditional markets. They will then expand their businesses into higher growth areas such as international electric utility businesses and other related non-core businesses. In search of higher growth, these companies will probably reduce their dividend payout ratios, depending on the degree to which they devote capital to these other non-core businesses. It is not unreasonable to expect utilities with significant investments in non-core businesses or electric utility businesses outside the traditional sense, will see payout ratios in the sub-70 percent range.

Another trend that may occur in dividend policy practiced by utilities will be a general trend away from setting dividends per share in light of expected earnings per share which are regular, predictable and sustainable. Clearly, this has been a sound strategy for creating a dividend policy. However, in an increasingly volatile business situation, utilities will no longer be able to count on the characteristics of regular, predictable and sustainable growth in earnings. Therefore, in giving recognition to the increased volatility in their business, utilities will be forced to consider other types of dividends such as special dividends and stock dividends. Also, companies will be much more willing to adjust their dividend payout targets in response to changing business conditions. In short, utilities will be forced to become a lot more creative in determining ways to compensate stockholders.

The Emerging Importance of Value Creation — In the past, utilities, recognizing their almost totally regulated environment, were especially focused on regulated concepts such as book returns. They established goals and measurements that reflected this environment. However, in the future, utilities will start to run their businesses much more like independent power producers and the rest of industrial America. They will rely less on book concepts and focus more and more on cash value concepts. In addition, because of largely deregulated markets, utilities will no longer be able to count with great assurance on significant deferred regulatory assets being recovered in the future.

Concepts of book return on equity (ROE) will become less and less important to stockholders and in response, utilities will focus on shareholder value as the driving force in determining corporate financial strategy. Corporate performance standards will evolve from ROE to measures like relative stock price performance with its competitors, relative market-to-book ratios and price earnings ratios.

Investor Relations and Changing Stockholder Groups — Future utility executives will have to deal with not only a changing business, but with a changing ownership of their business. Utilities of the future will cease to be traditional "low Beta" investments, both having low volatility of earnings and low risk characteristics. Ownership will drift away from largely individuals and conservative mutual funds and more and more be looked upon as riskier securities that have more volatile earnings statistics. As a result, utilities will have to contend with more aggressive owners, largely sophisticated institutional investors seeking more from their investment than receiving dividends for their retirement days.

As a result, it will be critical for utilities to increase their investor relations efforts, first, to communicate with these new ownership groups and second, to communicate the strategies of the company and how the company is responding to a changing marketplace. It is clear that during times of significant change, the need to communicate increases exponentially. As utilities move from their traditionally regulated environment to an increasingly unregulated competitive environment, utilities must consider specific investor relations strategies as a major cornerstone to their corporate finance strategies.

Another factor that must be taken into account and managed by utility executives will be a consolidation of companies as change evolves within the industry. Cost pressures will drive utilities to combine with each other, not only for efficiency purposes but also out of self-defense. Further consolidations will be prompted by different philosophical approaches to responding to competition. For example, some utilities will decide that they would rather not compete in the generating industry. Therefore, they may sell off significant portions of utility assets, retaining instead the marketing company concept. They may focus on buying their capacity from several different sources, selling to what will remain of franchise territories, and opportunistically attacking large commercial and industrial markets. As a result, not only will there be a consolidation of common equity in the utility market of the future, there will also be a changing of hands of significant portions of assets in the utility industry.

Liability Management — Liability management is a science that has evolved slowly in the electric utility industry, but one which will assume greater importance in a competitive marketplace. Utilities will recognize that within their capital structure they will be able to rethink the financings of the past (which have traditionally been fixed rate, long-term bonds and perpetual fixed rate preferred stock) and reevaluate ways to treat the balance sheet as a profit center.

Utilities will think of themselves more and more as companies that have as assets cash flow streams from major franchise customers and large commercial and industrial customers. As liabilities, utilities have cash flow requirements necessary to support the company's assets. Utilities will be able to model the streams of asset cash flow, as well as liability cash flow, and effectively perform a type of duration analysis designed to optimize the risk and return relationship within the firm. As a result, an asset/liability portfolio theory will emerge which will indicate that each utility has a measurable risk appetite that will be used to structure the capital in its balance sheet. Measuring the appetite for risk in the balance sheet and the expected returns that a utility must experience in order to be compensated for undertaking risks on its balance sheet will be of great importance to utility financial officers and will result in added value to the utility's shareholders. The manifestation of this strategy will be to optimize the term structure of the portfolio of debt and preferred stock.

The nation's financial markets will respond to an increasingly competitive environment by providing more creative corporate financial structures which optimally raise capital within acceptable risk parameters. Examples of this in the debt markets include: the emergence of floating rate or index debt, a trend towards varying maturities as opposed to significantly relying upon 30-year debt structures with single bullet maturities, and an increasing awareness of the values within debt structures of call options, improvement fund and sinking fund requirements and maintenance and replacement requirements.

With regard to preferred stock, new products have been introduced. They include adjustable rate preferred and auction rate preferred stocks. As liability management becomes more commonplace, change in the philosophy of selling preferred stock will emerge. Utilities will recognize the benefit of leveraging their common equity ratios with cheaper perpetual preferred stock by selling a maximum amount of perpetual preferred stock. The use of alternatives to perpetual (sinking fund or variable rate preferred) will be treated more like debt alternatives in the companies' capital structures.

In summary, in a truly competitive environment, even though utilities will probably carry higher levels of equity in the capital structure, for the remaining piece of the capital structures, utilities will become increasingly competitive and creative in designing cost effective, money saving strategies. Critical to the strategies will be the utility's ability to model technically the risk in the company's cash flow.

Relationships With the Financial Community — Utilities have traditionally relied upon long-standing investment and commercial banking relationships for strategic financial advice and to execute financial transactions. Utilities, as well as members of the financial community, have cultivated these relationships, especially for strategic financial advice assignments. It has been a "people" business, driven by trusted personal relationships. Even for the execution of rather generic transactions, such as the sale of fixed rate first mortgage bonds, the old line utilities have awarded the underwriting business to these same relationships and negotiated the pricing. The utilities of the future will likely continue to have important investment banking relationships, especially for strategic financial advice. But for transactions of a generic nature, utilities will rely more and more on competitive bidding as a means to obtain the most inexpensive financings possible. The spectrum of bidders will likely be broadened. Negotiated business between utilities and commercial investment banks will be much more focused and will be directed towards transactions of a more strategic nature—for example, merger and acquisition activities or how the utility can respond to the new competitive marketplace. Of course, investment and commercial banks need to be paid, and the compensation for advice will take the form at being awarded the sole or lead position in a transaction, like a merger. For advisory assignments which do not evolve into a transaction, utilities will compensate the advisor by awarding negotiated transactions.

Likewise, the financial community should find this industry to be especially attractive as it undergoes change in the future. There will be premium compensation available to firms who understand the complex changes, and as a strategic advisor to the firms, are able to recommend strategies which preserve and maximize shareholder value.

Because the marketplace will become increasingly competitive, investment and commercial banks may force themselves to take sides in cultivating long-term relationships with different utilities. In effect, a utility will be less likely to share its innermost secrets and strategies with an investment bank if it knows that the investment bank is calling on a potential competitor. Further, from the investment banking and commercial banking standpoint, there will continue to be a blurring of the traditional roles that these financial entities have played. With the emergence of some of the commercial banks into traditional investment banking roles, they will become an increasingly important and powerful force in executing financial transactions. In order to attract significant deal flow, investment banks are likely to be forced to be willing to use their own capital, becoming in effect, merchant investment bankers.

Growth and Diversification — As mentioned previously, utilities will evolve into two types of entities. One group will remain solely in the traditional utility markets of generation, transmission and distribution of electricity. There will be another group of utilities which will believe that the competitive marketplace will limit future earnings per share growth and will rely more and more on achieving growth in other areas. In effect, the first group will believe that because the market is so competitive, they cannot afford to invest in riskier, non-core, non-traditional electric utility activities. The second group will conclude that because competition is so great in the traditional utility business, they cannot afford not to invest in potentially higher growth non-core activities.

The track record of utilities entering into "diversified" activities has been laden with losers. However, utilities have been most successful in entering into diversification strategies that are closely aligned to their businesses. A tremendously increasing market for electric utility diversification has been the international arena. The U. S. electric utility industry is one of the most advanced utility industries in the world and there is significant value-added potential in taking their expertise across national boundaries. It is common in the international marketplace to find government owned and controlled utilities. Privatization of these entities makes a lot of sense for reasons of increased efficiency, as well as to alleviate international capital constraints. Clearly, the early focus for utilities has been the ownership of generating assets. However, the trend will evolve to include the ownership of international marketing companies as well as energy service companies, especially as they may interrelate with large industrial concerns.

Electric utility expertise and dispatching capabilities for companies that have dispersed production facilities could be a key ability for certain industries to compete in the future. Therefore, what is typically seen as internal utility strengths will become strengths that have tremendous value to other industries. Utilities will be able to capitalize on this expertise by selling energy management and energy brokering services to other industries in the future. As we have seen in the past, seeking future growth does not assure that growth will occur. Utility strategists must bear an acute awareness that with the increased risk they will be undertaking in pursuing these strategies, they are responsible for obtaining higher incremental returns.

A real skill is knowing when to cut losses and exit a strategy. The culture of the past has been that admitting failure was an action taken only as a last result, if at all. Utility managements that expand into non-traditional utility businesses will find that the ability to admit failure and cut losses at the earliest possible stage will have a tremendous benefit in value. Exit strategies are as important as entry strategies. These utilities will likely find that their investors appreciate these strategies.

With entry into diversified businesses and international marketplaces, the talent base of utilities must also diversify. In fact, companies must be willing to introduce outsiders into their staff, management, and executive ranks, including introducing talent on an international scope. As utilities diversify their businesses, a key to success will be attracting diversity of talent and blending this increasingly diverse group of employees into a common entrepreneurial company culture that has a highly molded focus for business success.

■ External Publics

"Credibility, Cooperation, Concern"

Changing Regulation in the Future

A continuing theme for electric utilities in the 21st century will be the restructuring of the industry. This same restructuring will impact the industry's regulators. For example, in the Energy Policy Act of 1992, FERC was permitted to order transmission access and set in place guidelines under which transmission capacity would be provided, including the cost of such transmission capacity. Wholesale transactions of electricity continue to be regulated by FERC, primarily on a cost basis, but as market dominance disappears and transmission access is permitted, FERC may allow the market to price capacity transactions between wholesale providers.

The advent of retail access will accelerate this transition from cost-based regulation to market-based regulation. The circumstance of market dominance will become increasingly rare. In fact, the market will push the change at a much faster pace than will arise out of changing regulation. As a result, the future influence of FERC will gradually diminish, and the transactions for power between utilities and ultimate retail customers will create a market in which true competition will take the place of regulated competition.

State commissions likewise will also come under increasing pressure. With the advent of retail access, state utilities commissions will come under pressure to allow cheaper market-based pricing to large commercial and industrial customers and to some extent, allocate the lost revenue requirements over to the remaining franchise customers. State commissions, as a matter of survival, must join with utilities in devising rate structures that will permit protection of buyers of electricity who do not have market power because of their size and fragmentation and yet still allow utilities to compete for large commercial and industrial customers. Failing to do so will put the commission under tremendous financial pressure. First, franchise customers, residential and small commercial, are very powerful constituencies to whom state public utility commissioners must be responsive. Second, if they completely protect their franchise customers and they do not provide a mechanism for utilities competing in the retail access marketplace, then utilities will find themselves losing tremendously valuable load and being forced to spread the same fixed costs over a continually diminishing group of customers, thereby forcing price increases or tremendously weakening host utilities. The answer, as mentioned previously, may be to allow some sort of modified rate cap regulation to the customers who have limited market power, and on the other hand, allow utilities a great amount of pricing flexibility for large commercial and industrial customers.

Flexibility is a key to a utility's ability to compete. The time necessary to get the "competition" rates approved must be eliminated or at least greatly reduced. As with the FERC, state public service commissions will for a large part be giving up their influence in regulating utilities. One area where state regulation may increase is in integrated resource planning. State commissions will enter into a planning partnership with the utilities they regulate which will take into account all of the economic variables of the service territory to solve the generation needs of the state. Potential providers of capacity will include utility-provided generation, generation provided by third party contracts (including independent power producers), power purchases from other utilities, and the incorporation of capacity-reducing demand side management programs.

In the capacity planning process, state commissions will realize that the market for generating capacity will become more volatile. In fact, given retail access and the ability for utilities that may be outside the state jurisdiction to come and sell capacity to large consumers of electricity, a form of regional regulation may arise. The primary focus of the regional regulation will probably be to coordinate the resource planning requirements of different states. Clearly, the advent of regional regulation and its role in displacing, to some degree, both the role of FERC and individual state public utility commissions will be a tremendously difficult transaction for all regulatory bodies as well as utilities to go through.

Utility's Role in Shaping Legislation and Public Policy

Utilities must address the reality that the market is likely to accelerate the pace of change in the industry much more than the speed at which regulators change the industry. As a result, utilities must have enough vision to understand not only that their own businesses must change in response to a more competitive marketplace, but that utilities must begin to work with their regulatory bodies well in advance of the impending change. Thus, when the change comes, the utilities will have the best chance to compete successfully. In fact, utilities that succeed in having credible relationships with their regulators will be able to work to educate their regulators. They will have a significant role in creating for themselves the best regulatory environment possible which will clearly increase their chances for success in the competitive future.

This shift will be a difficult transition for utilities to make. The protected markets of the past have been in many respects an attractive environment for utilities. In the past, utilities have focused on ensuring that enough capacity was in place to serve customers reliably. Utilities were run with a production/engineering mentality. As with many regulated industries, this environment tended to foster the growth of large bureaucracies and tended to distract utility managements from undertaking corporate strategies which focused on profound cost competitiveness and market sensitivity.

During the transition period, some utilities will hang on to the protected markets and the heavily regulated environment as a defensive strategy. Other utilities will understand the driving changes that are present in the marketplace and move ahead of the change in terms of designing regulation. That strategy will provide for cost competitiveness and market sensitivity. These utilities will likely prove to be those that become the most successful.

Successful utilities will recognize that indeed there is a fistfight in the future. They must prepare now for that fight through innovative regulatory mechanisms, cost-cutting and market-driven strategies. Clearly, a tremendous tension is created. What has made utilities successful in the past could hurt them in the future. The transition period may be especially difficult and may encourage the wholesale change of executive management and, with them, the adversarial philosophies of the past. A utility must take the role of a partner in dealing with its regulatory bodies. This new cooperative role, with utilities being partners with state and federal and perhaps regional regulatory bodies, will serve the interest of both the regulators and the utilities.

In shaping the future regulatory environment, utilities will need to become involved in shaping legislation, not only on the state level, but also on the federal level. It may be that legislation will evolve slowly, and, as a result, the changes during the transition period will be inconsistent and incomplete. Successful utilities of the future will take action now because they realize that the ultimate arbiter of value is the market. The sooner utilities get to the ability to compete freely in a market and have flexible, market based pricing, the better off will be all stakeholders of electric utility services—customers, employees, shareholders, as well as external publics.

Environmental Commitment and Proactivity

A necessary trend emerging among corporate America is a profound awareness of environmental stewardship. As large consumers of natural resources, utilities are often criticized for their lack of environmental sensitivity. However, most utilities today have a much better track record than they are given credit for. In fact, utilities must work not only to improve the environment, but also to improve the public perception of their commitment to environmental quality.

Successful utilities will devote significant resources not only to comply with, but to exceed environmental standards. There will be a primary focus on research and development activities that will look to the future to find better ways to harness the energy resources of the earth and deliver that energy to utility customers.

Beyond good citizenship, successful utilities will find that proactive environmental stewardship is good business. Successful strategies for utilities in the future will include having multi-fuel firing capabilities at their generating plants. Not only can the utility manage the environmental impacts on the service area, but as environmental issues evolve and impact the cost and availability of fuels, the utility will be able to react more quickly and effectively than its competitors.

Corporate Citizenship and Community Activities

Utilities have long been leaders in the communities they serve. This role will come under increasing pressure in the future because every expenditure of the utility will be examined critically in order to reduce cost as much as possible. There are likely to be two groups of utilities that will emerge in this future competitive marketplace.

Some companies may argue that the utility's franchise no longer exists and they will withdraw to a large extent from their community support activities as a cost-saving measure so that they can be as competitive as possible in the marketplace. In effect, these utilities will transfer the community service and charitable activities to its stockholders. That is, stockholders, through their companies which are active in the community, actually have less cash available to be paid as dividends or be retained in the business, providing a basis for future growth. These utilities will say that rather than the utility making the decision about where and to what degree they invest in the communities they serve, management will withdraw and allow their shareholders to make those decisions. Utilities that withdraw to some extent from their corporate citizenship and community service activities will probably be those who see as their primary markets the large commercial and industrial customers and those who invest significantly in related but non-core businesses as a primary means of achieving future growth.

Other utilities will continue to recognize that community service and charitable activities are still a fundamental part of a successful business. As a business matter, however, whether a utility falls into the first group or the second may depend to some extent on the mix of its customers. For example, utilities that continue to rely to a great extent on the traditional electric utility business and largely depend upon its continuing franchise, will certainly fall into the second category. Public support and perception of excellent citizenship contributes tremendously to differentiation by the public of a commodity product.

Internal and External Issue Management
For utilities in the future, issue management will emerge as an increasingly important business function. Public relations and external communications groups within utilities will develop this expertise and become an integral part of the company's ability to implement its strategic business plan. As with any company that markets a commodity product, packaging becomes extremely important. The packaging of electric utilities will essentially be done by these issue managers. They understand the strategy of the company and future needs of the company's markets and are able to create media strategies to maximize its chances for success. These issue managers will become involved in shaping proposed legislation, positioning the company's proactive responses to emerging environmental issues, and maximizing utility's investment in its community service and its corporate citizenship programs in the community. During times of change, those who are able to best verbalize their strategy for the future and are committed to communicating it relentlessly will be those who will be positioned for greater success.

While issue managers clearly have an important role to play in external communications, the role they play in internal communications will be critical to a utility's success as well. As suggested earlier, utilities will be attracting a much broader, more diverse group of employees into its staff, management, and executive ranks. Achieving a common corporate culture, one that is empowered and entrepreneurial in spirit, must have a common vision for the future and be able to act on that vision in a consistent manner.

Technologies such as company-wide video communication networks may prove critical to a utility's success in getting its employees to act on the right information as quickly as possible. Clearly, for utilities in the future, it is not enough for executive management to develop the strategy of the company. The communication of corporate strategies must be driven down to the lowest levels of the organization as effectively and as often as possible. Internal issue managers will be critical to the success of getting this message out to those who are able to implement it.

The Evolution of Utility Industry Associations

In the old protected environment, the electric utility industry and its industry associations were somewhat of a club. The Edison Electric Institute (EEI) and the other regional organizations such as the Southeastern Electric Exchange were really organizations which facilitated personnel from different utilities coming together to discuss common problems and issues. In a competitive marketplace, utilities may be much less willing to discuss their candid feelings on business issues. Further, the social aspects of membership in such organizations will likely quickly erode as cost pressures mount on utilities.

One common manifestation of change within organizations like EEI may be a further fragmentation of political support for industry change. As with the Energy Policy Act of 1992, the membership of EEI, because of its diverse base of interest, may be less effective in representing the industry at large. In the past, the electric utility industry was able to think about most legislation in terms of an "us versus them" mentality. In a truly competitive marketplace, utilities may see potential legislative changes as "us versus us" and therefore will be much less willing to work with other utilities who have conflicting interests. As a result, utilities of the future will rely less upon industry organizations such as EEI and rely more and more on their own political constituency and lobbying efforts in order to shape future legislation.

Another organization that will be undergoing the pressures of change will be the Electric Power Research Institute (EPRI). It may be that certain research and development activities will be extremely valuable to those companies that are able to understand and implement those advances to the marketplace first. As a result, there will probably be emerging within utilities in the future, proprietary research and development organizations. Such utilities will withdraw to some degree from active support of EPRI.

Conclusion

There is an old saying that the best time to fix a roof is when the sun is out. Clearly, utilities that are able to recognize that, in fact, there are storm clouds on the horizon will make every effort and act on the need to change now. The changes that these utilities will go through will be difficult and painful, but they will certainly be less painful for those utilities that plan carefully and act first. Those utilities that have the vision now to begin to change will find that their chances for success in the future are greatly enhanced.

Chapter Eight

PROGRESSIVE CHOICE: THE CUSTOMER AS REGULATOR

Terrence L. Barnich, Philip R. O'Connor,
Craig M. Clausen

"Freedom's just another word for nothin' left to lose."[1]

Janis Joplin, 1971

"Freedom's just another word for somethin' more to choose."

Terry & Phil, 1993

The late, lamented blues singer from Port Arthur, Texas had it a bit wrong, as the recently liberated populations of Eastern Europe might attest. Freedom, the ability to exercise choice, personal, economic and political, may not be easy, but it is better than not having any choices at all. If any unifying theme characterizes human development in the past several centuries, it has been the struggle between the individual's drive for greater freedom and choice and the desire of some to deprive individuals of their freedom and choice on behalf of some vague notion of collective good. This basic struggle now envelopes the utility industry.

In its day, the vertically integrated "natural" monopoly utility—telephone, gas and electric—delivered new and wonderful choices to people. Consumers had new options available to replace the telegraph and the mails, coal and oil for furnaces, and town gas for

---

Terrence L. Barnich is a member of the Illinois Commerce Commission. Philip R. O'Connor is Managing Director of Palmer Bellevue and of Demand-Side Resources, divisions of Coopers & Lybrand. Craig M. Clausen is Senior Policy Advisor for the Illinois Commerce Commission

[1] From "Me & Bobby McGee" written by Kris Kristofferson, (New York, NY: Columbia Records, 1971).

lighting (which, in its turn, had offered an alternative to candles and whale oil lamps). The regulated utility monopoly endured over the years precisely because it offered choices and options in keeping with the drive toward greater freedom and the enhanced quality of life that freedom of choice brings.

The past two decades of developing competition in the telephone, natural gas and electric industries have been elaborately discussed elsewhere and require no further attention here.[2] Suffice it to say with respect to all three industries, the process is well underway for the disestablishment of the vertically integrated utility as the sole legitimate model for the delivery of these services. AT&T's divestiture of the Bell Telephone Companies; the passage of the Natural Gas Policy Act of 1978; the Federal Energy Regulatory Commission's Orders 436, 500 and 636; and enactment of the Energy Policy Act of 1992 all represent official recognition and confirmation of that basic process.

The argument within industry and regulatory circles is no longer whether there will be increased competition but how that increase should be managed, what role regulators should play and how transition costs can be smoothly and fairly apportioned. For regulators, the ultimate challenge will be to replace profit regulation

---

[2] *See*, for instance, J. Dasovich, W. Meyer, and V. A. Coe. *California's Electric Services Industry: Perspectives on the Past, Strategies for the Future*, (San Francisco, CA: California Public Utilities Commission, Division of Strategic Planning, February 1993).

This report presents an outstanding history and analysis of developments in the electric industry the past two decades. The report also served as the centerpiece for a series of *en banc* seminars held by the California Commission to consider the range of possibilities for the reformulation of regulation and restructuring of the electric industry. Our chapter here is based on two separate papers presented at the invitation of the Commission as the keynote presentations for the first two seminars. On April 22, 1993, Mr. Barnich presented a paper entitled "Challenges and Opportunities: California's Electric Services Industry" and on May 25, 1993, Dr. O'Connor offered his paper, "Progressive Choice: A Model for Consumer Choice in the Electric Power Industry."

with customer choice as the central theme of utility oversight and the measure by which regulatory action is judged.

Premises For Change—Progressive Choice (PC)[3]

The underlying premises of the Progressive Choice (PC) model are simple. Evaluating any particular feature of a practical PC program is straight-forward, assuming that faith is kept with the underlying theory. A key PC objective is to distill the essential elements from a regulatory system that has become mired in minutiae. Regulatory initiatives or utility proposals to accommodate change have been entangled in much of the same sort of hair splitting and juridical sophistry that has come to characterize much of the nation's court system.

■ **The current regulatory framework is out of sync with competitive realities in the electric market.**

➡ Competition in the wholesale generation sector has brought about the demise of the vertical monopoly as the sole legitimate model for the utility.[4] Other elements of the "natural" monopoly, such as transmission and distribution, may also prove vulnerable in light of technological change and global

---

[3] Progressive Choice (PC) attempts, among other things, not merely to usurp the use of the PC initials but to merge the values of the Personal Computer and Political Correctness. Progressive Choice is fundamentally information-based, relying on individual customer decisions, driven by access to timely, accurate information (through relatives and descendants of the Personal Computer) to achieve Politically Correct results of lower prices, more environmentally conscious energy production and usage, and the exaltation of individual choice.

[4] A report by Bechtel Power Corporation, Outlook for U.S. Power Markets, (San Francisco, CA, July 1993), indicates that an increasing percentage of base load/cycling generation plants is already currently being built by nonutility generators (NUGs). Furthermore, Bechtel forecasts that NUGs will meet half the nation's generation capacity demands in the next ten years. This prognostication is not out of line with other forecasts in the industry.

competitive economic forces which give customers increasing choices to leverage utility services.

➡ Conventional regulation has distorted the relationship between underlying costs and ultimate customer prices. The regulatory process, often with the acquiescence or connivance of utilities, has inflicted significant rigidities on pricing that conflict with the notion of flexibility in a competitive market. Distorted price signals flowing between consumers and utilities obstruct optimal efficiency in operation, investment and consumption decisions.

➡ Inconsistent regulatory attitudes about the role of competition produce a hit and miss approach to the rules of entry and exit by electric market competitors. Barriers to both entry and exit inhibit the normal playing out of competitive pressures in the market.[5]

➡ Equity holders and investors of utilities, as well as those of new electric industry competitors, can increasingly find regulation a risk factor rather than a risk mitigator.[6] Market forces, the utility commission's role in planning, the fragility of deferred revenue recovery items and mandates for particular resource acquisitions converge to produce a volatile mix of regulatory and market risk.

➡ The mismatch between the rules of the regulatory game and the realities of the market encourage many customers and existing utilities to develop regulatory exit strategies.[7,8] Like people going over the Berlin Wall, customers and utilities seek

---

[5] Alfred E. Kahn, "Telecommunications, Competitiveness and Economic Development—What Makes Us Competitive?" *Public Utilities Fortnightly*, (13 September 1990).

[6] Philip R. O'Connor, "Utility Regulation in Illinois: Uncertainty as a Regulatory Product," *Twenty Years of Energy Policy: Looking Forward Toward the Twenty-First Century (Proceedings of the Twentieth Annual Illinois Energy Conference)*, (Chicago, IL: The Energy Resources Center, University of Illinois at Chicago, 1992).

the freedoms they have heard exist on the other side. Regulators should not accept employment as border guards. Instead,
their job should be to make the system attractive enough that
customers will not seek to escape.

■ Global forces are reshaping the electric business just as they have other industries, regulated and unregulated.

The list of developments driving basic changes in the world economy is long and varied. Running through any such list, however,
is the theme of choice and the customization of services through
the use of amazing advances in the creation, communication and
manipulation of information—all at the fingertips of hundreds of
millions of ordinary people and businesses.[9] The collapse of the
destructive communist experiment has spread both the "American" culture and the market ideal far and wide. Now, as it become
the world's "fuel of choice," electricity will be seen in the same
terms as other services—one that must be provided competitively
and tailored to meet individual customer needs.[10] The globaliza-
tion of finance and the relatively uninhibited flow of money

---

[7] See, Edward J. Tirello, Jr., "Traveling Light," *Public Utilities Fortnightly*,
(1 July 1993).

[8] As the electric industry has matured and competition has intensified,
margins have narrowed and authorized and actual returns on equity
(ROEs) have declined. Domestic energy companies have responded by
seeking to diversify in order to seek out profitable un-regulated
ventures abroad. Rigidities in pricing and other terms of service, all
controlled by regulators through elaborate proceedings encourage both
buyers and sellers to seek contexts in which greater freedom and
flexibility can be exercised. As larger customers seek to escape the
imposition of cross subsidy responsibilities, their ability to relocate, shift
production or to self-generate all present competitive pressures on local
utilities to offer concessions of various types.

[9] B. Joseph Pine, II., *Mass Customization: The New Frontier in Business
Competition*, (Boston, MA: Harvard University Press, 1993).

[10] Peter F. Drucker, *Managing For The Future: The 1990s and Beyond*, (New
York, NY: Truman Talley Books, 1992).

around the planet means that electric industry financing needs and opportunities must be on a worldwide competitive footing.[11]

■ The utility regulatory system requires a fundamental overhaul because mere reform cannot lead to the full blossoming of competition.

Only genuine competition, rather than simulations of competition, can actually deliver the fullest measure of consumer benefits. Utility and regulator forecasting techniques cannot possibly predict the combination of efficiencies and innovations that will emerge from a competitive environment. Government regulators, especially, lack complete information about the markets they are regulating. Regulatory and utility planning models tend to be linear and relatively undynamic, unable to accommodate the entrepreneurial response to the complex of risks and rewards which are characteristic of more fully competitive industries. Regulatory proceedings seeking proof of the precise consequences of a movement toward competition are a futile exercise, asking questions that can be answered only by time and experience.[12] The posing of such questions will often be less a sincere effort at inquiry than an effort to constrain competition within narrow bounds. Use of the impossible-to-answer questions is the regulatory ploy of those seeking to limit action to incremental reform around the edges rather than carrying out fundamental (and sometimes radical) change. The fundamental change we envision, which forsakes the central role of profit regulation and relies instead on competition, is justified by the same faith in competition on which we operate elsewhere in the economy.

---

[11] Philip R. O'Connor and Wayne P. Olson, "Global Challenges in Energy and the Environment," (Chicago, IL: Palmer Bellevue Corp., October 1992).

[12] Charles Stalon, "Decision Making, Information Overload and the Pursuit of Legitimacy," *Proceedings of the 103rd Annual Convention of the NARUC*, (Washington, D.C.: National Association of Regulatory Utility Commissioners, 1992).

■ **A plan for fundamental change should take into account the nearly immutable patterns of change in regulated industries as they move toward competition.**[13]

Incremental change — Fundamental change in the electric industry need not be one of blood and iron. Change in regulated industries has proven to be incremental. The system does not change overnight, but bit by bit. However, market forces cause them to do so at ever accelerating speeds, leading to a new model, which then itself achieves a certain stability. Regulatory bodies are unequipped with gear shifts and are unable (or unwilling) to accommodate their pace to the market driven change and thus, all too often, end up acting as a drag on the procession.

Entropic change — ntropy begins to characterize the system with the entry of brand new players who take slices of the market, eschewing the costly and impossible effort to replicate the entire range of services provided by the existing utility. Ironically, among the most important new players are the few existing utilities who decide quickly that change is coming and alter their business strategies in order to meet the competitive challenge. These incumbents also create the case for overruling the objections of more recalcitrant incumbents.

Moving prices to cost — The new players force prices to move toward cost. The system of cross subsidies, which characterize regulated monopoly, becomes unsustainable. Importantly, the subsidies themselves help unravel the closed market because once the new entrants' products and services become available, the customers paying the subsidies actively look for alternatives whose prices do not include subsidies.

---

[13] *See*, Philip R. O'Connor and Gerald M. Keenan. "The Politics and Policy of Access to the Electric Utility Transmission System," *Public Utilities Fortnightly*, (7 July 1988), for a more complete discussion of these four themes in the transition of the electric industry.

Resistance to change — Finally, many utilities and regulators resist change in an ultimately failing cause. In the process, the regulators tend to reinforce the subsidy system which increasingly disadvantages the regulated firms by providing advantages to their new competitors, who are more free to meet customer needs. Resistance does not merely delay customer choice, it is costly for the incumbent utility and inhibits its ability to offer choice even when the regime of choice achieves hegemony. For the regulator, resistance to change ends up disrupting the realization of the very social or political goals for which the subsidies were originally created as the incumbent utility is increasingly unable to respond flexibly, if at all.

The Principles Of Progressive Choice

Just as there are four premises for offering Progressive Choice as the mechanism for basic change, there are four principles on which a regulatory format of PC in the electric business is based. All four focus on regulator-led enhancement of choices to provide "protection" for consumers or investors, not regulator-based denial of choices.[14]

■ Percolate The Benefits Of Competition

Recognizing that competitive forces are not equally distributed throughout the electric market, a Progressive Choice program should focus on percolating or flowing through competitive forces from competitive market segments to segments in which competition is limited. This principle recognizes that many customers, especially larger ones, have the ability to extract concessions from the local utility—from a variety of options, ranging from demand side management (DSM) and process changes to relocation and the installation of self-generation. This is not a reason to forestall

---

[14] See, Philip R. O'Connor, "The Protection of Core Customers: Enhancing Customer Choice," Presentation at the Annual Convention of the National Association of Utility Regulatory Commissioners (Los Angeles, CA, November 1992), for a thorough discussion of the problem of "protection" as a counterproductive mindset for utility regulation.

competitive inroads, but rather, it is a reason to encourage their reach to an increasingly wider customer base.

■ Auto-Pilot The Change

Regulatory micro-management should give way over time to competition. The process of change itself should be designed to operate nearly automatically, with minimal regulator involvement in the "progress" of the movement toward competition once the process has started.

■ Facilitate The Movement To A Competitive Market.

In order to mitigate utility resistance, as well as to address equity issues in the transition to PC, regulators need to focus attention on important transitional issues that may have significant financial implications for existing utilities, such as depreciation rates for sunk investment.[15]

■ Rely Upon New Information Technologies

Communication and information technologies, rapid advances in which have been expansively cultivated by several utilities, lie at the heart of the ability of customers and electric service providers to exercise choice and to tailor services for specialized needs. PC assumes that reasonably priced information technology will be available to permit most customers to receive and act on real time pricing information.

---

[15] With the advent of the technologically driven competitive environment in the telecommunications industry, the regulated companies were, in part because of uneconomic depreciation policies, carrying on their books assets that were grossly overvalued. Beginning in 1980 the FCC responded by altering depreciation methods for the regulated companies to more accurately reflect realistic and timely capital recovery. This included accelerated depreciation for "inside wiring," allowing companies to "expense" all "inside wiring" in the year it was incurred. Uniform System of Accounts, 85 F.C.C. at 818.

The Grand Caveat

Progressive Choice has a "non-principle": that it does not depend upon retail wheeling as an essential feature.

First, there is every reason to implement the choice standard without the delay inherent in a bitter and insufferably consuming debate over retail wheeling and the way in which it would be regulated (or "refereed").

Second, dispensing with retail wheeling for purposes of the PC discussion does not mean the issue goes away. Some will continue to believe retail wheeling is just over the horizon, while others believe it is some considerable distance away. No doubt the debate will proceed. That debate will either accelerate or become quieter as average costs and long run marginal costs begin to converge in more places around the country.

Third, recognizing that the retail wheeling debate will proceed, there is a certain discipline to be imposed on the rest of the discussion of choice by undertaking it without it being held hostage by the retail wheeling issue.

Finally, disconnecting the retail wheeling debate from the broader question may make it easier to consider a wider array of multiple structural models for the industry.[16]

The Operating Features Of Progressive Choice

PC does not seek to replace one rigid system with another, similarly rigid one. Rather, PC is intended to be malleable and subject

---

[16] See, for instance, Ashley C. Brown, and Terrence L. Barnich. "Transmission and Ratebase: A Match Not Made in Heaven," Public Utilities Fortnightly, (1 June 1991), for a discussion of the potential for open access of transmission which would result from the "de-ratebasing" of transmission assets. One obstacle to retail and wholesale wheeling may be that transmission pricing has not yet matured to accommodate a competitive environment, perhaps due to the inclusion of transmission assets as an undifferentiated item in retail utility rate bases.

to change.[17] As time goes on, regulators can refine the basic design to assure continued and improved access to choices, given that there is likely to be a continued mix of monopoly and competition. However, PC would, at the outset, embody eight overarching principles.

■ An "Osmotic" Core/Non-Core Market Segmentation

PC would cure the most significant flaw in efforts to establish a bright line between "core" and "non-core" markets. It has not been clear whether the distinction between customer groupings has been based on "protecting" those customers who have limited choices, or limiting the share of the customer base that actually has access to choices. Certainly, many so-called "core" natural gas and telecommunications customers could have found better prices and services in the market than they currently receive under the protection of regulation, if allowed to do so. Their right to exercise choices would probably attract more competitors into the market to serve them and cause their utility to seek the flexibility necessary to satisfy these customers.

Under PC, those who start out in the core category are able, of their own volition, to move to the non-core category without having to seek regulator or utility approval. This process might be thought of as an "osmotic" flow of customers from the core to the non-core market through a "permeable membrane", a membrane purely economic in nature rather than regulatory. The ability to move through the membrane to non-core status would be a function of an individual customer's own belief in his ability to function in the non-core, more fully competitive arena. Available technology and a customer's evaluation of the economics of moving would govern these

---

[17] "Progressive choicers" can take a lesson from Karl Marx here. His notion of "praxis" provides for activist theory rooted in the principle that theory must be constantly revised by experience and practice. To the extent that the theory seems a bit "off" from reality then the theory may need amendment to address new found facts.

choices, as well as the willingness to forego the traditional set of protections of "core" status.

This "permeable membrane" could include some regulatory barriers to moving back to core status such as re-entry fees. But core customers would no longer be hostages, prohibited by law or rule from changing their status.[18]

The PC core/non-core distinction would not be uni-dimensional, centering solely on the characteristics of the consumer (such as residential versus industrial). Rather, as in the classification of some telecommunications services, the PC core/non-core (competitive/non-competitive) distinction would be at least a two-dimensional matrix of customers and services.[19]

---

[18] This sequestering of customers by characteristics has been somewhat provocatively called "regulatory apartheid" by Peter Huber, et al. (P. Huber, M. Kellogg, J. Thorne. The Geodesic Network II: 1993 Report on Competition in the Telephone Industry, (Washington, D.C.: The Geodesic Co., 1993), p. 1.27).

[19] Innovations in classifying services as competitive (and thus, non-core) irrespective of the class of the customer using the service, have been employed for some time in the telecommunications field. Most conspicuous has been cellular telephone, which many jurisdictions simply have deregulated. PBX and Centrex services for small business customers are largely deregulated and Integrated Services Digital Network (ISDN), to the extent it is deployable, will follow suit. In mid 1993, Indiana Bell Telephone filed an alternative regulation plan called "Opportunity Indiana," which allocates services to various categories; competitive, discretionary and basic. In addition, rates for basic services for residential customers would be guaranteed to rise at a rate somewhat lower than general inflation.

The movement toward full competition within the local telephone exchange is well underway. The first articulation of a state regulatory strategy to accommodate this movement appears in Terrence L. Barnich, Craig M. Clausen, and Calvin S. Monson. "Telecommunications Free Trade Zones: Crafting a Model for Local Exchange Competition," (Springfield, IL: Illinois Commerce Commission, January, 1992). On August 3, 1993, the Federal Communications Commission moved another step closer to completely opening the access portion of the local market through its switches access interconnection order (FCC Order 91-141).

■ Unbundled Services at Negotiated Prices

With some customers having the increasing ability to extract concessions from the local utility, the relationship between the non-
core customer and the utility should become characterized by
flexibility and negotiation. Non-core customers and all energy
service providers (including the utility) should be permitted to
negotiate the prices and terms for all services. This negotiating
process will lead to the unbundling of current services and the
offering of new ones. Services which start out as bundled and core
can be unbundled and offered competitively to some customers
while continuing to be offered as bundled core services to others.

In a competitive market, the idea of unfairly discriminatory prices
should be considered only in the narrowest of terms. Mere differences in price among similarly situated customers, even large differences, should not form the basis for intervention. Only where
differences are based on invidious and genuinely unacceptable
reasons (such as those addressed in civil rights laws) should government intervene.[20]

---

[20] *See,* Phillip Areeda and Donald Turner, "Predatory Pricing and Related
Practices Under Section 2 of the Sherman Act," *Harvard Law Review.*
Volume 88: pp. 697-733 (1975). Predatory pricing, wherein a supplier
sets prices below his actual cost in an effort to run his competitors out
of business and recoup his losses by imposing monopoly prices later
on, is a basis for anti-trust law and a traditional touchstone for unfair
trade practice allegations. However, this concern results in turning a
blind eye toward the welfare benefits that flow from competition's
rigorous discipline to move prices downward. Confusing price and
policy change in a competitive market for monopoly behavior is a
prescription for higher prices and lower service quality over the long
run. *See,* Robert H. Bork, *The Antitrust Paradox: A Policy At War With
Itself,* (New York, NY: Basic Books, 1978).

Alfred Kahn once commented that "[o]ne of the most damning
condemnations of motor carrier regulation was the demonstration that
of all the motor carrier pricing decisions made by the ICC during one
year, 95% involved complaints that the prices were set too low and only
5% the setting of ceilings." Thus Kahn shows empirically that traditional
"protect the consumer" regulation sets the whole public policy basis of
competition on its head.

Under PC, the initial group of non-core customers would be identified by their ability to negotiate with the utility. Size, demand
characteristics or traditional class grouping would not necessarily
be the defining elements. More important would be the characteristics which would indicate that choice already was or soon
could be an important part of the relationship between the utility
and the customer. Customers who can easily self-generate, switch
fuels, shift production to other locations or potential customers
who can decline to come into the market area all have bargaining
power. There would be a premium on creating an initial group of
customers which would begin to define a different relationship between the utility and its customers. This initial process of classification could be made complicated if regulators, utilities and
intervenors choose to make it so by requiring enormous amounts
of analysis to determine the membership of the first non-core
group. The criteria should be simple and straight-forward. In addition, the first couple of years of membership in the non-core
group could be on a trial basis as a way of encouraging customers
to volunteer for non-core status at the beginning of PC.

■ Real-Time Pricing

Currently, most customers have little sense that electricity costs
more or less to make depending on when it is produced. Regulated
prices obscure this fact. Even larger industrial customers on time-
of-use tariffs tend to see only gross price/cost relationships in their
billings. Average cost pricing just does not move pricing signals
back and forth between customers and the utility quickly or accurately enough for the needs of a modern, competitive and information oriented market place. This lack of information is a key cause
of the poor load factors which characterize many utility systems.
Poor pricing undercuts the implementation of cost-effective, sustainable DSM. One effective way to begin breaking through this
barrier to customer choice is to make real-time pricing available
across all customer groupings—at the election of the customer.

Micro-electronics and inexpensive methods of communication can
enable customers to control their usage and to shift load, automat-

ically or with little direct action, in reaction to different price levels. It is by no means essential that customers have absolutely precise production cost information as long as they know the price they will be charged at any specific time. A pyramided price scheme with seven differentiated levels for each day, would be a dramatic improvement over the single price now applied to most customers or the two or three prices larger customers now might see in the course of a 24-hour period.[21] If electric utilities are reluctant to make the information infrastructure available for real-time pricing, local telephone and cable TV companies as well as Radio Shack will probably be interested in doing so.[22]

Real-time pricing can also be used to move core customers into the use of non-core services and eventual passage into complete non-core status. Core customers, whose prices may be otherwise under a tandem pricing plan (described below) could opt for real-time pricing as a non-core service.

Real-time pricing could have major environmental benefits, under the sorts of smog precursor (emissions) trading schemes that have been developed in southern California by the South Coast Air Quality Management District (SCAQMD) and in the Chicago area by the Illinois Environmental Protection Agency (IEPA). The

---

[21] Already, important real-time pricing experiments have been conducted or are ongoing around the country, including ones at Niagara Mohawk Power Corporation, Georgia Power Company, Consolidated Edison Company, Entergy Corporation, American Electric Power Company (AEP), Pacific Gas & Electric Company and at Southern California Edison Company. All of these real time pricing programs have been strictly experimental, limited in scope, directed at a variety of customer groupings (including residential in the case of Entergy and AEP) and have produced mixed results. Taken together, however, they are harbingers of things to come. Technology is rapidly moving to allow customers to inexpensively acquire current pricing information, alter consumption and to have that change measured in real time.

[22] Even now projects such as the venture with First Pacific Network and Entergy are under way to bring fiber optic electronics to the home using the electric utility rights of way to provide "smart" energy management for Entergy's residential customers.

internalization of environmental costs through specific trading mechanisms might well be reflected in real-time pricing of electric power since smog related emissions' effects on the local environment are so time specific. Movement to an aggressive real-time pricing program can be accompanied by aggressive marketing of associated electronics and DSM services carried out under a PC regime of competitive, unregulated prices.

■ Tandem Pricing[23]

Price cap regulation is intended as a way of weaning traditional regulation from its obsession with profit and returning regulation to its roots, eliciting fair prices for desired service.[24]

---

[23] Tandem pricing is partially inspired by the concept of "leveraged pricing" first developed by Dr. J. Cale Case of Palmer Bellevue Corporation. Leveraged pricing was first advocated for application to pricing of core telephone services for residential customers, linking the pricing of individual residential services to unbundled service offering prices in the competitive, non-core market, where the services have similar underlying costs. Tandem pricing, while perfectly capable of linking prices on a service-to-service basis, is more centered on accommodating the linking of baskets of services with one another, accepting some greater disparity in the underlying cost relationships. See, J. Cale Case, "Leveraged Pricing: A Better Alternative For Telecommunication Regulation," Proceedings of the Sixth NARUC Biennial Regulatory Information Conference. Volume III: Telecommunications, Water and Transportation Papers, ed. David W. Wirick, (Columbus, OH: The National Regulatory Research Institute, 1988).

[24] Thomas K. McCraw in his book, *Prophets of Regulation*, (Cambridge, MA: The Belknap Press of Harvard University Press, 1984) shows that utility regulation did not have its roots in complicated profit regulation. It was intended to focus on assuring the maintenance of prices which were fair in relationship to the service being provided. The departure from this standard and the gradual adoption of rate-of-return regulation predicated on the regulation of profit on investment in property grew up in response to court decisions around the turn of the century. Utility regulation has often been the effort to reconcile financial and economic theory and practice with notions generated in the courthouse.

Price caps, based on initial just and reasonable rate levels are set and then indexed to an inflation measure, less a defined productivity factor, thus creating incentives for cost control.

While price caps represent a significant advance over rate of return regulation, it still represents an effort to simulate market forces rather than injecting a significant dose of direct market medicine.[25] A more direct way would be tandem pricing, in which price caps would be based upon an index measuring prices in the non-core market. Therefore, price change developments in the competitive market would move prices in the core markets as well. Rather than requiring regulators to choose an appropriate productivity factor as a discount to the inflation index, tandem pricing lets the competitive market select the productivity factor. Tandem pricing can assure that core customers get many of the benefits of competition, with little utility or regulatory dilution.

In the simplest model of tandem pricing, prices would be initially set for core services provided to core customers, on a just and reasonable basis. At the same time, a benchmark price level would be ascertained for the non-core market. Thereafter, core and non-core prices would move in correlation with one another. Prices need not to move up or down on a one-for-one basis. Prices in the core market could move at a one-half or three-fourths rate compared to changes in the overall basket of non-core prices, since the full measure of competition is not likely to exist at each level of the market. In addition, not providing full flow-through of non-core market price changes to core customers will encourage those customers on the cusp between core and non-core markets to choose to move into the non-core market. Tandem pricing should act as a nearly auto-pilot pricing mechanism for the transition from regulated to competitive pricing *as technology and the market* require.

---

[25] *See*, Terrence L. Barnich, "The Challenge for Incentive Regulation," *Public Utilities Fortnightly*, 15 June 1992.

■ The Devolution of Rate Base Assets to Competitive Status and the Role of Affiliate Transactions[26]

To the extent that utilities and customers are given the freedom to exercise the choice to convert their relationships to market-based rather than regulated ones, it is also reasonable to allow a utility sufficient freedom to organize its assets (including the capital structure associated with those assets) so as to better conform to competitive market behavior. Form should follow function.

The Energy Policy Act of 1992 wisely left to the states the authority to determine whether a currently rate based generation asset could be devolved to exempt wholesale generator (EWG) status. With prior approval, a utility can transfer ownership of a generation unit (presumably for consideration under state commission oversight) to an affiliate EWG company. While the use of tandem and real-time pricing might diminish the interest of a utility in devolving generation, the option should be clearly articulated and the regulator's open mindedness expressed in the development of a PC program. Core customers are not disadvantaged by devolution under PC since the utility would be obligated to move core prices in tandem with non-core prices.

The corollary to permitting devolution of rate based assets and to the general principle of encouraging flexible response by utilities is an open mindedness to affiliate EWG transactions between utilities and their affiliate EWG companies. One important aspect of

---

[26] The use of the word "devolution" for the movement of utility rate based generation assets (first appearing in Philip R. O'Connor, *Competition on the Electric Utility Industry: Sunset Series Monograph #15, (Springfield, IL: Illinois Commerce Commission, 1985)* is intended to provide a looser concept than that implied by use of the word divestiture under which the generation assets would move out of the corporate family of the utility into independent ownership. The 1992 Energy Policy Act amendments to PUHCA explicitly provide for devolution, regrettably without use of the word, by which utility rate based generation can be spun off to exempt wholesale generator (EWG) status, as long as state regulators agree.

such affiliate transactions may well prove to be more comprehensive than customary energy service deals between utilities and their industrial and commercial customers. For instance, under PC, regulators ought to be open to deals in which industrials serve as hosts and partners for cogeneration or other power plant developments by utilities.

■ Competitive Selection of Supply and Demand-Side Resources

One area of conflict that is bound to become sharper if there is a movement toward PC is the role of regulators in integrated resource planning (IRP) and mandated resource acquisition and demand side programs. If government mandates particular investments and expenditures, the costs of many such mandates are likely to exceed those that would have resulted from competitively driven choices.

PC's underlying philosophy is that market forces result in better decisions than government intervention. But there may well be important goals that can better be achieved by a combination of government goal setting and/or prescription of method. PC allows for such intervention and prescription, but with the caveat that there is no free lunch and that the price distortions should be kept to a minimum and social responsibilities be spread as widely across the market as possible.

PC ought to offer a better future for DSM than the current mode of regulation. Regulatory pricing would no longer shield customers from the actual costs of particular patterns of demand and consumption—including the real time costs of environmental impacts. Conventional rate-of-return pricing has the perverse effect of pricing power too low when there is not enough and pricing it too high when there is too much. Various states have gone so far as to ban the inclusion of construction work in progress (CWIP) from rate base, thus exacerbating the situation. More accurate pricing through competitive and market forces would move DSM investment into the portions of the load curve which is in need of capacity. To the extent that kilowatthour conservation is most valued by the market, then that is where resources would go. Similarly, to the extent capacity is needed, load shifting and peak shaving strategies can be implemented in a cost effective way.

■ PRISM Contracts (Price Responsive Industrial Marketing Contracts)[27]

PC could employ a subset of competitive market resource acquisitions that would give the local utility the opportunity to exercise its classic value-added role of aggregating and blending different resources to serve disparate customer power needs in an environment characterized by competition. A Price Responsive Industrial Marketing Contract (PRISM), would be one in which the utility acquires a specific set of power resources that can be packaged, blended and priced to match an identified set of customer demands. Through PRISM contracts, utilities could acquire new resources through contracts with EWGs or other third parties, but the sales contracts would be balanced with a specific portfolio of complementary contracts on the customer side. Individual customers could avoid many of the risks and complexities involved in arranging bilateral purchases from other utilities or from PURPA-Qualifying Facility (QF) units.[28] Instead, the utility would play its traditional "blending" role.

---

[27] Depending on how this particular idea develops it seems possible that other meanings for the PRISM acronym might be developed which convey slightly different notions, such as Portfolio Reflective Incentive Sales Marketing contracts.

[28] The Energy Policy Act of 1992 amendments to PUHCA, which created the category of exempt wholesale generators (EWGs), prohibits an EWG from engaging in retail sales. Therefore, this entire class of power producers would not be directly available to customers but would have to have their supplies mediated through a utility, either the one that served the area in which an industrial customer was located or one that somehow arranged for retail wheeling through a local utility to a specific customer. The PRISM contract, because it relies on the value-added blending role of the utility, avoids transgressing the Act's prohibitions on sham EWG retail transactions.

The genius of the founding giants of the American utility business is not to be found solely in their scale-up of power plants and their financial creativity (such as the open-ended mortgage bond).[29] It was also the recognition that a variety of power plant types could be brought together and coordinated to serve ever changing customer needs that would, over time, become fairly predictable in their aggregate pattern of demand. One of the critical complications today in moving toward a competitive market in electricity is that our conventional model of the vertically integrated local monopoly electric utility compensated the electric company for its integrative (blending) role through the grant of monopoly status and subsumed the financial benefit into the return on the hard dollar investment rather than a service fee that reflected a profit.[30] Just as profit centers have moved from hardware to software and service in many other industries, so too should that transition be made in the electric business.

PRISM contracts are an outgrowth of a simpler idea in which utilities could be expected to engage in "accountant's wheeling", re-

---

[29] Sam Insull, the unfairly maligned genius who, as much as anyone, built the modern electric utility, created new financial mechanisms that allowed the rapidly developing technology and its associated efficiencies to be reconciled with the need to raise large sums of capital for the development and deployment of a vast network of electric power infrastructure. *See*, Forrest McDonald, *Insull*, (University of Chicago Press, Chicago IL. 1962).

[30] Participating in the May 25, 1993 panel discussion at the California Public Utilities Commission in San Fransico, Jeanine Hull, Vice President and Counsel of LG&E Power Systems, Inc. of LG&E Energy Corp., the independent power affiliate of Louisville Gas & Electric Company, opined that the idea of a profit margin or mark-up for the local utility on purchased power represented an unnecessary tax on EWGs. While perhaps true in a basic sense, the labeling of that mark-up as a tax does not solve the problem inherent in the loss of profit potential for local utilities in the provision of commodity electricity to distribution customers. That loss deters some utilities from seeking out purchased supplies in lieu of owned generation. However, providing a profit opportunity by specifically pricing the "blending" task is one way of reconciling customer and utility interests.

flecting "mirrored" contracts with third party suppliers and with individual large customers. Mirrored contracts would be simple in the sense that a mirror is, just reflecting an image. PRISM contracts would contain far more complex elements, including commodity electricity and a variety of other services.

The major difference between PRISM contracts and the old fashioned utility role of meeting many differing needs with bulk resources will be twofold. First, the PRISM contract will not rely on franchise rights to underwrite the purchase, but will rely instead on customer contracts and merchant relationships which underpin the purchase commitment. Second, PRISM resources would be acquired with much lighter oversight, if any, by state regulators. *Post hoc* used and useful prudence reviews would be unnecessary since the resource acquisition would be undertaken pursuant to corollary customer contracts. The newer integrated resource planning (IRP) processes in the states could be revised to accommodate PRISMs by merely taking the implications of PRISMs into account when resources for the non-PRISM customer base are considered.

■ Management of Transition Costs—Accelerated Depreciation

Conventional rate making and the related accounting techniques may be increasingly unsuited to current industry conditions. Assumptions about monopoly have led to overestimates of useful economic life and excessive optimism about the ability of a utility to recover deferred revenues. The willingness of regulators to address the more arcane areas of rate making accounting may have important implications for the ease or difficulty with which we cope with the order of the new world.

Some of the most important transitional problems in regulated industries involve accounting practices or conventions unsuited to competitive markets. These artifacts of regulation trap assets into vintage valuations which have little or nothing to do with their economic value. Regulated enterprises, during periods of transition are often expected to continue the commitment of "undervalued" assets to customers at vintage prices while being free to price only their most expensive assets at market rates.

By identifying particular parts of the asset base for which some sunk costs could be recovered on an accelerated basis, regulators could significantly reduce resistance by existing utilities to important competitive changes—perhaps even retail wheeling. The precedents are there and demonstrate that the process can work. For instance, at the federal level and in several states, telephone inside wiring was depreciated off the books within just a few years, eliminating a whole category of utility investment from regulatory attention and treatment.

Southern California Edison Company's (SCE) suggestion that its interest in the San Onofre and Palo Verde Nuclear Generating Stations receive accelerated depreciation treatment was directed toward this problem.[31] The plants have come to be viewed as assets whose useful economic lives may be shorter than the accounting life for rate making purposes. Whether the reasons involve the contemplation of large investments to keep the plant in good operating order or excessive increases in operating costs due to federal nuclear regulatory mandates, the company has a different view today of the likely future for the plant than that which it and regulators once had. SCE, like other electric utilities, is seeking the financial flexibility to meet a more competitive environment which almost everyone sees coming.

---

[31] In early 1993, Southern California Edison Company petitioned the California Public Utilities Commission to permit an "additional capital recovery" of about $75 million annually for SCE's interests in the San Onofre and Palo Verde nuclear stations. Central to the rationale for the accelerated recovery is that new generation technologies will soon be coming on line at $500-$800 per installed kilowatt while these nuclear stations have embedded capital costs of $1,350 and $1,900 per kilowatt, respectively.

Progressive Choice And The Pace Of Change

Many may subscribe to the notion that the utility industries are subject primarily to long, slow change rather than abrupt change. While change is indeed incremental, it can nevertheless come quickly in relation to the industry's expectations. The past decade alone demonstrates how dramatic change can be in utility industries. The telecommunications business is fundamentally different today than just ten years ago, prior to the divestiture of the Bell Telephone companies. Numerous competitors are entering the local exchange market, as they have the long distance business. There is a real question as to where the action actually will be in telecommunications. Will customers soon control the network through sophisticated end-use equipment and software, dipping into a global network of networks to extract the desired information and signals?[32] Or will the network be the manipulator of information in addition to delivering information to right place?

Ten years ago, virtually every molecule of natural gas that moved in the interstate market was owned by the interstate pipeline transporting the gas and sold at prices regulated by FERC. Today, pipelines do not own gas at all, although their marketing affiliates may, and no gas now sold in interstate commerce is subject to federal economic regulation. Other important aspects of the gas market have changed dramatically as well, including the use of storage, the role of end-use customers and marketers arranging gas supplies in competition with local gas distribution companies.

In the electric industry ten years ago, there was a huge backlog of utility built and owned generating capacity which was driving rates up far faster than the overall rate of inflation. Independent power was available in small increments and accounted for just a

---

[32] George Gilder has suggested that the future of telecommunications will be characterized by huge capacity "dark fiber optic" pipes into which vast amounts of information will flow to its intended recipients pursuant to the commands originating within the end users own computer-like equipment. *See*, George Gilder, "Into the Fibersphere," *Forbes ASAP*, January 1993.

small percentage of the capacity under development. Today, more than half of all new generating capacity is independent, and the law has been changed to allow independent developers and utilities to compete on a level playing field in the generation development market. The generation industry is now largely wide open to competition.

If all of this is not enough change in just ten years for someone, then perhaps only such years as 1492 and 1945 would satisfy such aficionados of paradigm shifts.

Implementing PC does not necessarily require a single dramatic regulatory decision. Pieces of PC can be undertaken on an individual basis over the space of as little as two years if the process begins now. In that space of time, customer choice could largely replace regulatory and monopoly dictates as the fulcrum for electric industry structure, prices, products and customer service.

Chapter Nine

THE FUTURE OF INTEGRATED RESOURCE PLANNING

John H. Chamberlin

Integrated resource planning (IRP) is today the principal means used by electric utilities to identify new resources. It has also become a key vehicle for state regulatory commissions and intervenors to understand and influence the planning process. As the process has grown and evolved, it has come dangerously close to being regarded as synonymous with strategic planning—that is, as the vehicle by which the key market decisions of a company are determined. As the energy service market becomes increasingly competitive, the IRP process leads to increasingly nonstrategic results. Thus, a critical conflict is growing, one that will ultimately lead to the demise of either the IRP process as it is employed today, or to the demise of the utilities themselves.

The chapter outlines the development of IRP, discusses the forces at work which are having the greatest effect upon the operation and outcome of IRP and, finally, speculates about the evolution of IRP over the rest of the decade.

What Is IRP Today?

Integrated resource planning as practiced today is the continuous process of identifying and evaluating combinations of demand-side and supply-side resources that will achieve specified objectives and meet forecasted demand. Through this planning process, the utility and other participants seek to find the least-cost manner in which loads can be met, or modified, while meeting constraints such as maintaining a given level of reliability and customer service.

Dr. John H. Chamberlin is Executive Vice President of Barakat & Chamberlin, Inc.

Although long-term planning has long been a critical activity for the electric utility (in part due to the size and lead times of central station power plants, and in part to the need to anticipate the transmission and distribution systems required to support community growth), traditional electric utility planning consisted largely of matching expected customer load growth with new generating capacity or energy purchases. During the 1980s, as the costs associated with that planning approach rose, utilities and others became interested in expanding their planning methodologies to consider opportunities to modify customers' use of electrical energy. Planners no longer took the level and timing of customer demand as a given, but as a variable that could be modified by demand side management (DSM) programs.

The principal development in resource planning over the past decade has been the movement from a linear process to one in which feedback is explicitly considered. As first employed, IRP proceeded as a series of discrete steps. First, analysts forecast customer purchases of electricity for a lengthy period into the future, e.g., 20 years. Then, computer models simulated the operation of existing generation units and considered the addition of new units when required to maintain the reliability of the system in the face of sales growth. The costs of operating the system and adding new units of various kinds were calculated, and the size, type, and timing of new units determined. Next, the marginal costs associated with the operation and expansion of the system were calculated for the selected plan, and these costs were compared with the costs of modifying sales growth via DSM programs. DSM actions that proved less expensive than the selected generation plan were then identified and substituted into the resource plan.

As experience with the process developed, two deficiencies became clear, and the process evolved to mitigate them. First, it did not capture the dynamic interrelationship between demand side and supply side options. Differences in the size, type, and timing of DSM programs produce differences in the preferred mix of generation resources; these differences in turn affect marginal costs, and thus the type, size, and timing of DSM programs. The process had to be modified to capture this interaction. Change occurred either through expanding the generation planning model to select both supply and demand side options, or by iterating back and forth between the generation plan and the DSM plan until convergence is obtained. Thus IRP now generally involves the systematic iterative evaluation of alternative sets of resource options conducted in order to select a "best set."

Second, it did not incorporate the interaction of changing resource plans, rates and sales. Changes in resource selection have an impact upon the overall level of costs, and thus upon rates; these impacts in turn affect the level of sales, and thus the need for resources. The second modification of the IRP process was therefore to incorporate the effects of changing resource plans upon the overall level of sales in some sort of simultaneous process.

These changes have significantly expanded the complexity of IRP. They are not, however, the only forces increasing its complexity. The strategic importance of electricity to the national economy, the rising capital costs of generating plants, wider availability of energy-efficient technologies, and greater choices of fuel suppliers all have made electricity planning a topic of public scrutiny, intervention, and legislation.

Over the past ten years IRP has helped utilities to think about how to expand their service offerings, to improve the quality of the plans adopted, and to minimize confrontations with ratepayers, environmental advocates, and others through a collaborative process. The process is now under pressure, however, from deregulation and competition, technological change (microwave heating and drying, ultraviolet curing, membrane separation, and other recent electro- and gas technologies), and economic change (e.g., trade agreements, global competitive pressures). The remainder of this chapter describes the pressures on utility planners, describes the forces now at work that are changing the nature, purpose, and outcome of the IRP process, and suggests two views—short-term and long-term—of how IRP is likely to evolve.

Driving Forces

IRP came into prominence rapidly. In less than a decade it became the leading edge planning tool for utilities and commissions that wanted lower costs, more efficiency, and environmental improvement. It is now just as quickly becoming obsolete. Three forces are driving this trend: increasingly sophisticated public participation, an expansion of the functions encompassed by IRP, and competition.

■ Public Participation

IRP has offered a way into utility planning for individuals and organizations concerned about rates and/or environmental issues (e.g., natural resources, emissions, and wastes). Having learned from experience, utility customers and other intervenors are becoming increasingly sophisticated, better funded, and more active. In most states they are having an ever larger impact on decision-making. The effect of public participation in regulatory matters has been in many cases informative, creative, and constructive and has led to better planning and more options. Increasingly, however, the effect of intervention has been to stymie the planning process—to so complicate and prolong it that before a plan has been agreed upon, the utility has necessarily made day-to-day decisions that may have made portions of the plan irrelevant. In states where collaboration drives the planning process, a single IRP "cycle" lasts for more than a year and costs millions of dollars. In short, IRP can become so complicated, detailed, time consuming, and costly that it is not a viable decision-making tool.

Further, intervenors do not necessarily share objectives. All want the process to satisfy their goals, but these goals are increasingly diverse. Industrial customers and environmentalists, for example, tend to drive the process to opposite poles as the battle over increased efficiency versus lower rates and reduced interclass subsidies heats up.

■ Expansion of the Process

Commissions and other parties to IRP want to expand the scope of the process. Commissions, for example, may want to consider investments in transmission and distribution as part of the plan; or the impacts of prices on sales forecasts; or the effect of more DSM, cogeneration, and purchases from qualifying facilities on avoided costs. Where such "vertical" expansion has been tried, the process has been cumbersome and both computationally and organizationally difficult. One utility in the east, for example, now needs six to seven months to do the required calculations for a plan that must be filed annually. Yet another consideration is whether, when, and how to incorporate bidding into the IRP process. Should the utility complete its IRP and then put out its request for bids? Or should it be able to consider the bidding resources available as part of the plan? Thus far the question has not been satisfactorily answered. The process has expanded "horizontally" as well, as participants weigh DSM versus power plants, DSM versus additional transmission facilities, DSM versus distribution system facilities (a geographically complex task).

A current trend in regulation is to reflect in the planning process costs that heretofore were considered external to the energy system. Yesterday, air pollution from power plant stacks was viewed as an unfortunate price of progress borne by society at large—not just by energy consumers. Today, through clean air legislation and regulations, the cost of reducing this pollution is falling first on the utilities and ultimately on consumers in the form of higher rates. The rationale for incorporating the cost of "externalities" in energy rates is that it promotes economic efficiency. When energy prices reflect all legitimate and relevant costs, consumers allocate their dollars more efficiently to satisfy energy and other—competing— needs. Yet, with little agreement on the correct approach, or the boundaries or values of these external costs, the IRP process has become increasingly politicized.

■ Competition

With deregulation and increased competition in the airline and telecommunications industries as examples, and with the impetus provided by PURPA, power producers of all kinds are seeking to expand their markets. With retail sales of electric power becoming increasingly deregulated, the number of potential competitors will greatly increase. They will offer lower rates, more appropriate or more comprehensive services, "greener" power, etc.

From a competitive or strategic viewpoint, IRP has two critical conceptual weaknesses: (1) it focuses upon cost minimization as the only goal of the planning process, and (2) it assumes that customer loads are predictable and that customers in a given area will be served only by the "host" utility. Competition undermines both the assumption that lowest cost is equivalent to greatest value and the expectation that customers are made dependent, and therefore relatively predictable, by the fact of geography.

Utilities already find themselves facing new competitors, and should expect that others will soon abound. Competition may come in the form of:

➠ Substitution of gas for electric power

➠ Substitution of other products for current end uses (e.g., insulation for heating, fiber optic light source for light bulbs)

➠ Energy service companies that provide DSM measures and charge a share of the savings

➠ Independent power producers

➠ Cogeneration (on-site self-generation)

➠ Utilities that draw customers to other territories by offering lower rates

➠ Other countries that offer lower electric rates and less expensive labor

➡ Direct utility competition via transmission access

➡ New entities (or differently structured utilities) that package financing, equipment, maintenance, operations, and energy

What is the value of a planning process that identifies a "least cost" resource plan, only to find that competitors are serving the demands which drove the plan in the first place?

What's Next For IRP?

Changes in the utility industry, chief among them the virtually unstoppable trend toward more competition, will continue to drive changes in resource planning. In the short term—the next one to three years—utilities will step back from IRP (as some are doing already) in response to the pressures described above. They will use the documented resource plan as a showcase for the adopted planning strategy, not a means by which to develop it. Or they will find ways to adapt the process to produce the desired results, broadening the definition of IRP to include competitive positioning. This means an increasing emphasis on consideration of the rate impacts of alternative strategies, on increasing flexibility for the company, and on some means to reflect customer value (not just cost) in the resource strategies.

■ The Next Generation in Utility Planning

The next generation of IRP will be a full integration of customer service planning with system planning, pricing, and evaluation. Operating under an obligation to meet a forecasted load led utilities to develop the least-cost, reliable resource plan. As they become market oriented, the focus of their planning will become external rather than internal (customer needs rather than utility loads). Instead of driving the IRP process, power supply issues will be only one of a number of considerations.

The shift of focus will come about as both commissions and utilities extend the standard practice tests of cost-effectiveness to reflect customer value. The current tests examine the changes utility programs produce in the electricity market (i.e., the market for Kwh). But the value of energy service to customers is not confined to the electricity market: customers value energy services, such as cooling, heating, lighting, and motor power. The value of these services is measured in the market for energy services, not the market for electricity. The standard practice tests are insufficient in a deregulated market where customers have the power to choose among services and suppliers; they must be extended to address the energy services market if value to customers is to be reflected in assessments of cost-effectiveness.

As utilities recognize that customers value end-use energy services, not kilowatthours, they move away from expenditures on programs that yield energy savings but inconvenience their customers (for example programs that require them to apply for rebates, agree to interruptible service, incur financing obligations, or accept performance risks). Higher lumen levels, higher precision, better reliability, and even the possibility of buying *more* cooling, heating, lighting, etc., owing to efficiency, to name a few examples, will become criteria for program selection.

To date, most regulators do not formally recognize customer value as a basis for planning utility services; but for utilities to ignore customer value increases their risk of losing market share to other energy providers. Assessing program options from the perspective of customer value within the IRP process provides planners with additional potentially powerful decision-making information. Those utilities that are already beginning to do so will have a competitive edge.

■ Beyond IRP

In the longer term—five to seven years—utilities will step away from the IRP process altogether, and replace it with a strategic process that is sensitive to the market. Utilities will evolve into commodity suppliers, with cost minimization strategies, or into energy service suppliers that seek to serve customers well beyond their existing geographic territories by using a value enhancing strategy. Some utilities will attempt to adopt both strategies. Structurally, electric utilities may change in two possible directions:

➡ They will disaggregate into their component parts—generation, transmission, distribution (as in the deregulated telecommunications and gas industries), with the distribution company being the point of contact with the customer; or

➡ They will split into regulated and deregulated market segments (similar to "core" and "non-core" customers of gas utilities)

In either case, electric utilities will no longer be the energy service providers that they are today.

Utilities that once provided the same service throughout their territory will take varying transmission and distribution costs into consideration in their DSM marketing and will package different services by community to take advantage of varying profitability. They may even offer entirely new services, such as a solar or wind-generated resource, to a community. And they will compete in neighboring—or even distant—service territories by offering brokered sales of independent power producer (IPP) power, dispersed generation, and other fuels (including oil, kerosene and propane), as well as DSM services.

Similarly, the industry itself will face competition from service providers not now considered to be in the energy market. Telephone companies, cable TV, and other services connected to customers' homes and businesses will offer "Smart Home" and "Smart Business" services that include energy and load management options such as sophisticated heating, ventilating, and air conditioning (HVAC) thermostat programming and remote control, and detailed end-use energy usage feedback mechanisms that provide customers with concise information about the benefits of efficient equipment.

It is evident that customer service will be the key to survival in a fully competitive marketplace. A new breed of educated, informed energy consumers will demand a selection of energy types, rates, and service options requiring a revitalization of utility marketing departments, and a larger role for marketing in system planning and supply-side issues. Utilities will offer a menu from which customers can customize their service, valuing individually the importance of cost, time-of-use, reliability, power quality, design assistance, and environmental concerns. Since customers' energy-using equipment will become much more sophisticated, with state-of-the-art, highly sensitive electronics, power quality and reliability will become much more important. Customers will be savvier about their power purchases, expecting different grades of power at different prices. Along the lines of recent developments in the cable TV industry (which are expected to allow consumers to choose from among five hundred different channels of programming using add-on scheduling, program description, and selection options), utility customers will choose their bundle of energy services and will even pay to have their options analyzed for them.

To thrive in a competitive market, utilities must both understand their customers' business objectives and assess their own capabilities and constraints in order to determine which needs they can most efficiently and most profitably meet. Customer intelligence is the key to understanding customer value; competitor intelligence is the key to identifying what customer needs a utility can fill competitively.

When and if full-scale competition (or retail as well as wholesale wheeling) exists, utilities will have become a different business. They will not simply bring power to customers' meters, but will also provide information and expertise in all processes and equipment using energy (including interfuel trade-offs) and will provide financial assistance when needed for equipment changeovers. In some cases, this expertise will be provided by utility staff, and in more specialized cases by utility-endorsed energy service companies.

End-use service providers—which could be utilities or entirely new entities—will sell light, heat, and motor power directly to the customer. For example, a midwestern utility has already announced plans to own and operate motors in a factory assembly line. Another utility plans to own, install, maintain, and operate the lighting and HVAC systems in commercial buildings. This approach removes the last barriers to energy conservation: building managers or factory owners have no further worry about payback from investments in efficient equipment, because they will get immediate payback in the form of lower bills. Further, and probably more significant, the utility has an incentive to install the most efficient equipment in order to maximize profit.

How does IRP fit into this picture of the future? Does a planning process developed partly in response to regulatory pressure—and based on an assumption about who the customer is—have a role in a deregulated market for energy services? Certainly the time has passed when simple linear regression models were adequate to forecast demand for power and the price of electricity was not the key variable in the equation projecting customer usage. This change has two implications for IRP: first, existing planning methods will not provide meaningful information about a market that cannot be counted on to be there. A few years ago, newly added DSM made historical trend information invalid for forecasting. Although the fragmenting of the customer base does not invalidate the end-use forecasting methods that are the current state of the art, it will add complexity. Sales forecasting will evolve into market share forecasting. Second, given that customers consider attributes and price together in forming their perceptions of value, functions that are often separate in regulatory-driven planning (such as resource selection, services planning and implementation, and ratemaking), must have a single focus—the customers in the utility's chosen market niche.

Competition inherently changes the relevance of IRP. In a competitive market, consumers will choose their energy suppliers on the basis of the value received for dollars expended. To be competitive, therefore, all energy suppliers must be free to consider customer value explicitly in developing their energy service offerings. Regulators cannot require utilities to rely upon traditional IRP without putting them at a competitive disadvantage.

In competitive markets, traditional IRP will lead to incorrect conclusions because it does not look at the full set of legitimate costs and benefits. In other words, it does not take into account customer value. It will lead to financially disastrous conclusions because customers in a deregulated market will gravitate to suppliers who provide the most value; thus a utility that does not incorporate customer value into its planning process will be at a dangerous disadvantage. Greater market power arises from customers' greater ability to tailor energy services (and service providers) to their unique needs.

In short, beyond IRP is market-based planning that does not just *include* customer value but that *focuses* on customer value. The new questions that utility planners (who will be market planners as well as system planners) must ask are not, "What is the least cost way of meeting my sales forecast?" but, "How big is the market? What are my niches? and How can I maximize market share and earnings in those niches?"

Chapter Ten

THE ENERGY POLICY ACT OF 1992: WHAT DID IT DO?

John L. Jurewitz

The Energy Policy Act Of 1992

When the Bush Administration began assembling its "National Energy Strategy," a diverse constituency of utilities and independent power developers lobbied for repeal or substantial modification of the Public Utility Holding Company Act (PUHCA). Originally passed in 1935 along with the Federal Power Act (FPA), PUHCA was intended to protect the public by controlling and restructuring the financially unstable gas and electric utility holding companies that had developed during the 1920s. The provisions of the Act are among the most complicated of any piece of American legislation. While perhaps well suited to the industry of the 1930s, by the mid 1980s it was clear that the provisions in PUHCA were significantly inhibiting the development of competitive generation markets by placing severe restrictions on anyone owning diverse utility properties in various states under a holding company structure. In brief, any corporation holding generation assets was a utility under the meaning of PUHCA, and any corporation holding generation assets in diverse locations in multiple states risked being designated as a registered holding company by the Securities and Exchange Commission (SEC). Qualifying facilities (QFs) under the Public Utility Regulatory Policies Act (PURPA) had been granted an exemption to PUHCA, but non-QFs enjoyed no

John L. Jurewitz is Manager of Regulatory Policy for the Southern California Edison Company and Economics Instructor at Pomona College. The views expressed in this paper are purely the personal and tentative observations of the author. They are offered here to advance the open discussion of a complex subject. They do not necessarily represent the corporate viewpoint of the Southern California Edison Company. A version of this chapter was previously published in the *Electricity Journal*, June 1993.

such exemption. As a result, both utility and nonutility entrepreneurs were not very interested in pursuing stand-alone non-QF generation ventures. PUHCA was also inhibiting American investors from freely pursuing power development projects in the increasingly active international electricity markets.

■ PUHCA Reform

The Energy Policy Act of 1992 (the Act) creates a new class of wholesale-only electric generators—"exempt wholesale generators" (EWGs)—which are exempted from PUHCA. An EWG must be engaged exclusively, either directly or indirectly through affiliates, in the ownership or operation of "eligible facilities". An "eligible facility" is an electric generation facility with output sold only at wholesale. An eligible facility includes the interconnecting transmission facilities necessary to deliver this wholesale power to the local utility.

EWGs differ from QFs in several significant ways. Utilities are not obligated to purchase power from EWGs. EWG status is not subject to restrictions relating to fuel type, maximum size, or eligible technologies. Utilities may own all of an EWG; their ownership is not limited to a 50% share, as with a QF. Unlike a QF, an EWG may sell power generated by others, along with the power it generates itself. Also unlike a QF, whose purchase prices are regulated by state commissions, the prices paid to EWGs remain subject to regulation by the Federal Energy Regulatory Commission (FERC) under the FPA.

The Act permits facilities currently in a utility's rate base to become owned or operated by an EWG, but only with explicit approval of all relevant state commissions. The Act also permits, with state commission approval, the creation of "hybrid facilities" where a portion is an eligible facility held by an EWG and the remainder of the facility is included in a utility's rate base.

The Act prohibits utilities from purchasing power from an affiliated EWG unless such purchases are approved by the state commission on a case-by-case basis. The state commission must find that it has sufficient access to information, books and records, and that the transaction is in the public interest and is not the result of the exercise of any unfair competitive advantage. The Act gives states federally derived authority to examine the books and records of electric utilities under their jurisdiction and the books and records of any EWG selling to such jurisdictional utilities as well as any *utilities or holding* companies affiliated with these EWGs.

In an exemption separate from the EWG exemption, the Act exempts "foreign utility companies" from PUHCA. A foreign utility company is one owning electric or natural gas facilities, whether for wholesale or retail sales, that are not used to serve U.S. retail consumers. In the case of investment in foreign utility companies by affiliates of utilities or utility holding companies, state commissions must certify to the SEC their ability to protect ratepayers from possible adverse financial consequences of failed foreign investments. Utility companies are also generally prohibited from pledging their credit to support investments in foreign utility companies.

■ Transmission Access

The Energy Policy Act of 1992 also provides the FERC with broad authority to order utilities to wheel power for wholesale electricity market participants. These participants include other utilities, federal power marketing authorities, QFs and EWGs. A request for transmission service must first go to the prospective transmitting utility who then has 60 days to respond. After 60 days have passed, or the utility has issued an unacceptable response, the requestor can apply to the FERC for a wheeling order. The FERC may issue a wheeling order if it finds that such an order is in the public interest and would not unreasonably impair reliability or result in retail wheeling.

In issuing its wheeling order, the FERC may direct a utility to undertake expansion of its transmission facilities to enable the wheeling service to be offered. If, after making a good faith effort, the utility is not able to acquire the required permits and property rights necessary to expand its facilities, the FERC must modify or entirely revoke its original wheeling order to the extent such actions are necessary to avoid unreasonably impairing the utility's reliability.

The Act provides for pricing to allow transmitting utilities to recover all costs incurred in connection with the wheeling transaction, including an appropriate share of all "legitimate, verifiable and economic costs" (a clear, though implicit, attempt to recognize the legitimacy of opportunity costs). The transmission charge is to reflect any benefits to the system of providing the service, as well as the costs of any needed enlargement of transmission facilities. These rates are to be just and reasonable, not unduly discriminatory or preferential, and should promote the economically efficient transmission and generation of electricity. To the extent practicable, the applicant for the wheeling order—not a utility's other wholesale and retail customers—is to pay the costs incurred in providing the transmission service. The precise meaning of all these complex pricing provisions is left for the FERC to implement.

Life After the Energy Policy Act

■ Electric Resource Markets

The creation of a class of EWGs free from PUHCA restriction is the single biggest impact of the Electricity Title of the Act. Despite FERC's initiatives to facilitate the development of stand-alone non-QF generators through its proposed independent power rulemaking in 1988 and subsequent case law implementing "market-based" rate regulation, PUHCA restrictions have effectively stifled development of all but a small handful of stand-alone non-QF generators. The Electricity Title sweeps away this barrier, enabling a potentially huge new economic interest to develop free from the technological restrictions constraining PURPA QFs. Although most observers believe these generators will be heavily skewed toward developers of combined-cycle, gas-fired technologies, unlike QFs there are literally no constraints on the range of generation technologies EWGs can adopt.

First, a few brief points:

➡ The Act does not fully "deregulate" EWGs; it merely (but importantly) frees them from PUHCA's restrictions. All generators selling power at wholesale remain "utilities" under the Federal Power Act, subject to rate regulation by the FERC when selling for resale in interstate commerce.

➡ Under the Act, EWGs may not sell their power at retail.

➡ Any price "deregulation" of EWG power sales will be shaped by the policies adopted in FERC cases and rulemakings, and by the rulings of federal courts on appeal. In recent years, FERC has shown considerable commitment to advancing such "deregulation" in the form of its market-based pricing initiatives. With no effective constituency in sight to oppose this trend, and with a new and growing constituency to support it, the FERC's administrative "deregulation" of EWG power sales will undoubtedly continue.

➡ The Act does not "mandate" any specific result in generation markets, but increases supply opportunities available to utility resource planners and state commissions. Acquisition of resources remains the utility's responsibility, with a heavy and growing exercise of oversight authority by the state commissions and, in some states, other resource oversight bodies. The following issues and trends seems likely to surface as utilities and state PUCs proceed with resource planning and selection in the new era.

■ Wide Variations In Resource Procurement Processes Will Remain

During the past decade, state commissions have followed widely differing courses in implementing PURPA, with dramatically different results in terms of nonutility generator development. These differences are undoubtedly the result of many factors—regulatory philosophies, state law, cogeneration potential, the persuasiveness of some individuals, and sunspots. The Act does nothing directly to standardize or impose any restrictions on these state resource planning and procurement processes.

The most important resource procurement question for states is the degree to which they allow utilities latitude to negotiate agreements with independent producers. As procurement processes continue to evolve, they will fall along a continuum between two polar models: on one hand, highly stylized and structured auctions intended by their creators to mimic commodity markets; on the other, processes that more closely resemble the "industrial policy" approaches of "social democrats," with state commissions more directly partnering with utilities to achieve state development objectives. These latter processes will be very much like principal-agent exercises, with utilities acting as agents implementing state energy and economic development policies.

A fundamental difference between these two approaches is the degree to which third-party suppliers will politically "capture" the process and secure a greater share of the economic rents of resource development. In spite of the textbook model of commodity spot markets which seems to underlie the highly rigid auction model, long-term generation contracts have many complex dimensions. Under the highly structured auction approach, the design of the standard contract and the multi-dimensional selection algorithm for determining bid winners become intensely complex—a dense forest of technical concepts and terms impenetrable to all but the most determined and gifted policymaker. Under this approach, the results of the "competitive" process are more likely to be a pork barrel for supplier interests than a boon for electricity customers. By contrast, the principal-agent model offers far greater potential for capturing a greater share of the economic rents of resource development for electricity customers.

No doubt there will be wide variation in the procurement processes adopted by the various states and in the degree to which the increased competition benefits electricity customers.

■ FERC's Role Will Increase, and With It the Potential for State/Federal Friction

The Energy Policy Act of 1992 does nothing directly to extend the authority of FERC in generation markets. However, its *indirect* manner of doing so is likely to be substantial. By enabling the creation of EWGs, the Act strongly reinforces the state jurisdictional trend toward competitive resource procurement (whether patterned as an auction or as a principal-agent exercise). During the foreseeable future, very little new utility-owned generation will be developed and almost all new non-QF generation will be developed by EWGs. The pricing, terms, and conditions of these contracts will become a source of friction between state and federal jurisdictions. In many cases the terms and conditions of contracts will be initially overseen, if not designed and approved, through state jurisdictional procurement processes. The prices will be determined through competitive auctions or negotiation processes overseen and approved by state commissions. However, the FERC will ultimately have exclusive authority to approve, and possibly modify, these wholesale power contracts.

The FERC, through its administrative oversight of wholesale rates and its market-based rate initiatives, holds an important key to the evolution of electric industry structure. There is no reason to believe the FERC will turn away from its support for market-based wholesale generation rates. However, as it attempted to do in its 1988 competitive bidding Notice of Proposed Rulemaking, it may use its leverage over approval of wholesale generation rates to pursue objectives that it has little or no authority to achieve directly. If it does so, it will certainly stir up federal-state regulatory tensions.

For example, the FERC may try to influence the design of state procurement processes by narrowly defining those procurement structures it deems sufficiently "competitive" to be worthy of "market-based" rate approvals. Here, FERC's pursuit of a competitive national power market (or, at least, large regional markets) is likely to come into conflict with some states' implementation of energy/environmental policies (for instance, through resource set-asides, or externality adders) and other states' direct or indirect attempts to design competitive procurement processes that exploit the purchasing power of utilities to capture supplier rents for the benefits of electricity customers.

A second source of potential conflict involves the treatment of utility affiliates in market-based rate applications. The Act leaves states to decide whether utilities can purchase power from affiliated EWGs. However, it also assigns to the FERC the responsibility to assure that wholesale rates paid to affiliates are not preferential or discriminatory. This gives the FERC further leverage over the design of state jurisdictional resource procurement processes, and effectively over the state decision to allow affiliate purchases. The FERC could implement rules placing such restrictive conditions on the design of procurement processes sufficient to permit "marketbased" rate approval of affiliate purchases that states would be discouraged from allowing such purchases in order to avoid any perceived adverse effects of these additional federal restrictions.

A third source of potential state-federal conflict involves FERC rules governing market-based rate treatment for utility affiliate sales to other utilities in the same bulk power market area. Prior to the Energy Policy Act of 1992, FERC case law denied market-based pricing to affiliates of utilities selling power to other utilities in the same market area unless the parent utility essentially had an open-access transmission tariff filed with the FERC (e.g., see the *TECO*, *Terra Comfort*, and *Nevada Sun-Peak* cases). The Energy Policy Act of 1992 gives the FERC remedial authority to order a utility to wheel power at wholesale for an eligible requestor, but it does not require utilities to file open-access tariffs with the FERC. To the extent FERC remains interested in encouraging the filing of open access tariffs (a requirement that was linked to FERC approval of mergers or market-based rates in earlier drafts of the Act), it may use its authority in granting market-based rates to affiliated EWGs selling power in the same geographic market area as the parent utility to require as a pre-condition that the parent file an open-access transmission tariff. However, some state commissions may not regard such tariffs as being in the best interest of a utility's retail customers if they reduce the utility's ability to fully exploit its own system or, alternatively, to collect opportunity costs.

Finally, despite attempts along the road to its passage, the Act does nothing to institutionalize the so-called "*Pike County* doctrine." This doctrine holds that state commissions may disallow costs of a wholesale power purchase as "unreasonable," even though the purchase price and terms were determined by the FERC to be "just and reasonable." (This lower-court doctrine has yet to be recognized by the U.S. Supreme Court.) With regulatory approval of most new non-QF generation contracts now headed for federal jurisdiction, the validity and "legs" of the *Pike County* doctrine will likely become a source of future tensions between state and federal regulators.

■ Conflicts with Demand Side Interests Will Grow

As demand side conservation and load management advocates become more aggressive, they will encounter increasing conflicts with nonutility supply side interests. This is already happening in California, where QF interests have accused demand side interests of offering not "nega-watts" but instead ethereal "vapo-watts.". Such rhetoric will escalate as these nonutility supply interests, as well as large industrial customers who see themselves subsidizing other customers' participation in demand-side programs, put DSM programs under increasing pressure to justify themselves through more rigorous measurement protocols.

Even if measurement controversies are overcome (which does not seem likely) the conflict between demand side and supply side programs will continue because the two types of programs have differing impacts on rates and are fundamentally impossible to compare in a non-controversial way, even when all the facts are known with certainty.

■ Pressure Will Build to Modify PURPA

As EWGs develop, the rationale for maintaining a privileged class of QF generators will erode. It seems likely that most QF privileges (especially, the unilateral right to obligate utilities to purchase a QF's power and pay full avoided costs) will eventually be statutorily revoked or administratively modified. However, statutory changes, if they ever come, will take many years. PURPA will be guarded as the flagship that began the process; sentiment, if nothing else, will prevent its repeal or modification unless certain of its provisions are widely regarded as causing serious distortions relative to the efficient development of competitive supply markets.

In the meantime, state administrative actions will minimize the privileges available to QFs and attempt to place them and EWGs on equal footing to the maximum extent allowable under PURPA. Indeed, many states have already taken the largest step in this direction by adopting competitive procurement processes which essentially allocate fixed amount of long-term utility capacity payment obligations to low bidders—whether QFs, EWGs, or other utilities. This leaves the right to receive as-available energy payments as the main privilege retained by QFs. Though valuable to QFs, and potentially distorting to competitive markets, this seems a rather limited privilege and legislators may be reluctant to revoke it.

■ Organized Regional Spot Markets Will Emerge

In creating EWGs, Congress specifically provided that they be allowed to buy and sell power purchased from others. This somewhat obscure and seemingly innocuous provision may be the "sleeper" in the Act. It may prove to be similar to the QF provisions in PURPA in terms of having largely unexpected and far-reaching implications. This single provision could superimpose on the present industry structure a huge number of power brokers. This may eventually lead to much more active, well-publicized and organized spot and futures markets in electricity, such as are already being discussed and explored by the New York Mercantile Exchange and the Chicago Board of Trade. If and when an active, well-organized market develops in spot and futures contracts, regulators will increasingly use these prices as a benchmark for reasonableness reviews and a basis for designing innovative performance-based regulatory initiatives, as some regulators are now contemplating the use of gas spot market indexes as the basis for evaluating utility gas procurement.

■ The Role of the Utility and Its Affiliates In New Generation Will Be Controversial

In recent years, many state PUCs have begun struggling with the issue of how best to integrate new utility-owned resources into the utilities' competitive procurement processes. They have confronted several difficult and controversial questions. How should the choice be made between third-party procurement and new utility-provided supplies? Who should make the decision? Are there unmeasured values in utility-owned resources? In third-party resources? How do you compare a third-party contract resource with a utility rate-based resource? Should the utility-owned resource receive cost recovery as if under a contract? If so, why not require that it be organized as a below-the-line, arms-length subsidiary? Should utilities be permitted to purchase power from their own subsidiaries?

The Act does nothing to resolve these questions, reflecting the implicit judgment that they are inherently state jurisdictional issues. In fact, an initiative to impose a federal structure on these issues by banning affiliate transactions (a provision passed in the House version of the Act) was dropped in the final version of the Act in favor of delegating this decision to the state PUCs.

■ Some Existing Generation Assets May Be Spun Off Into EWGs

The success of possible utility initiatives to remove existing utility generation from rate base and create a below-the-line EWG will also depend, in part, on state laws governing disposition of capital gains on transfer or sale of utility properties. Utilities will find the greatest potential benefit in disposing of assets whose market values exceed book values, but only if their shareholders can capture at least some of the gains of such transfers. In many states, utility law precludes the transfer of such assets to below-the-line affiliates except at market values, with the gains credited to rate-payers. This makes such transfers far less appealing from the utility's perspective.

In the final analysis, utilities and regulators must cope with the legal regimes in which they operate. Regulators will act to block windfall gains to shareholders from transfers of utility assets by either denying such transfers or by requiring that ratepayers be compensated at market values.

This will substantially reduce, but not totally eliminate the frequency of such transfers. Indeed, utilities and their state regulators may increasingly see mutual benefits in using the EWG structure as a means for implementing so-called "incentive regulation" for individual generating units. This approach would take the essentially unenforceable "social compact" of an incentive regulation agreement between a utility and state regulators and convert it into an enforceable wholesale power contract subject to FERC oversight. Riskier provisions in incentive regulation structures may be far more acceptable to utilities if they believe the full range of possible gains and losses will be disposed of fairly once the structure has been established. Utilities will feel far more comfortable with an enforceable contract than with an unenforceable political compact.

Likewise, the option of "hybrid" facilities may provide an appealing structure for dealing with repowerings. Some fraction of the repowered unit could remain in utility rate base while the remaining fraction becomes an EWG with a contract to sell power back to the utility. Utility ratepayers would essentially receive in-kind compensation for contributing their equitable claims to the benefits of the existing site, and utility shareholders would take most of the risks on the incremental capital investment. It would essentially be a joint venture between ratepayers and shareholders with the agreement enjoying some degree of contract protection and FERC oversight.

■ Bulk Power Transmission

Future trends in regulatory institutions and ownership patterns involving bulk power transmission facilities are among the most difficult results of the Act to forecast. These changes will be driven by the new economic interests unleashed by the Act, possible utility interests in corporate restructuring along functional business lines (e.g., generation, transmission, and distribution), and regulatory responses to these basic economic forces and initiatives. The fundamental questions are: Who will get access to transmission? How will transmission services be priced? What transmission ownership patterns will evolve? How will new transmission capacity be planned and coordinated?

Wholesale Transmission Access

Prior to passage of the Act, the FERC had very limited authority to order a utility to wheel power for another utility. The system was fundamentally voluntary. One of the few clear results of the Act is the broadening of the FERC's authority to order wheeling under a very wide range of conditions. Although utilities were already voluntarily providing a tremendous amount of wholesale transmission access before the passage of the Act, the new access provisions are likely to have a significant impact on future provision of transmission services. Wholesale transmission service will now be much more readily secured by applicants. Providers now have a clear obligation to make a good faith effort to expand facilities where necessary. And the FERC now will be the ultimate arbiter of how much access can be provided on the existing system before reliability is "unreasonably impaired."

Transmission Pricing

Before the passage of PURPA, when the electric industry was still clearly vertically integrated, getting transmission pricing "right" was not quite so important as it is today. Location of generation on the vertically integrated utility system was influenced by transmission costs—not prices. Of course, intersystem power sales could be, and were, influenced by transmission pricing. But provision of transmission services was voluntary and, consequently, serious economic distortions were avoided for the most part by utilities simply declining to wheel for others when opportunity costs were too high. In short, price signals were not the sole vehicle, nor even the main one, for determining the allocation of transmission resources.

The Act changes all this. In the new mandatory access environment the need for more accurate transmission pricing increases tremendously. The location of new generation resources as well as choices among competing generators may now depend critically on transmission pricing. In this setting, it will be especially important to get the transmission pricing right.

Under the Act, the FERC retains complete jurisdiction over pricing of transmission services. But lobbyists on both sides of the pricing issue were not content to leave it at that. Each side jockeyed for position and created a confusing combination of language that will take a good deal of time and effort for the FERC (and, perhaps, the courts) to sort through. However, on the brighter side, the Act does state reasonably clear principles supporting the objectives of economically efficient pricing and protection against shifting the costs of providing transmission services to a utility's other customers. With specific implementation of price regulation now squarely with the FERC, it seems the agency may want to manage this process through a policy statement or rulemaking rather than through the cumbersome and less certain process of developing policy through individual case law.

Recently, when the FERC found itself wanting to encourage increased transmission access but not having the authority to directly order it, it encouraged utilities to provide greater transmission access by liberalizing its regulation of transmission pricing to recognize the legitimacy of opportunity costs and stranded investment concepts. But now that the FERC has the authority to order directly what previously it could only encourage, it may revert to more heavy-handed pricing principles and interpretations.

The philosophical objective that will continue to drive transmission pricing policy at FERC is the encouragement of competitive generation markets. Based on past speeches, the FERC staff may take the viewpoint that, to avoid the risk of having the tail wag the dog, it is better to err on the side of underpricing transmission services and risk resource distortions in excess transmission capacity additions rather than risk losing increased generation efficiencies. This policy will find considerable political support among the new economic interests in generation as well as the traditional constituency of transmission "have-nots," such as most municipal utilities. The result would be at least slightly underpriced transmission services, some unpredictable mix of over-investment in transmission or reduced system reliability (depending largely on the willingness of local regulatory authorities to authorize transmission expansion), and some shifting of costs to a utility's other customers in the form of either increased rates or reduced system reliability.

Coordinated Transmission Planning and RTGs
While the Act clearly mandates wholesale transmission access and appears to favor efficient development, it does not change the historic fragmentation of regulatory responsibilities over transmission siting and pricing between state and federal jurisdictions, and adds nothing to address the coordinated planning of interstate transmission networks.

Under the new regime, the FERC retains jurisdiction over transmission pricing and access, while state commissions retain jurisdiction over approval of transmission construction and investment, occasionally exercising some degree of responsibility for intrastate transmission planning and coordination. To the extent there is coordination of interstate transmission network expansion, it is the result of voluntary cooperation among utilities through power pools and the regional reliability councils of the North American Electric Reliability Council (NERC).

The siting of new transmission facilities and upgrading of existing transmission lines is likely to become an increasingly politicized activity. So long as transmission remains a cost-of-service regulated activity (as it almost certainly will), the main beneficiaries of the transmission grid will be electricity generators and retail customers. Therefore, third-party generators and representatives of retail customer interests (i.e., mainly retail utilities and utility regulators, rather than consumer advocates) will shape the development of institutions governing planning and siting of new transmission facilities.

Partly in an effort to design alternative institutions and avoid heavy-handed government directives, both investor-owned and publicly-owned utilities will continue to pursue the formation of Regional Transmission Groups (RTGs). The FERC's current rulemaking on RTG issues may become quite instrumental in shaping the development, viability, and scope of these associations. Successful development of RTGs could in turn become very instrumental in reducing the political pressure for legislating interstate transmission planning agencies.

Retail Wheeling

When the Energy Policy Act was debated in the 102nd Congress, utility interests wanted to preserve and strengthen the perceived federal preemption against retail wheeling. They lobbied for a clear federal ban that would have precluded state initiatives. On the other hand, state commissions lobbied to preserve their authority, whatever it might have been. The result was several clear victories for utilities, but also some rather murky language regarding state authority to order retail wheeling.

First, the Act clearly precludes the FERC from ordering retail wheeling. *Second*, language was included to attempt to prevent so-called "sham transactions"—wheeling transactions that, although technically wholesale, are essentially retail in nature. *Third*, EWGs were clearly precluded from making sales directly to retail customers. However, the Act also includes this equivocal provision:

"Nothing in this subsection shall affect any authority of any state or local government under state law concerning the transmission of electric energy directly to an ultimate consumer"

This language was apparently a compromise skillfully phrased to duck the federal preemption issue and preserve everyone's ability to fight another day. Advocates of a state's right to order retail wheeling will cite the language as evidence of Congress' intent not to have the Federal government completely occupy the field and to recognize the legitimacy of a separate state role. Advocates of the view that states were previously preempted from ordering retail wheeling can continue to argue that states had no preexisting authority and, therefore, continue to have none.

Whether and how fast retail wheeling progresses beyond isolated experiments will depend on the economic interests of the various players, which are diverse and locality-specific. Large industrial customers will be the greatest advocates of retail wheeling; they will push political "hot buttons" when they argue the need for industrial competitiveness and regional development. At a minimum, these large customers will use the threat of retail wheeling legislation at the state level to keep downward pressure on large customer rates. Some supplier interests will also favor retail wheeling. These will include the least expensive independent generators and possibly even some low-cost utilities who are willing to break ranks with their brethren.

On the opposite side, a long list of constituents can be expected to line up *against* retail wheeling. This list includes most utilities, small consumer advocates, environmentalists, many independent generators, and perhaps even state regulators. Utilities, especially those with embedded generation costs and long-term contract commitments exceeding current market prices, will see their ability to recover these embedded costs as being threatened by retail wheeling.

Advocates for small consumer interests will oppose retail wheeling because they will reasonably expect the patterns of income redistribution experienced in the gas and telephone industry restructuring to be repeated under retail electricity wheeling. Environmentalists will oppose retail wheeling because they will see it seriously eroding the substantial inroads they have made in recent years influencing state commission electric resource planning processes. Under retail wheeling, customers could be expected to choose among alternative suppliers based only on direct costs. Environmentalists would then be forced to pursue environmental policies in the more difficult state and federal legislative arenas through taxes, subsidies, or command-and-control restrictions.

Many independent generators will oppose retail wheeling because they see themselves (correctly) as being able to secure a larger market share through the current highly politicized resource planning process. For instance, in California, utilities are being required to purchase additional QF resources not because of a forecast supply-demand imbalance, but because development of certain QFs is expected to displace current production from gas-fired and coal-fired resources, thereby creating environmental benefits in reduced air emissions. Under retail wheeling and the free-for-all markets it would bring, this "political market" would disappear, as would the one created by set-asides or environmental adders favoring the development of otherwise high-cost renewable technologies.

Reaction to retail wheeling by state utility commissioners and their staffs will be mixed. Their responses will be driven both by regulatory philosophy and self interest. Philosophically, they will split between "free-market" advocates and those favoring more politically driven state energy planning.

■ Industry Restructuring

The Energy Policy Act of 1992 mandates no electric industry restructuring. A best guess is that any restructuring will be gradual and incremental, but this forecast must be offered with a good dose of humility. Larger forces than we realize may be set in motion by the creation of EWGs and mandatory wholesale transmission access. It is at least interesting to speculate about some possibilities.

Generation

New generation will be developed almost exclusively by QFs and EWGs which of course will include existing utilities building for wholesale sales outside their service territories. In certain circumstances, utilities will be able to put together political constituencies supporting construction of some new utility projects—especially repowerings and upgrades to existing facilities. But regulatory approval for development of "green field" utility projects will be much more difficult to obtain. For the most part, utility regulators will require that to the extent utilities pursue new projects, they do so under an EWG structure subject to a power purchase contract.

Most existing generation will likely be retained under state jurisdictional rate base. State regulators will be unwilling to devote significant hearing time to determine the size and allocation of any capital gains or losses resulting from generation restructuring, and associated design and valuation of power sell-back contracts to the utility to assure adequate power supplies to meet its utility service obligations. Utilities will see little benefit to determining these values through market sales or spin-offs of facilities if all capital gains go to ratepayers; utility regulators will see little benefit if capital gains go to shareholders. Exceptions will involve EWG and hybrid facility status to deal with repowerings, incremental facility upgrades, and the application of incentive ratemaking to troubled generation units.

Transmission

With the exception of radial lines developed for delivery of third-party power, new transmission will be constructed and operated by traditional utilities, under traditional ownership patterns, involving increasingly complex patterns of entitlements.

It is not clear why utilities would benefit from vertical de-integration of transmission. However, to the extent utilities pursue vertical de-integration, it would seem that bulk power transmission facilities would be organizationally aligned with the local distribution function. If the greatest value of transmission were wholesale "wheeling through" transactions with neighboring transmission systems, an alignment of transmission with existing utility generation might make more sense because the future expansion of the system would be designed to maximize the value of this wholesale wheeling function. Such an alignment might also make sense to the extent that artificial economic and political forces were causing an uneconomic balkanization of the distribution function (e.g., see the discussion of municipalization that follows).

Ignoring these potential forces, integration of the distribution function over a wide area would seem to be warranted by scale economies. Assuming the main value of the bulk power transmission system is to deliver and integrate generation to the load center, organizational economies will be best served by aligning transmission and distribution functions over a wide area. In any event, an organizationally separate bulk transmission system does not seem to offer any clear advantages to current transmission owners.

Mergers

The Energy Policy Act of 1992 does nothing directly to encourage or discourage mergers. However, by imposing mandatory wholesale transmission access, the Act removes one of the major anticompetitive concerns of regulators in approving mergers, namely the alleged expansion of monopoly power over transmission. This would seem to facilitate regulatory approval of mergers.

Consolidation of small distribution and transmission systems over wider areas could improve cost efficiencies, especially in individual cases. It would not be surprising to see an increase in such mergers without substantial regulatory opposition up to a 4,000 to 5,000-MW merged system. Mergers may also be motivated by increasing the purchasing power of the merged system. Although the latter motive may raise public policy concerns with some regulators, such concerns should be regarded as misplaced. Exercise of purchasing power by local distribution systems will merely affect the disposition of the locational rents of suppliers, potentially shifting them from suppliers to consumers, with little or no inefficiency implications. Nonetheless, populist and economic democratic philosophical inclinations will still cause many regulatory staffs to oppose mergers.

Municipalization

There can be not doubt that the Act facilitates the municipalization of investor-owned utility distribution systems by assuring wholesale transmission access to the resulting municipal utility. Whether this results in a flood of new municipalizations will depend on many factors.

For the most part, municipals will have the same opportunities to purchase new generation resources as investor-owned utilities. Therefore, their motives for municipalization may be based largely on avoiding high embedded sunk costs of utility-owned generation and expensive utility long-term power purchase obligations (e.g., with QFs), and on avoiding state commission resource procurement processes to the extent they cause utilities to purchase expensive new and sometimes unneeded generation. This "bypass" of the political process of resource procurement is possible because, in most states, commissions have no jurisdiction over municipal resource procurement.

The amount of new municipalization that may occur will also be affected significantly by state laws governing compensation in municipal condemnations. In states where utilities can receive "fair market value" or "going concern value" rather than "reconstruction cost new less depreciation" or "original cost less depreciation," there will be far less interest in forming new municipal utilities.

FERC's rules implementing pricing of transmission services could also have a significant impact on the economics of new municipalization. In case law during the past year, the FERC has recognized in principle the inclusion of "opportunity costs" and "stranded investment" costs in transmission service pricing. Full implementation of these principles would serve to reduce the incentive for new municipalization. However, as noted above, now that the FERC has clear expanded authority to order wheeling, it may adopt rules that err on the side of underpricing transmission to foster competitive generation markets. Such as pricing would encourage new municipalizations.

Regardless of whether there is a trend toward new municipalization, the Energy Policy Act of 1992 gives municipalities increased leverage over their local investor-owned utilities in franchise negotiations. In a world of diminishing local revenue sources, cities will be hard-pressed to forsake these opportunities. Again, variations in local and state laws, especially those governing condemnation valuation, will determine the degree of increased leverage a city has. In any event, there is likely to be an increase in the types of conflicts experienced recently in Albuquerque, Las Cruces, and Chicago. Most cities will not actually be interested in forming municipal utilities, but will use the threat to increase utility franchise fees and extract other concessions.

Diversification and Foreign Investment

Currently, roughly 60 percent of utility investments are in generation resources. In many states, utilities will be effectively precluded from replacing these capital investments as they are depreciated. This will create an internal generation of cash that regulators may try to transfer to ratepayers through tighter regulation and lower allowed rates of return. Utility management will be faced with two choices for disposition of this internal cash generation: dividend the cash back to shareholders, or diversify into other activities. With the prospect of low or negative growth in utility rate base investment, utility management will be under heavy pressure to preserve stock prices predicted on continued growth; many will pursue the diversification option.

Based on the recent unfortunate experiences of utilities diversifying far from their traditional areas of expertise, utilities will "stick close to their knitting" in future diversifications if for no other reason than fear of an adverse capital market response. As a result, diversification will take the form of subsidiaries and affiliates to pursue development of EWGs, demand side energy service companies (ESCOs), fuel procurement, and foreign investments in new generation and distribution systems. This will cause a shift in regulatory focus to a host of new issues such as self-dealing, cross-subsidies, anti-competitive impacts, and protection of ratepayers from adverse financial impacts of failed diversification ventures.

A great deal of regulatory attention will be focused on the appropriate role of the utility during the next 20 years. At one extreme, some regulators will argue for a nearly complete roll-back of utilities to the "wires business"—i.e., simply transporting power from increasingly independent generators to the customer's meter. Utilities and some regulators will seek a more expansive role for utilities. Especially in a time of diminishing public sector capabilities, progressive regulators will form alliances with utilities to invest their cash in the development of social infrastructure at the margins of traditional utility activities including infrastructure for waste management, electric transportation and customer-side-of-the-meter investments in demand side investments. Specific regulatory actions will influence the outcomes. How private interests respond to these actions will make the future occur.

Chapter Eleven

THE IMPORTANCE OF THE ENERGY POLICY ACT

Judith B. Sack

The Energy Policy Act of 1992 is not a crucial event in defining the future of the electric utility industry. It is the most important energy legislation of the last 15 years but, in and of itself, it will not make much difference to the industry's likely structure in the next decade. To put the Energy Policy Act of 1992 in perspective, it is helpful to focus on several questions:

➡ Are Laws More Important Than Market Forces?

➡ Is a utility management's success rate likely to be higher when focused on managing the business or when reacting to changes in legislation?

➡ What is the relative value of market share, pricing power and regulatory edicts?

➡ Are utility shareholders likely to benefit more when a utility exploits a legal loophole or legislated opportunity, or when the utility supplies service demanded by the market?

These questions are not difficult: market forces always overpower regulations. The market forces at work in the electric utility industry far outweigh the impact of legislation. The Energy Policy Act of 1992 simply recognizes market forces already underway and is intended to eliminate restrictions that are making the marketplace less efficient. Twenty years ago, increases in the cost of doing business changed the industry's economics. No longer did economies of scale make ever-larger, more efficient generating plants possible. Astronomical increases in new plant costs forced regulators to

---

Judith B. Sack is an Advisor to Morgan Stanley & Co. Inc.

grant dramatic rate increases required to maintain individual utilities financial condition, even to stave off bankruptcy. Customers rebelled: as prices increased, price elasticity caused demand to decline. Capacity that had appeared necessary to meet demand suddenly became excess. No one wanted to pay prices for power from new, expensive capacity that covered its cost. Regulators responded with liberalized accounting procedures that made utilities look financially viable while they were bleeding to death and forced companies to promote conservation just as expensive new capacity came on line.

As price differentials among utilities widened, customers of high-priced utilities looked to neighboring utilities and nonutility generators for cheaper power. But high-cost excess capacity could not be abandoned: market realities required that capacity produce revenues. Electric utility fixed costs are high and variable costs low: electricity sold in the wholesale market at any price above its variable (fuel) cost can add desperately needed revenues to a cash-starved utility. All that is needed is transportation to a willing buyer. Thus arises the importance of the transmission system and access to it.

This simple market force—excess capacity—mandated enactment of the Energy Policy Act of 1992. In the harsh world of capitalism, it is not the Act itself which matters. Market forces—in place long before Congress began its deliberations—will affect the electric utility industry much more than any legislation.

Changes in the rules regarding generating capacity and transmission access mandated by the Energy Policy Act simply exacerbate the competitive threats. Exempt wholesale generators (EWGs) will not be encumbered by the restrictions of the Public Utility Holding Company Act of 1935. These EWGs can compete with existing utilities and nonutility generators for market share. The Federal Energy Regulatory Commission (FERC) can now order wholesale access to transmission systems. Authority over retail access resides with the state commissions.

Other broad issues considered by the Energy Policy Act include energy efficiency, integrated resource planning, demand side management, renewable resources, environmental research and development and alternative transportation fuels. But these issues are merely given philosophical encouragement and not much else. Nuclear licensing reform will not mean much until a new plant is ordered. Dealing with nuclear waste is a far more serious and growing problem with great potential to wreak havoc in the next decade and this legislation will provide desperately needed forward progress. However, responsible corporate managers will be required to provide their own—probably very costly—interim solutions until a more permanent solution is found.

Many issues are not resolved in the Energy Policy Act. Rational transmission pricing must be established to assure that access is meaningful. Regional Transmission Groups may help solve transmission problems, but the definition of "market power" is not resolved by the legislation.

The new Clinton Administration and the appointees to FERC are decidedly more interventionist and have a pro-consumer bias. Federal/state disputes will arise and will not be readily resolved. State regulators could become less important. One key consideration for regulators will be "stranded investment." Will these costs be charged to ratepayers—a Republican solution—or to shareholders—a Democratic approach? Market forces have already proven that the electric utility business is no longer a monopoly. Rate base rate of return regulation does not make sense. Incentive regulation is only an interim, stop-gap solution. In a competitive marketplace, pricing and profitability are crucial to an electric utility's success, to its very survival.

The real challenge is to create a system where market-based pricing schemes send the right signals, where transmission access and pricing methods are designed to allow the markets to work efficiently. Prices and services must be unbundled. Each individual service must be priced separately and users must be able to choose the services they are willing to pay for. Cost-plus pricing is irrelevant in a market-driven, competitive economy. In the United Kingdom, the electric utility industry was restructured and privatized in 1990. Customers with a peak load exceeding 1 MW (about 30 percent of the total load) were permitted to buy either from a generating company or a distribution company at the current market price. By 1992, 50 percent of these customers were buying directly from a generating company—bypassing the distribution company entirely—at a 20 percent discount to prior rate schedules. But more importantly, customers who had not switched from their distribution company were paying the same price as those who had. A plausible reason is that customers were willing to switch for as little as a 1 percent price difference.

America's electric utilities need to learn how to price their product—to deal effectively with rate subsidy, pricing and product issues which they have not faced before. Their "obligation to serve" may not be the relevant question in the new world. More important are questions such as, "What does the customer want?" and "Where will corporate earnings growth come from?"

It is imperative that a better understanding of this business be developed. How it does operate? What controls it? What is the product? Who buys the product and why? What is it worth to them? Management must learn to price the product correctly and efficiently manage each facet of the business. Customer needs must take a high priority, and each utility must become much closer to its customers.

Technology, economics and customer demand drive the electric utility industry—not laws or regulations. The danger in assuming that electric utilities are different because they are regulated must be recognized. In the past, managing a utility was really managing a rate case factory. Rate cases were the industry's most important product in the 1970s and 1980s. But the 1990s are different. Market forces have been set in motion and cannot be stopped. The industry must look to core business principles to be successful in the new era—not opportunities created by laws or regulations. Tomorrow's focus must be on technology, economics and customers.

Chapter Twelve

HOW UTILITIES ARE RESPONDING TO THE NEW REALITIES

Roger W. Gale

Competition is no longer just nibbling around the edges of America's electric utility industry. According to survey results released by the Washington International Energy Group in early 1993, senior utility decision-makers increasingly believe that broadened wholesale—and, perhaps, retail—transmission access threatens to allow competitors to chomp deeply into electric utilities' traditional business.

While environmental issues, including implementation of provisions of the Clean Air Act and electric and magnetic fields (EMF) remain major concerns, there is a significant shift in attitude among respondents to the Washington International Energy Group's annual survey away from a concern about "issues" toward a very pronounced concern about bedrock business performance.

Nineteen percent (328 people) of those who received questionnaires responded, a surprisingly high return. The survey was conducted before passage of the Energy Policy Act of 1992 and the election of Bill Clinton as President. Eighty-seven percent of the respondents work for investor-owned utilities, 12 percent for public power. Eighty-five percent of the respondents were over 41 years old; none was under age 30. Over three-quarters of the respondents identified themselves as being in "senior management," suggesting that the survey results successfully capture the views of corporate decision-makers.

Roger W. Gale is President of the Washington International Energy Group. This chapter was written with the assistance of the entire Washington International Energy Group staff, in particular, Art Dunning, Karen P. Humphrey, and Karin A. Santoro.

The findings of the survey are consistent with informal interviews among the Washington International Energy Group's clients and other utility executives, most of whom believe that with the signing into law of the Energy Policy Act in October 1992, utilities will have to be prepared to compete like other unregulated corporations, even though they remain heavily regulated compared to other industries. Utility executives increasingly recognize the seriousness of competition, but most do not yet have a long-term strategy for recreating themselves for success in the 21st century.

Downsizing, which 66 percent of the respondents say their company has tried, is one indication of the growing trend toward utilities emulating the example of IBM and other "blue chip" companies that have been forced to take draconian action in the face of fierce, unforeseen competition.

Controlling operating and maintenance costs (O&M), especially in nuclear operations is one of the industry's unsolved problems—as the survey results highlight. The electric utilities' predicament is reminiscent of the problems that plague the telecommunications and other "old-line" industries, despite multiple rounds of downsizing.

As one interviewee put it: "It's beginning to dawn on utilities that 'business as usual' really means fighting to make a profit, and risking catastrophic failure if you don't succeed. The era of being guaranteed a profit by state regulators has been an historic exception to the laws of nature." And, he added, "It just could be that the shattering of the mainframe computer market in the face of the onslaught of the distributed PC culture has an electric utility analogy."

Competitive Scenarios

Nearly all respondents (85 percent) expect nonutility generation to grow, and half (51 percent) intend to put new generation of their own into service before 2000. After the year 2000, nearly two-thirds (63 percent) expect to build new generation, but there is no consensus among respondents nor a high-probability accorded to the introduction of new technologies (such as Integrated Gasification Combined Cycle [IGCC], fuel cells, or photovoltaics) other than clean coal. This suggests that the American electric utility industry doesn't yet have a clear vision of the extent to which the electric utility business will remain centralized or move, like many other industries, into a more distributed mode.

When asked an admittedly speculative question about the direction of the utility industry by the year 2010, there were fewer respondents who envision international electric transmission links tying together much more of the world (33 percent) than the number who believe more electricity will be produced locally (59 percent). Clearly, these are not necessarily mutually exclusive scenarios .

Other Conclusions

➠ There is a strong consensus among utility executives that transmission access is the most important issue facing the industry today. Transmission access was also considered the most important issue in the Group's 1992 survey. It is probably safe to assume that the mandatory wholesale access provisions in the new Energy Policy Act only heighten this issue's perceived importance to the industry.

➠ Many utility executives continue to believe that "it is the other guy's problem." When asked, for example, whether their own company "needs to change its priorities and management style," only about half (54 percent) said "yes." But, when asked whether utilities "in general" need to change, there was a much more robust consensus (79 percent). Even more striking, when questioned about ordering nuclear power plants, only 17 percent said "yes," their company would consider ordering a new nuclear power plant. When asked the more generic question, "Do you think there will be a resurgence of nuclear power in the U.S.?" however, 42 percent answered in the affirmative.

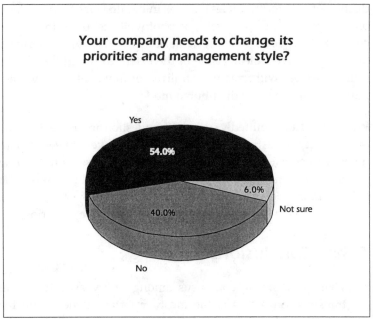

Washington International Energy Group 1993 Electric Utility Survey

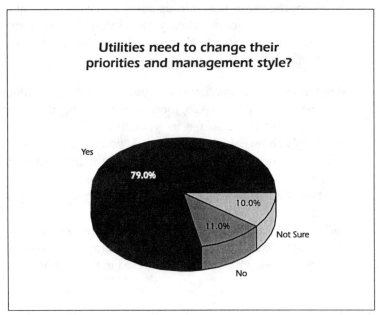

Washington International Energy Group 1993 Electric Utility Survey

➠ Nearly one-third (31 percent) of U.S. utility executives expect reliability to decrease in the near future.

➠ "Internationalization" and, what most foreign utilities consider one of the biggest issues, "global warming," remain the least important issues for most U.S. utility decision-makers. This is a very unexpected finding—although consistent with the results of our 1992 survey—considering the huge interest that has emerged in international development and investment opportunities and the active involvement of some utilities and their subsidiaries, such as Mission Energy, Southern Electric International, and PSI Resources, Inc.

➠ EMF has—for now—moved down the charts by 21 percentage points compared to last year.

➠ Enthusiasm for demand side management (DSM) is flagging. Last year, over three-quarters of the respondents said that they believed DSM was "an effective approach;" this year only two-thirds agree. And, perhaps most important, half of the utility executives surveyed do not believe that DSM is a "long-term" alternative to building new generation.

➠ Only 11 percent of the utility executives surveyed believe that utilities and their customers should be required to internalize all environmental externalities associated with utility power generation.

➠ There is no consensus on a trend toward more industry mergers and acquisitions (M&A), despite the activity in recent years. Twenty-one percent of the utility executives surveyed said that their companies are involved in M&A activity this year, compared with 30 percent last year.

➠ Compared to 1992, more utility executives expect to build generation in the future. This year, half of the respondents indicated that their companies plan to build new generation by 2000; 63 percent expect to put new generation into operation after 2000. In 1992, 24 percent expected to build within five years; a third expected to build new generation within ten years.

UTILITY OPINIONS

■ The Most Important Issue

The five top issues (as indicated by the number of respondents identifying them as "very important") facing the electric utility industry today are: transmission access (71 percent); improving revenue and earnings (62 percent); competition (58 percent); cutting O&M costs (53 percent); and amending the Public Utility Holding Company Act (PUHCA) (47 percent).

The Big Five	
1993	1992
Transmission Access	Transmission Access
Improving Revenue and Earnings	Clean Air Act Compliance
Competition	PUHCA Amendment
Cutting O&M Costs	Improving Revenue and Earnings
PUHCA Amendment	Electric and Magnetic Fields

Transmission access is the most important issue this year for utility decision makers, as it was last year, even though at the time they were polled, Congress and the White House had not yet enshrined mandatory wholesale access into law.

Competition and cutting O&M costs are new to the top five this year, replacing Clean Air Act compliance and electric and magnetic fields (EMF), indicating a heightened sensitivity to bread-and-butter business concerns. Clean Air Act Amendment compliance was probably higher on the list of top issues last year because it had just become law. But, the prolonged economic recession, the recognition that competition is here to stay, and a growing concern about ever-increasing O&M costs—especially at nuclear stations—conspire to make senior executives increasingly concerned about performance. Competition was rated 22 percentage points higher over last year, a very clear indication of the changes now afoot in the U.S. electric utility industry.

Especially with Bill Clinton and Al Gore in the White House, it is hard to imagine that environmental issues will become a lesser concern during the rest of the 1990s, making it even more significant that utilities are increasingly concerned about core business issues. Yet, those judging Clean Air Act compliance a "very important" issue dropped 19 percentage points; EMF was down by 21 percentage points.

Just as important as what utility executives believe to be the most important issues are what they perceive to be the *least* important issues. This year—consistent with last year—internationalization was chosen by respondents the fewest times as a "very important" issue. Despite the competitive vulnerability most other U.S. industries feel, and the seemingly dramatic increase in utility investment overseas—as measured by such factors as number of bids on projects, the number of conferences on the subject, U.S. government-funding, etc.—most utilities apparently retain a very local orientation.

Global warming, seen by some as one of the all-time environmental mega-issues, and an issue that is high on the priority list for utilities in Japan and Europe, remains a relatively low priority for U.S. utilities, having declined slightly from last year. Time will tell whether that is a prudent judgment, especially when over one-third (35 percent) of the utility community surveyed is convinced that the federal government will legislate carbon or other energy taxes.

■ PUHCA and Transmission Access

Now that Congress has amended PUHCA and mandated wholesale transmission access in the Energy Policy Act of 1992, survey questions concerning PUHCA and transmission access illustrate important points, especially considering only a minority in the industry supported these changes. Among the respondents, personal support for PUHCA reform did not quite comprise a majority (45 percent) and just 38 percent of the utilities favored congressional action. Mandatory wholesale transmission access was favored by only a third of the individuals who participated in the survey. Only 26 percent of the respondents indicated that their companies support mandatory wholesale transmission access.

Although the likelihood of Congress passing legislation was uncertain at the time the survey was circulated in late summer 1992, a majority of respondents had already guessed right despite their personal opposition. More than three-quarters of U.S. utility executives (80 percent) believed PUHCA would be amended and a very appreciable majority (73 percent) had already conceded in their own minds that Congress would also include some form of mandatory transmission access in the new energy law.

■ Nonutility Generation

There is no longer any question about the prominence of the nonutility industry—85 percent of the survey respondents believe that both the number of independent power producers (IPPs) and affiliated power producers (APPs) in the U.S. will grow.[1]

When asked if they purchase power from nonutilities, two-thirds of the survey respondents responded affirmatively, with more than half of them (55 percent) planning to increase their purchases from nonutility generators in the years ahead. Still, only one out of three utilities have established their own nonregulated generation subsidiary. Among them, 60 percent want the option—which has

---

[1] There remains considerable confusion about the terminology to apply to generating units that are not built under traditional rate base approaches. The term "nonutility generation" is inaccurate considering the large number of units built and operated by utility subsidiaries. The terms—"IPPs" and "APPs"—used in the survey have no legal standing. The term electric wholesale generator (EWG) was given legal definition in the Energy Policy Act of 1992, and the Federal Energy Regulatory Commission approved the first EWG status application on November 25, 1992.

since been granted them under some circumstances—to purchase power from their own subsidiaries.

Even though there is a growing trend toward larger but fewer generating units, more of which are owned and, typically, operated by utility subsidiaries, only 44 percent of the senior utility managers surveyed are convinced that non-rate base generation is reliable; a sizable portion (24 percent) say they are not sure. Based on extensive interviews conducted by the Washington International Energy Group as part of proprietary studies for various clients, it had been assumed that with some notable exceptions, qualifying facilities (QFs) and IPPs had been quite reliable. In at least some cases, QFs have maintained a higher capacity factor than the utility's own units.

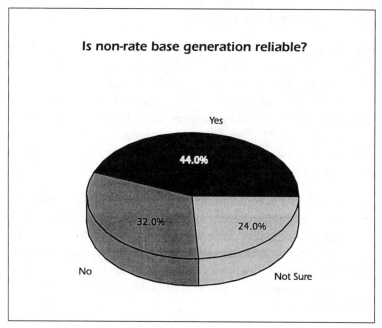

Is non-rate base generation reliable?

Yes
44.0%
32.0%
24.0%
No
Not Sure

Washington International Energy Group 1993 Electric Utility Survey

It is possible that in questioning the reliability of non-rate based generation, some respondents defined "reliability" as the long-term ability of a utility to build its supply scenarios around purchased power, as opposed to current operating performance.

■ Demand side Management/Environmental Externalities

As already mentioned, despite the increase in DSM expenditures and the projected impact of demand side management programs, faith is sagging; as seen in an eleven percentage point decline in confidence over the past year (down from 77 percent last year to 66 percent in this year's tally).[2]

This year, the survey asked the utility industry a very blunt question: "Do you think of DSM as merely a way to appease regulators?" Two-thirds (66 percent) do not think of it that way, but an appreciable 28 percent claim that they feel DSM programs serve only to make regulators happy.

Importantly, half of those who responded do not believe that DSM is a long-term alternative to building new generation (41 percent believe that it is, and 9 percent are undecided). If these figures capture current thinking, there is a real possibility that despite DSM, utilities will have to build more generation than is currently in the planning process. It cannot be determined from the responses, however, whether utilities believe they will have trouble meeting those supply requirements in a timely fashion.

Few issues breed as broad a consensus as the negative feelings that abound about environmental externalities. A notable 69 percent of the senior electric utility decision-makers surveyed do not feel utilities and their customers should be required to internalize all environmental externalities associated with utility power generation. Only a small minority (11 percent) think all externalities should be taken into account.

---

[2] For an excellent analysis of current thinking on DSM, see a series of articles on "Reconsidering DSM" in *The Electricity Journal*, November 1992.

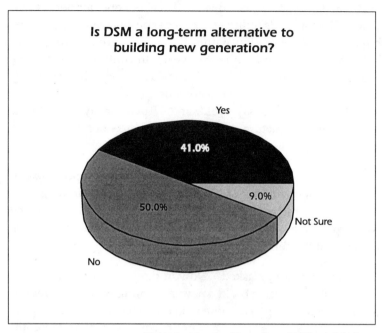

Is DSM a long-term alternative to building new generation?

Yes
41.0%

9.0%
Not Sure

50.0%
No

Washington International Energy Group 1993 Electric Utility Survey

■ New Generation and Transmission Capacity

It has been the Washington International Energy Group's judgment for some time now that whatever the advantages of nonutility generation, and no matter how successful that industry turns out to be in the 1990s, many utilities will find it in their interest to build their own generation, whether in the traditional rate-based mode or through arms-length transactions with their own affiliates. This judgment appears to be on the mark, although the results may not capture whether some utilities may do most of the building or whether a broad spectrum of utilities will get back into the construction business someday. (As argued in this year's Outlook, our assumption is that generalizing about utilities will become increasingly difficult as companies choose dramatically different paths and seek to capture niche markets, including generation).

Last year's survey results indicated that about one-quarter (24 percent) of the country's utility executives expected their utilities to be building new generation within five years; a third expected to build new generation within ten years. In contrast, this year respondents are almost evenly divided when asked if their company has made plans to put new generation into operation before the year 2000: 51 percent say "yes", and 47 percent say "no." In the next century, the picture changes with 63 percent of the utility industry surveyed assuming it will build again.

In short, compared to 1992, more utility executives expect to build generation in the future. This is an important trend, although it is not clear from the survey results the extent to which this increased intent to build generation will be traditional rate-based generation or nonutility generation.

This year, the survey asked, "Do you think it possible that your utility will never again build a new generating station?" Over one third (37 percent) agreed; more than half (55 percent) remain convinced that their company has not permanently abandoned the construction business.

On transmission, almost three-quarters (74 percent) say that their company plans to add capacity before the end of the century, while two-thirds (67 percent) expect that new transmission capacity will be built after 2000. (In 1992, 42 percent of the respondents indicated they were currently building transmission, 40 percent expected to be building transmission in five years and 21 percent expected to be building transmission in ten years).

■ Utility Status

There is no doubt that the electric utility industry is undergoing changes of historic proportion and, as the industry leaders indicated in their ranking of the most important issues, financial performance is of growing concern. Yet, a consensus remains elusive on the broad implications of the competitive pressures that are inextricably altering the face of the investor-owned and public power industry.

Despite the magnitude of the changes now underway, 62 percent of the industry senior decision-makers surveyed are certain that public confidence in the utility industry will remain the same for the rest of the 1990s; only 14 percent believe confidence will decline. And, 21 percent think it will improve during the remainder of the 1990s.

What does this indicate? Considering the utility industry's own penchant for believing that it has lost public support over the

Utility Trends

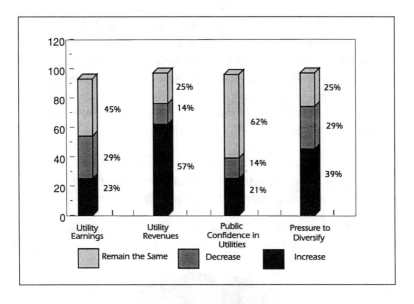

Washington International Energy Group 1993 Electric Utility Survey

years, and its generally adversarial relationship with regulators, consumers, and environmentalists, the results may indicate that the vast majority of the industry (83 percent) believes that utilities have faced the worst.

In keeping with this assumption, more than half of the industry (57 percent) expects *revenue* to increase. Only 14 percent predict revenue will decline during the rest of this decade, with a quarter of the respondents assuming that revenue will remain about the same. At the same time, however, despite the prospect of increased revenue, nearly half (45 percent) of the industry's managers expect *earnings* to remain the same, with the rest of the industry about evenly divided about the prospects of earnings increasing (23 percent) or declining (29 percent).

The confidence that earnings can be sustained or increased is somewhat surprising in view of the declining margins that most other industries have experienced as competition and price-cutting have intensified. (Look, for example, at the airlines and the personal computer industry today). With transmission access a reality, it is more likely than not that transmission prices will tend to be squeezed on a downward spiral as industrial customers demand access and many sellers are forced to offer lower wholesale-level prices. The recent Jersey Central case is a prime example of the emergence of a trend toward price squeezing.

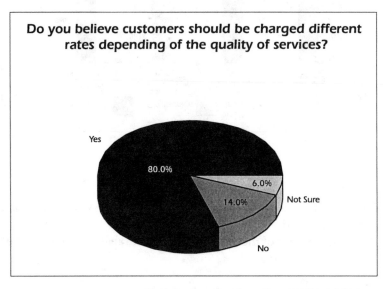

Do you believe customers should be charged different rates depending of the quality of services?

Yes — 80.0%
6.0% — Not Sure
14.0%
No

Washington International Energy Group 1993 Electric Utility Survey

■ Diversification, Mergers & Acquisitions

Despite the increased discussion "on the street"—exemplified by the sudden interest in overseas opportunities—there is no consensus among executives on a trend toward utilities moving pell-mell into diversified businesses. A robust 54 percent either expect pressure to diversify to decline or remain about the same as it is today during the rest of the decade; however, 39 percent expect increased pressure to diversify.

Nor is there a consensus on a trend toward more industry mergers and acquisitions (M&A), despite all the activity in recent years. Compared to last year, when 30 percent of the industry claimed to be involved in some kind of undefined mergers and acquisitions activity, only 21 percent say they are involved in such activities this year. What about the most likely scenario for the rest of the decade? Exactly half of the industry assumes that the number of M&As will increase over the next ten years, but a notable one-third (34 percent) of the industry is convinced of just the opposite.

There is no arguing the fact that the fate of the nuclear power industry in the U.S. is uncertain. Passage of the Energy Policy Act of 1992, which included a number of pro-nuclear provisions, gave the industry a boost; however, the presidential election replaced George Bush, a nuclear power advocate, with Bill Clinton, a president less apt to be a proponent of nuclear power.

As far as the utility industry is concerned, the outlook for the nuclear industry is mixed. On the subject of operating reactors, 73 percent of the survey respondents expect that most nuclear power plants will remain in operation at least through their initial 40-year license period. Fewer than half (47 percent) expect licenses for most nuclear power plants to be extended.

On the subject of new orders, 42 percent of the industry continues to believe there will be a resurgence of nuclear power in the U.S., while slightly over a third (36 percent) think not. Nearly a quarter of the industry (22 percent) is unsure. The more telling reply, however, is that only 17 percent of the respondents think that their

219

company would ever consider ordering a new nuclear power plant. Presumably, if new plants are ordered it will be by the "other guy," or, conceivably, by the government.

Even with the industry's legislative success in 1992, last year's results were more optimistic with 68 percent of the industry's senior decision-makers convinced that there would definitely or probably be a resurgence in the industry.

■ Fuel Resources

Survey participants were asked to indicate whether they expect a significant increase in use of various fossil fuels to generate electricity. As expected, a substantial proportion of utility executives, 74 percent, expects a significant increase in the use of natural gas to generate electricity. Conversely, 92 percent do not anticipate a significant increase in the use of oil. The future of coal is not as clear; 37 percent say "yes" they expect more coal to be used to generate electricity, while more than half (56 percent) say they do not.

■ Global Warming Policy and Energy Taxes

In order to highlight any differences between the individual opinions of the respondents and those of their companies, the survey requested that executives indicate their personal opinion on specific legislation compared to their company's view. They were also asked to judge the likelihood of federal action.

As might be expected in a country where nearly 60 percent of electricity generation is coal-fired, a small number of utility executives (12 percent) and their companies (6 percent) favor global warming legislation. Such legislation would presumably make it more expensive to generate electricity, especially from fuels with higher carbon content. Nonetheless, one-third of the utility industry (34 percent) believes that the federal government will adopt such legislation. Just about the same number of executives are convinced that the federal government will adopt a carbon tax or some other energy tax, generally considered the most likely means of stabilizing or reducing carbon dioxide and other greenhouse gas emissions.[3] (Last year's results were almost identical).

When asked if the global warming issue has an impact on the way their company makes decisions, one-third of those surveyed responded "yes." Nearly two-thirds (60 percent) believe that the U.S. policy of opposing targets and timetables for greenhouse gas reductions was the correct course of action at the United Nations Conference on Environment and Development (UNCED), and nearly half (46 percent) are convinced that complying with the Clean Air Act will also contribute to a reduction of greenhouse gases. (The survey did not ask why they think so).

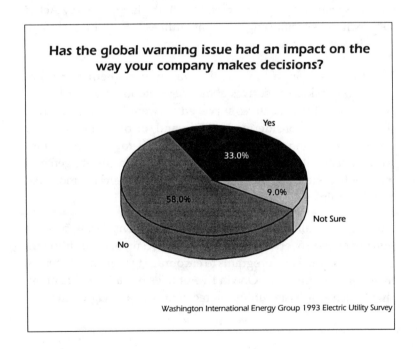

Has the global warming issue had an impact on the way your company makes decisions?

Yes 33.0%

Not Sure 9.0%

No 58.0%

Washington International Energy Group 1993 Electric Utility Survey

---

[3] For a detailed analysis of the current policy, economic and scientific understanding on global climate issues, see the Washington International Energy Group's December 1992 report *Global Climate Change: What Is Known, An Update.*

Although not a utility issue *per se*, the Washington International Energy Group asked how many of the respondents personally support a higher federal gasoline tax. The result? Survey respondents are personally more in favor of a higher gasoline tax than carbon or other new energy taxes. Almost half (43 percent) answered "yes," that they support higher gasoline taxes, even though fewer than one third (29 percent) believe Congress will actually raise gasoline taxes.[4]

■ Internationalization

As privatization of national power systems sweeps the globe, many U.S. utilities have been actively seeking involvement in the overseas power development market. In fact, the Energy Policy Act of 1992 includes specific language that outlines U.S. utilities' eligibility to invest in overseas power development.

Based on these opportunities, the Washington International Energy Group asked executives about their intentions. Only 17 percent of the utility executives surveyed answered that they or their subsidiaries are considering building and/or operating a power generation station overseas. When asked if foreign companies would eventually own a significant portion of the future generating plants built in the U.S., about one fifth (19 percent) indicated that they think so.

Although a small percentage (17 percent) are considering plans to build or operate overseas, nearly half (44 percent) of the utility companies surveyed have programs to encourage foreign investment in their own service areas. One in five utilities has a formal relationship—such as a "sister utility" agreement with a foreign utility.

---

[4] A recent Fortune magazine poll of CEOs found that 50 percent of them favored a gasoline tax if taxes had to be raised. *Fortune*, December 14, 1992.

■ Technology

Respondents were asked to offer their opinion regarding the kind of contribution four emerging technologies will have on overall generating capacity in the future. The results:

⟼ Almost half (47 percent) believe that pressurized fluidized bed combustion (PFBC) will become a commercialized component of the future utility generation mix.

⟼ IGCC is considered important by nearly a third of the respondents (32 percent).

⟼ Regarding dispersed generation, while a quarter of the industry (26 percent) expect fuel cells to become a significant part of overall generating capacity, only 14 percent believe photovoltaics will have the same impact.

Although these numbers may appear to signify little confidence in three of the four technologies, as many or more respondents answered "not sure" to whether they expect these technologies to become a significant part of utilities' generating capacity: 49 percent answered "not sure" about IGCC; 30 percent about PFBC; 25 percent about fuel cells; and 19 percent about photovoltaics.

Outlook

Based on the industry's views expressed in the survey, interviews with clients and other industry, government and environmental leaders, combined with the Washington International Energy Group's own judgments, this year's *Outlook* makes long-term predictions about the North American electric utility industry.[5]

To act with confidence today, utility decision-makers need to know what to expect of the future. While a "picture" of the utility world

---

[5] It is important to look at the future from a North American point of view because of the U.S. Canadian Free Trade Agreement and the likelihood of the North American Free Trade Agreement being adopted.

of the 21st century will inevitably remain elusive, there are a number of increasingly well-defined trends emerging that point toward the future and should allow utility decision-makers and others in the electricity industry to begin making long-term decisions.

There are two means by which utilities can address global changes that are now underway: they can merely adapt at a point when many options have already been precluded or they can strive to stay ahead of the curve through a process of continued renewal and improvement. The latter will require tough, painful decisions that over time will change the very soul of the electric utility as we know it today. As management consultant Peter Drucker notes in a recent article on the organization of the future, "Every organization has to prepare for the abandonment of everything it does. Managers have to learn to ask every few years of every process, every product, every procedure, every policy, 'If we did not do this already, would we go into it now knowing what we now know.' "[6]

When one looks at the electric utility industry from the vantage of what may need to be abandoned, what do we see?

■ New Realties

First, we see that the generation of electricity is no longer either a "natural" technical or economic monopoly. In fact, in both the United States and Canada, the state or provincial-level utility is increasingly less likely to build new generation directly under its own aegis and for its own customers. To the extent that utilities remain in the power plant building business, their largest markets are likely to be outside of their own service areas.

To assure adequacy of supply, some utilities will build new generating plants, but for many utilities in North America that have not initiated the process of designing and building new generating facilities since the mid 1960s, it is difficult to argue that power plant

---

[6] Peter Drucker, "The New Society of Organizations," Harvard Business Review, September-October 1992.

construction remains a viable corporate capability. Many utilities have, in fact, already implicitly abandoned this role.

Second, during the next decade, broadened and larger-volume wholesale transmission access—a trend which began to grow more than a decade ago in North America—will inevitably lead to a blurring of the distinction between "wholesale" and "retail."

As has been the case in nearly all other consumer businesses, the traditional retail seller faces stiff competition from "discount" and "off-price" sellers whose strategy is to cast as naive any shopper who pays "retail" for products that can be bought at closer to wholesale price. The danger may not be—as it is usually portrayed—so much "retail access," as it is the pricing of end-use power at wholesale rates. Industrial and municipal customers, in particular, have a powerful financial incentive to push for retail access *and* wholesale pricing. North American utilities that have not yet considered the possibility of being abandoned or "blackmailed" by large industrial customers and municipals, are at risk.

Third, while in some cases retail wheeling may actually encourage longer-distance transmission, at the same time distributed and dispersed generating technologies are also coming of age—a development which will eventually allow many customers to move away from the "hard-wired" utility grid, a remnant of the 19th century. If the reliability of these new technologies can be proven over the next decade, many customers could eventually move off-grid, relying on the transmission-distribution infrastructure only for infrequent backup. Even backup could eventually be provided by other local dispersed generators and storage operators, leading utilities and their customers to abandon one another.

Aero-derivative gas turbines are the first in a stream of new small dispersed technologies. The fuel cell—which has been on the "verge" of commercialization for more than a decade—is, at least in Japan, likely to reach a competitive price soon. If gas companies continue their aggressive pursuit of fuel cell research and development, it is more likely that a descendant of today's gas companies will control the 21st century marketplace. Photovoltaics will also

225

become increasingly common in specialized settings. Eventually, the artificial distinction between "demand side" and "supply side" technologies may also break down as batteries, flywheels, and other storage devices become practical at the commercial and residential level.

Fourth, while the trend toward greater reliance on distributed and dispersed generation will grow, modular, factory-built central station technologies will also become more common for large utilities as well as for non-traditional generators.

Larger fuel cells located at switching stations, combined-cycle gas turbines, pressurized fluidized-bed combustors, and other technologies in the 50-100 MW and up size will proliferate. Although utilities and their nonutility subsidiaries are likely to build and operate many of them, manufacturers, end-users, and independent developers are also likely to be big players—as they are becoming in the U.S. and Canadian markets.

Fifth, while demand side management is currently viewed by the Washington International Energy Group as having a limited life once relatively quick improvement measures are in place, the demand side service business could become a prime source of revenue for some contenders. But, competition with energy service companies already exists and can only be expected to intensify as many U.S. state regulatory commissions consider requiring utilities to rely on competitive bidding to acquire demand side resources. Utilities need to be prepared to abandon their supply side mentality and their reluctance to engage customers—or risk losing both demand and supply side roles.

And, finally, there is nuclear power. Nuclear power—a safe source of energy that ought to have a brighter future—will be with us at least through the third decade of the next century (barring some sort of catastrophic failure). But the prudent energy planner needs to assume that there will be few, if any, new orders—at least in the United States. The regulatory hurdles over which utilities and other developers would need to jump—even if they are streamlined—add time and expense to an inherently expensive technology that only a small "priesthood" is capable of safely operating. Waste disposal and decommissioning loom as massive political problems in North America and elsewhere.

Further sealing the fate of the nuclear option in the U.S. is a growing likelihood that some operating reactors will be shut down before the end of their current 40-year authorized license periods due to high management and operating costs, costly upgrades, and seemingly more cost-effective options including demand side management and gas-fired turbines. Nuclear power is too complex, large-scale, and unforgiving a technology to play a role in an increasingly decentralized world.

In 1991, the average size of all new generating units coming into service in the United States was only 137 MW. This is probably the nadir, as utility affiliates will be putting a large number of 200-400 MW units into service over the next five years. But, with the end of the era of the 1,000 MW unit in the U.S. and the growing predominance of standardized units, more players will be able to participate in the generating business—many of whom will be meaner, leaner, and more competitive than even the leanest of utilities. Not to mention that regulated utilities will retain their obligation to provide reliable service to marginal urban or rural customers.

A substantial number of North American utilities have already begun addressing the future through downsizing, initiating frequent management reorganizations, instituting quality and productivity enhancement programs (sometimes referred to as the "corporate philosophy of the month" approach), and creating nonutility subsidiaries directed to pursue both domestic and international opportunities.

■ Drastic Changes

But, if the present industry trends are correctly described, utilities need to be prepared to make far more drastic changes than those so far conducted. While more than two-thirds of U.S. utilities have downsized and more than half have made what they call fundamental changes in their way of doing business, this may turn out to be little more than fine tuning compared to the metamorphosis that they have not yet even begun to contemplate.

Unless utilities are able to shift from their traditional role as generators of electricity to providers of whatever services and products the marketplace needs (or can be stimulated to need), the 21st century could witness the demise of many of today's utility corporations.

First and foremost, utilities need to be prepared to abandon their historic role as the primary generators of electricity if they are to survive as viable corporate entities into the next century.

This is particularly true since, for the duration of the 1990s, many utilities are likely to be faced with static revenues and declining earnings. During the last major cyclic utility turndown in the 1970s and early 1980s, utilities often diversified into unfamiliar and unrelated businesses in search of new sources of revenue. In almost every case, these ventures failed. This time, as utilities are once again facing increasing pressure to diversify, the creation of independent power subsidiaries is often the typical response. Many utilities are counting on these subsidiaries to provide the bulk of the parent company's revenue and earnings growth during the latter half of the 1990s.

Despite the large number of generating projects underway in the United States and Canada, and the prospect of some successful ventures overseas, intense competition—sometimes resulting in ten or more bids per megawatt solicited—has raised the level of risk for the losers as well as lowered returns for the winners. This competition has encouraged some U.S. developers to pin their hopes on potentially higher-profit margin projects in the United Kingdom, Australia, New Zealand, Portugal, and other parts of the world where power demand is growing or privatization initiatives are underway.

But, for a number of utilities, generating ventures are not going to prove a prudent, profitable course of action. Competition will remain intense, and, more importantly, many utilities—as good as they may be at operating plants—have little recent experience in designing and building plants. In many cases, even when utilities were building generation, they relied heavily on architect—engineering firms. For many utilities that launched large nuclear power plant building projects in the 1960s, it has been a quarter of a century since they last put pen to paper to-design a new plant (in the era when pen and paper, not CAD/CAM, was the way it was done).

For some utilities, the abandonment of the construction business has already taken place, even if the corporation has not explicitly recognized this shift. Heavily staffed with engineers, some companies have a natural reluctance to face facts. For these companies, as well as for some municipals and other local distribution companies which have little or no generating experience, their future, if there is one, lies elsewhere.[7] But where?

◾ Scenarios

Frankly, for some companies there may be no long-term future. The trend toward an increasing number of mergers and acquisitions has not been as pronounced as some predicted, but is likely to be one means of cutting costs and optimizing comparative advantages.

For those utilities—public or private—located strategically along major transmission corridors or intersections, some may find the combination of transmission ownership and such a location to be an increasingly valuable asset if they can make money as a toll collector.

If it becomes even more difficult to site new green field plants, existing sites located along prime transmission corridors could become valuable assets. Repowering of older units, squeezing new

---

7   We are likely to see municipals and others with little or no generating experience build generating units as a means of breaking their dependence on traditional suppliers whose role is no longer considered vital or in the local distributor's best interest.

units on existing sites, or continuing to run old, amortized units may be the name of the game for some companies.

Some utilities may find it advantageous to sell off generating assets, even if the profits from selling amortized units flows largely to the ratepayer. As has become common in the real estate business—some new unit sales are leased-back— utilities may "flip" assets for speculative purposes, while actual management and operation continues under contract by the former owner.

For many companies, the future will entail abandoning their current role as a vertically-integrated entity in favor of becoming a services-only company that owns, leases, and operates small dispersed units for its customers, provides storage, backup and non-interruptible capabilities, and, perhaps, moves to the "other side of the meter" supplying energy equipment for "Smart Houses."

In some cases, we might see the appearance of international networks of service companies, either the descendants of the giants like U.S. General Electric or the descendants of some present utility companies. Some utilities might reposition themselves as niche companies, specializing, for example, in packaged cogeneration, fuel cells, photovoltaics, or energy storage. However, chances are coal, natural gas, and other fossil resources, like oil sands, will also remain essential into the future. Companies in British Columbia, Alberta, and Saskatchewan, for example, could manage huge energy "parks" that produce energy shipped by superconducting cables to major urban markets in North America.

In the future, North American utilities will be increasingly integrated into the world-wide marketplace. Between now and the beginning of the next century, many analysts estimate that 100,000 MW of new generation will have to be built outside of the United States and Canada to meet burgeoning demand in Southeast Asia and elsewhere. The abandonment of the Chernobyl-type RMBKs and earlier WER reactors in Russia, the republics and Eastern Europe could also create a need for many new fossil-fired plants in that region. At least 11 investor-owned utilities, as well as a number of rural cooperatives, are engaged in international utility development projects. At least two Canadian utilities have also entered the international marketplace.

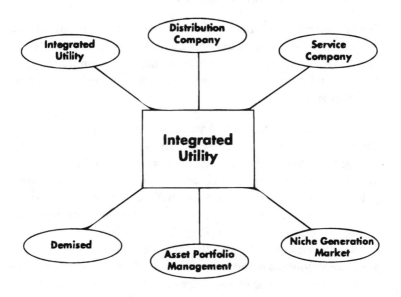

Washington International Energy Group 1993 Electric Utility Survey

As has been the case for the last two decades, meeting the basic infrastructural needs of developing countries will require the largest single pool of capital, even if nations are not forced to drastically improve the performance of their units. If the World Bank and other multilateral and bilateral lending agencies begin requiring environmental directives, such as emission controls on coal-fired plants in China and other countries, the bill will increase 25 percent or more.

These urgent needs are, however, only prefatory to the real internationalization of the world electric utility markets. By the early 21st century, standardized, module, factory-built, one-kind-fits-all power plants are likely to become commonplace. As mentioned above, the gas turbine is the first of these technologies. In

231

the developmental phase are the same dispersed technologies that are likely to move into commercialization in North America during the next decade—fuel cells, photovoltaics, fluidized-bed combustors, and energy storage devices.

The successful developers and marketers of these products and services will, like Coca-Cola and the other multinationals, compete in a single marketplace. It is by no means certain that today's utility corporations will be nimble enough to be major players in this market.

We are in the midst of a world-wide movement toward privatization that, at present, is bypassing only two of the world's major economies—those of the United States and Canada. In Europe, the former communist bloc, Asia, and Latin America, state-owned utilities are being privatized through either outright sale of government-owned assets or through increased reliance on privately owned nonutility generation. There is every reason to believe this trend will continue. Although there is no evidence that a well-run, government-owned enterprise need be any less efficient than a privately owned utility, the experience outside of North America and Western Europe is that state-owned enterprises have often been corrupt and inefficient.

It remains to be seen, however, whether corporations—public and private—can make the tough business decisions required in Peter Drucker's scenario of the company that coldly evaluates and, perhaps, actually abandons whole segments of its business every few years. If public and investor-owned utilities follow the experience of other industries, they will have to recreate themselves into lean market- and niche-driven companies equipped to create multiple profit centers, quick to sell under-performing assets, and able to build world-wide marketing organizations. Utilities that do not take this course must recognize that many of the banks, airlines and telecommunications companies which faced a similar predicament, no longer exist.

■ Bottom Line

The bottom line is that by early in the next century, the electric utility as we know it today—a heavily-staffed, engineering-oriented, vertically-integrated organization—may well have died. For those utilities that plan their future based on this premise, the future is likely to be more secure than for those who delay. It will be, at best, a difficult transition so long as the obligation to serve remains and the typical residential customer has no choice but to rely on the local utility for a reliable supply of electricity. At some point, when dispersed generating capacity has become reliable and cost-effective and access to transmission relatively open, the small customer can be safely set adrift to make his/her own decisions—freeing the utility, like other industry corporations, to "sink or swim."

North America's utilities are entering a new era characterized by profound technical, organizational, and financial change. For those leaders who see this as an opportunity, success is more likely than for those who bank on the status quo.

Chapter Thirteen

THE ELECTRIC UTILITY INDUSTRY AS SEEN FROM THE PERSPECTIVE OF LARGE POWER USERS

Maurice Brubaker

This chapter begins with an identification and characterization of large power users (LPU) and a description of their participation in the regulatory process. Next is a discussion of current characteristics of regulation that have contributed to some of the more serious problems faced by utilities, regulators and customers. This is followed by a review of the results of the current regulatory approach. The chapter concludes by outlining a prescription for change.

Large Power Users

LPUs are predominantly, but not exclusively, within the industrial sector. Some are highly energy intensive enterprises, with electricity accounting for 10 to 50 percent of manufacturing costs. Others are not as energy intensive, but use electricity for a variety of purposes in a multitude of facilities—with the result that electric power costs run into the hundreds of millions of dollars. The significant increase in the cost of purchased electricity that has occurred over the last two decades has served to focus management attention on electric power issues, regardless of the degree of electric intensity of the manufacturing process.

LPUs operate in competitive markets. These markets are increasingly competitive as a result of the breakdown of state and national economic boundaries. Typically, LPUs no longer operate only in a local or regional market, but face a global market characterized by ever increasing competition. Economic survival

Maurice Brubaker is Chief Operating Officer for Drazen-Brubaker & Associates, Inc.

depends upon the ability to control and manage costs and produce at the lowest possible cost.

LPUs have been active players in regulatory and legislative arenas. They routinely participate in utility rate cases, hearings on integrated resource plans and a variety of other regulatory proceedings that have the potential to affect electric rates. Most states have industrial intervention and/or legislative organizations. Many LPUs also belong to national organizations such as the Electricity Consumers Resource Council (ELCON). They have grown increasingly disenchanted with the regulatory process, and with the attitudes of both regulators and utilities.

Characteristics of Regulation

Regulation, as we know it today, has fostered a "cost plus" mentality on the part of both utilities and regulators. This is not true in all cases, but is far too prevalent. The all too common attitude seems to be that rates should simply be increased to reflect costs incurred, without sufficient attention to whether those costs were necessary, prudent, reasonable, and resulted in the construction of facilities that are used and useful.

Utilities and regulators simply do not pay enough attention either to the necessity for incurring the costs or the effect on rates. This is particularly evident in states such as California which have adopted a myriad of balancing accounts, adjustment clauses and regulatory proceedings. These mechanisms seem to LPUs to be designed primarily to *ensure* that the utilities recover their costs. Although there are "reasonableness reviews", it is extremely difficult for commission staffs and intervenors to effectively challenge the claims of the utilities. The utilities have the information and the resources, and certainly the motivation, to defend as reasonable all of the costs they incur. The cost to the utility of doing so is treated as a business expense and recovered from customers. The focus of utilities has been more on "approvability" than on implementing the efficiency improvements required for competitive success. Thus, utilities have created multiple rate mechanisms that foster cost pass-through to customers. Proceedings are numerous and the human and financial resources required to participate effectively in all of them surpass the ability of most LPUs.

Another factor contributing significantly to the cost plus mentality is the inclination on the part of many regulatory commissions to micro-manage utilities. All too often in proceedings such as those which address integrated resource planning, the commission makes the final decision, and approves the type and timing of new resources to be acquired by the utility. The commission cannot be held accountable for the consequences of these decisions if things go awry. Unfortunately, neither can the utility if it is simply responding to directives set out by the commission. This type of micro-management removes both responsibility and accountability from utilities, and leaves customers—LPUs and others—holding the bag.

Another undesirable characteristic of regulation as we know it today is the tendency to view electric rates as an engine for social change, rather than as a means to recover appropriate costs and provide proper price signals. All too often rates are used to provide subsidies to selected groups or classes of customers (primarily residential) with funds derived by charging LPUs prices that exceed the cost of service. Similar phenomena include the across-the-board collection of costs associated with demand side management (DSM) activities that benefit only a few customers, and the recent introduction of "environmental externality" considerations into the planning process.

Results of Regulation

The current regulatory approach has fostered a situation in which utilities do not behave competitively. The cost plus mentality and the ability of utilities to persuade their regulators to allow rates to be increased to recover all kinds of specific costs, regardless of whether other costs have decreased, have greatly diminished the incentive to be efficient. Only in an environment where most customers are viewed as "price-takers" (or as "ratepayers" instead of as customers) can this approach work.

If utilities were required to compete for customers, as most other businesses must do, the incentive to minimize costs and operate efficiently would be greatly increased. As a result of the non-competitive structure created by regulation, rates are too high. They are designed to recover costs that are in excess of what is necessary to provide the required services; and customers are often required to take services they do not want or need. While the rates of all customers should reflect greater efficiency on the part of the service providers, the problem is especially acute for LPUs as a result of the overcharges they are frequently required to endure in order to subsidize other customers.

More Competition is Required

It is clear that the existing regulatory structure is broken, or at least seriously damaged, and in either event requires replacement or major rehabilitation. From the perspective of LPUs, the key is competition. Utilities and commissions must replace the cost plus mentality with a competitive attitude, wherein the needs and desires of customers receive paramount attention. There also must be more real competition introduced into the supply of services; the provision of new power supplies, and in the provision of service at the retail level. Only if the forces of competition are allowed to work will it be possible to change existing utility and customer behavior. When competition is present, all existing and potential providers are given a strong economic incentive to perform in a manner that is both responsive and efficient. Competition usually brings enhanced services at lower prices, which is beneficial for the entire utility industry and *all* of its customers.

LPUs were at the forefront of introducing competition into the natural gas industry. For years, regulators, pipelines and gas distributors viewed customers as captives and as a place to collect money. The pipelines entered into high priced gas supply contracts that proved not to be marketable. Competition from alternate fuels, the availability of alternate natural gas supplies delivered under transportation contracts, and the bypass of local distribution companies and/or pipelines by LPUs provided much of the impetus for the major reforms that continue to take place in the natural gas industry. The lesson is clear. The existence of a business enterprise is critically dependent upon the ability to provide needed services at a reasonable price. Change may be painful, but the failure to change is often fatal. The electric industry should learn from the experience of the gas industry.

Many state commissions have sowed the seeds of change in the power industry and have now adopted competitive bidding or other strategies designed to implement competitive acquisition of new generation supplies. This trend, coupled with expanded wholesale transmission access that is a result of the Energy Policy Act of 1992 and ongoing initiatives at the FERC, is certainly a step in the right direction. However, it must be a full step, and not a half-step. In too many states, the competitive procurement process is micro-managed through the use of heavily litigated regulatory proceedings in which the commission ultimately directs which resources are to be procured.

A companion problem is the clamor of many electric utilities for formal preapproval of cost recovery by the commission, and guaranteed cost recovery. These are both steps away from a competitive process. If the utility is to be held accountable for the consequences of resource procurement decisions, the utility must ultimately make the decisions about whether to build or purchase, and if to purchase, from whom to purchase and under what terms and conditions. Regulatory commissions should resist the temptation to intrude into the details of the resource selection process. The regulatory commission should insure that the process is fair and unbiased and leave the contracting responsibility with the utility. Only if the utility has the responsibility can the commission later hold it accountable for the consequences.

Similarly, utilities should not be granted preapproval or guaranteed cost recovery. The utility must be required to prove the prudence of its decisions and its administration of both purchased power contracts and construction activity. Only under such a structure can we expect competitive forces to work, for only then does the utility have a financial stake in the outcome of the decisions.

Customers Should Have More Choices

LPUs also believe that customers should have more choices. For example, customers should not be required to participate in DSM programs, and in no event should they be required to fund DSM measures that primarily benefit other customers or other customer classes. A competitive market would not tolerate these subsidies.

LPUs are, for the most part, sophisticated practitioners of energy conservation. They are far more capable than are most utilities of assessing and implementing process efficiency improvements that hold the greatest potential for improved efficiency at most LPU facilities. Utilities may be able to play a useful role in the dissemination of information and in financing to facilitate the installation of new measures, but should not otherwise be involved.

To the extent that a utility participates extensively in the implementation of DSM programs for other customers, the costs of such programs should be recovered from the participating customers, or from the customer class of which the participant is a member. Only with this approach will cross-subsidies be avoided.

Retail Wheeling

No discussion of the utility industry from the perspective of LPUs would be complete without mention of competitive sourcing via what has come to be known as retail wheeling. Retail wheeling is probably the "hot button" of the decade. Millions of words have been written about retail wheeling, and a full discussion is well beyond the scope of this chapter. Retail wheeling is not only a potentially cost-effective alternative to new generation resources for the host electric utility, but also provides the customer an opportunity to secure more competitively priced power.

The willingness of a particular customer to provide its own power supply removes from the utility and its other customers the risks associated with the availability, price and need for that power. These risks are assumed by the contracting customer. To the extent that the end-use customer is willing to contract for a different period of time, a different level of reliability, or a different price structure, the result should be a more efficient transaction than if the utility made the arrangements on the basis of the perceived needs of its overall customer base in the aggregate.

Many LPUs have become disenchanted with the ability of electric utilities to secure power resources in amounts required at reasonable costs. This is not surprising in light of the experience with nuclear plants during the preceding decade. In the increasingly competitive global environment in which LPUs must operate, the ability to manage and control the costs of all important manufacturing inputs is critical. This is why many of the most energy intensive LPUs (particularly chlorine manufacturers) have installed their own generation facilities. Many others are expected to seriously consider installation of their own generation since the Energy Policy Act of 1992 has made this option more feasible. While customer ownership of generation facilities entails risks, the customer has an opportunity to manage those risks. The customer is not faced with monumental cost increases that result from decisions that not only are made by others, but are driven by different objectives. Securing a power supply from a source other than the local electric utility, and having the power wheeled is not without risk; but the risks assumed are manageable.

Many electric utilities and regulators have recognized that retail wheeling, in some form and at some level, is inevitable. This is an important step, but the next step is even more important. The next step should be to act on those realities and create a structure in which the potential benefits can be captured. Those in the "just say no" camp are fighting the inevitable. This attitude is a demonstration of the monopoly mind-set in which protection of existing territory is of paramount importance, and satisfaction of customer needs is secondary. Competitive alternatives are too often dismissed as cherry picking or cream skimming. Utilities that take this attitude and fail to accommodate to changing circumstances are missing significant opportunities and will be ill-prepared to function in the new world.

Regulation Should Be Streamlined

LPUs also believe that the regulatory structure should be streamlined and the number of proceedings minimized. The existence of a multitude of regulatory proceedings is not only burdensome and inefficient, but in concert with the numerous balancing accounts and automatic adjustment clauses used by many utilities serves to greatly reduce the incentives for utilities to control costs and to behave in a manner consistent with the increasingly competitive market in which they find themselves.

Elimination of most of the balancing accounts and associated regulatory proceedings would go a long way toward inducing competitive behavior because the utility stockholders would have a much greater stake in the outcome of utility decision making. There is a disturbing trend toward increasing the number of automatic adjustment clauses to cover such items as environmental clean up and DSM costs. Some have gone so far as to institute mechanisms that decouple profits from sales levels. These mechanisms represent a giant step backward into a cost plus regulatory regime because they remove much of the incentive to be efficient. If rates are not automatically adjusted, utilities have an increased incentive to minimize the level of costs incurred because a reduction in costs improves stockholder returns. The result should be not only lower rates but also potentially greater stockholder returns because of improved efficiencies.

Most LPUs would agree, at least conceptually, that superior performance should be rewarded and that substandard performance should be penalized. However, implementation of such an incentive structure is far from straightforward. Sometimes incentive mechanisms are prescribed for utilities that are performing at a substandard level and are designed to provide stockholders with rewards for improving to levels that are merely satisfactory. Satisfactory performance should be the minimum acceptable level, and certainly should not be accompanied by rewards. In addition, there is a high potential for unintended consequences unless incentives are comprehensive and properly balanced. For example, incentives that reward performance in one area (such as DSM) without consideration of performance in other areas are dangerous. They induce a focus on particular objectives without considering the overall consequences on, or the performance of, the overall operation of the utility.

Conclusion

LPUs want their electric utility suppliers to recognize the competitive pressures which they face, the need for choice, and the need for lower rates. Reforms designed to introduce more competition into electric utility regulation, resource procurement, and regulatory philosophy are all steps in the right direction. As a part of this reform, both utilities and commissions must recognize that a competitive environment will not tolerate cross-subsidies and other uses of the electric utility rate structure as vehicles to achieve social objectives. LPUs also expect utilities and regulatory commissions to recognize that social rate-making does more harm than good, and to take steps to eliminate cross-subsidies.

Chapter Fourteen

LARGE POWER USERS: FROM COST ALLOCATION TO QUESTIONING COSTS

Barbara R. Barkovich, William H. Booth

A major focus of large industrial customers who have been active in state electric utility regulatory proceedings has been cost allocation. Cost allocations in many states have resulted in cross-subsidization by industrial customers of other customer classes. This was true in California until the California Public Utilities Commission (CPUC) began to revise its cost allocation policies in the mid 1980s. Since then, the CPUC has made great progress in moving toward fair, cost-based allocation of electric utility revenue requirements between customer classes. Large industrial customers have been gratified by the success achieved in reducing the cross-subsidies between customer classes evident in the rate design of 10 years ago. That success, however, has not resulted in a reduction in the electric rates paid by large industrial customers, as substantial revenue requirement growth has far outstripped gains arising from more appropriate inter-class allocation.

Large industrial customers and their representatives have necessarily come to the conclusion that a fair allocation of a utility's revenue requirement will not result in fair and competitive rate levels if the costs underlying that utility revenue requirement are too high. Large electricity users have begun to address revenue requirement issues as well as cost allocation in rate proceedings. Recently, industry has also begun to encourage the state commissions to address the big picture of the future of the electric power industry in their states and the high overall level of electric rates facing all classes of customers in many states. Large customers are increasingly emphasizing that competitive factors and regulatory improvements must be brought to bear to create downward

Barbara R. Barkovich is a Principal with Barkovich & Yap, Inc. William H. Booth is an attorney with Jackson, Tufts, Cole & Black.

pressure on rates and upward pressure on the efficiency and productivity of electric utility companies.

The existing utility regulatory framework, and the processes embedded therein, were developed to address fundamentally different issues than those which currently face utilities and their customers. Concern about the impact of inflation on the cost of fuel and capital (and, in may areas, rapid customer growth) has had a major impact on regulation over the last twenty years. But the fundamental monopoly nature of the electric utility industry was not seriously challenged until fairly recently. In contrast, during the last decade, increasing competition has been introduced in the telecommunications and natural gas industries (also regulated by state public utilities commissions) and has had some positive impacts on customer options and cost reductions in those industries.

Currently there are large interregional (not to mention international) differences in the price of electricity faced by large and small customers alike. Prices are driven by differences in resource mix, recent plant construction and purchase power decisions, environmental regulation, and legislative and regulatory policy decisions about using utilities to meet social objectives. These differences have led to average costs for producing electricity that far exceed marginal costs in many states. The resulting price differences can and do have a significant impact on the competitiveness of industrial companies, especially those which are electricity-intensive. Facing highly competitive markets for their own products, industrial electricity consumers tend to see increased competition as being a desirable component of the electricity market of the future—as a means of driving prices down and increasing consumer choice. They increasingly regard this competitive trend as inevitable and urge regulators to minimize the disruptions and maximize the benefits to be achieved for all customers from such changes.

Electric utility regulation, as it has developed over the last 20 years in California and in most other states, is well suited to reducing utility risk and permitting social experimentation by regulators. It is less well suited to providing customer choice, offering incentives for efficient operation or creating competitive pressure on utilities. Further, the elaborate complex of routine proceedings designed to regulate each utility's rates and services (general rate cases, fuel and purchased power cost recovery cases, and resource planning cases in most states, cost of capital cases, inflation adjustment filings, demand side management cases, etc.) increasingly render impossible complete and effective intervention by representatives of most groups of consumers. All of these potential intervenors have a legitimate, often vital, interest in such matters. On procedural grounds alone, change is needed in many states to afford due process to all customer groups.

The need for procedural reform is real. The fundamental question facing the state commissions, however, is whether and how increasing competition in the electric power industry will follow such competition in the telephone and natural gas industries.

Competitive Alternatives for Electric Utility Customers Are Overstated

In its excellent recent report entitled "California's Electric Services Industry: Perspectives for the Past, Strategies for the Future ," the CPUC's Division of Strategic Planning concludes that "the utility now competes for a significant portion of its market share, often negotiating directly with large consumers over price and services delivered." This statement, and related comments, (e.g., that there is a "market" for retail services currently enjoyed by a limited number of large customers) imply that customers have more market power than is presently the case. While the number and extent of competitive alternatives is on the rise for customers, and while the rate of that change is not entirely within the control of any state commission, the report may overstate the current situation.

What service options does a large electric customer have presently? It may buy firm power from the utility under current tariff rates. It may sign a contract to take nonfirm power, with the associated risk of interruption and the continual uncertainty regarding the level of incentives available. It may be able to self-generate if it

247

can resolve often thorny questions of air quality regulation, space, standby rate levels, and fuel supply. It may choose to perform a costly study to demonstrate the feasibility of self-generation in order to provide a basis for negotiating a contract with a utility for a special rate (this is a requirement in California), for whatever period of time a commission deems appropriate (i.e., not more than five years in California). It may choose to shut down its operations and/or move out of state to a utility service area with lower rates or more willingness to negotiate special contracts. While the large industrial customer has some alternatives, certainly more alternatives than the residential or commercial customer has, there are definite limits and the monopoly nature of the utility/customer relationship is largely intact. Even large, sophisticated industrial customers do not currently enjoy the option to buy power from the nearest municipal utility or from a cheaper source in another region, nor can they seek to negotiate a competitive rate except under very limited circumstances.

A large electric utility customer has very little leverage to affect its relationship with the utility which serves it. In California and some other states, the threat of leaving the system, either through self-generation or shutting down, does not affect the utility directly because the revenue shortfall will be spread to all other customers through California's Electric Revenue Adjustment Mechanism (ERAM) or some similar mechanism for decoupling revenues from sales. Furthermore, not all customers have the option of self-generating, and those who do not can only threaten to leave. At present, this does not provide a pre-approved basis for negotiating a special contract. If regulators were to decide that a showing of inability to stay in business in California at current large power rates provides a basis for a special contract, what would be the burden of proof and who would be charged with carrying it forward? This is not an easy thing to prove.

Large industrial customers located in some states have a more accommodating audience in utilities whose revenues are at stake and whose regulators are more amenable to special contracts as a way of assuring a greater ability to spread fixed costs. But special contracts are a mixed blessing. In California, large customers have tended to be wary of schemes calling for the negotiation of contracts with utilities, precisely because of their lack of market power. They have instead preferred to pursue tariff opportunities for reducing rates, such as interruptible service. These tariffs allow all customers who qualify and are willing to take on the inherent risks to take part.

It is instructive to consider the experience gained in California's attempts to restructure the natural gas industry. There the CPUC permitted non-core gas customers (those with substantial gas use who could buy gas from sources other than the local utility) to negotiate gas transportation rates with the utilities. A maximum rate was set by the CPUC and downward negotiation was permitted, although at a loss of revenue and some loss of return for the utility. Not surprisingly, the utilities essentially refused to negotiate a rate below the maximum rate for any customer who could not demonstrate a viable alternate fuel. Even then, the utilities tended to negotiate a transportation charge on a "net back" basis such that the net cost to the customer of using gas was equivalent to that of using the alternate fuel. In short, the best the customer could do was to pay the same price to use gas. This is not market power.

Of course, the CPUC was trying, in the context of the natural gas market, to maximize revenue from large, non-core customers in order to reduce the burden on smaller, more captive core customers a frequent regulatory or legislative goal. This burden includes so-called transition costs, e.g. the local distribution company's share of the additional costs incurred by pipeline companies to renegotiate contracts with gas producers. Once true market alternatives become available, however, any commission's ability to maximize contribution in this way is constrained. In fact, the very act of trying to maximize revenues from non-core customers in order to spread the burden of transition costs made it most attractive for an interstate pipeline like Mojave to provide a bypass option that would allow non-core customers *to opt out of all transition costs.* Only in the face of the threat of bypass of the gas transportation tem entirely have the regulators indicated their willingness to allow utilities to negotiate special gas transportation contracts.

While there is currently no Mojave Pipeline equivalent for electric customers, the continuation of high, noncompetitive electric rates that are well above potential alterative sources will greatly encourage customers and entrepreneurs to seek out new alternatives to utility service. Those customers who are unable to find lower-priced alternatives will become increasingly less competitive in their own industries. Eventually they may find that they no longer have any need for electricity. In either event, lost sales to large industrial customers will make more difficult the burden of large fixed costs of electric utility operations on the remaining customers. These transition costs on the electric side include both the costs associated with non-economic or noncompetitive resources (e.g., high cost nuclear power or qualifying facility purchased power under contracts which do not reflect current market conditions) and the costs associated with social programs (e.g., funding the development of an infrastructure for alternative-fuel vehicles through utility rates). If these costs are not large, or if the cost of electricity represents a relatively small percentage of a customer's total costs, and if the risk or transaction cost associated with alternatives to buying power from the local utility are high, the customer will prefer to stay on the utility system. However, if the costs are large, (i.e., if the state has deemed it appropriate to incorporate significant social costs in utility rates, or there are some relatively recent nuclear plants or nonutility generator contracts at high costs on the system compared to neighboring utilities or states), or if electricity represents a large percentage of a customer's total costs (e.g., certain industrial processes involve electricity as an input representing over 20 percent of the cost of production), then this will significantly affect the ability of some customers to stay in business at tariff rates.

Regulators Should Explore Fully All Alternatives To Make Electric Rates More Competitive

A number of things could be done immediately to make rates more competitive. Many of the alternatives, however, create varying degrees of conflict between the perceived social contract embedded in the business-as-usual approach and the questionable long-term viability of the current system of regulation in keeping most customers on the utility system. One obvious solution to the problem of high utility rates would be to write down the value of utility assets (eg., nuclear power plants) to competitive levels, which is precisely what a competitive business would have to do. However, the issue of who would pay for the write-down (i.e., shareholders or ratepayers, or what combination of the two) raises the specter of violating the perceived agreement that the costs of all certificated projects, once past a prudence review, are properly recoverable in rates. Along these lines, Southern California Edison Company has recently requested authority to accelerate depreciation of its nuclear assets.

Price levels in many qualifying facility contracts in California are expected to fall later in the 1990s. The CPUC has often expressed its commitment to the sanctity of the existing contracts, but in the meantime they will continue to contribute to the overall high level of electric rates. (One might note that in the mid 1980s, the FERC decided that the sanctity of contracts should not stand in the way of restructuring the interstate natural gas industry. Shareholder risk was limited and consumers are still paying for that decision through obligations that find their way into transition costs.) While industrial customers have not advocated revision of the price terms of existing qualifying facility contracts, they have clearly expressed their opposition to efforts of some parties to extend beyond their term the fixed priced provisions in such contracts, further shielding some nonutility generators from competitive market pressure.

Some utilities have realized that their rates are too high and their bureaucracies too cumbersome. After receiving a substantial rate increase (effective January 1, 1993), a result achieved through proper channels of litigation at the CPUC, Pacific Gas and Electric Company announced a voluntary effort to reduce both its costs and its staff, and to pass through some of the benefits to customers. Indeed, out of concern about the impact of such rate increases on large industrial customers, PG&E offered them almost a 6 percent rate reduction to be recovered from cost savings and/or shareholders, not ratepayers, for a period of 18 months. The fact that business-as-usual regulation led to rates that even the utility recognized were too high is a demonstration of the fact that the business-as-usual system of regulation is not working very well under present conditions.

For this reason, the status quo is not a very useful guide for future regulation. The time has arrived to reexamine the value and purpose of automatic inflation adjustments and other incremental additions to the existing cost base. Such adjustments were a product of a period of very high inflation. Now that inflation is no longer a current threat to utility financial health, regulators could communicate much better signals to utility management by exposing the companies to the risk of increasing expense levels and the opportunity to increase earnings through increased productivity. Utilities, like all companies, need incentives and opportunity to perform efficiently; automatic cost recovery mechanisms rob them of both.

It may also be time to consider a non-cost-of-service approach to ratemaking, such as the price cap option. However, if a price cap approach is to be considered, it is very important to ensure that the base or starting prices should not be so high that they are already causing non-economic bypass or prompting customers to leave the system for lower rates elsewhere. The equivalent of zero-base budgeting in this context is likely to be defined by a competitor without the same baggage of non-economic former investments and social costs of existing utilities. Incentive ratemaking may well help bridge this gap, but it is not likely to be sufficient without attention to existing resources, goals beyond the provision of utility service, and the costs of competitive options as they arise.

It may also be time to reconsider the usefulness of broad-based decoupling mechanisms. California's mechanism for decoupling revenues from sales (the ERAM) does not isolate the source of the disparity between forecasted and actual sales. The disparity could be due to weather, energy conservation, recession, introduction of new technology, or any other factor one can imagine. While such a broad-based mechanism eliminates disincentives for utility demand side management (DSM) activities, which is certainly consistent with integrated resource planning goals, it does not discriminate between load reductions due to increased efficiency and those due to the loss of customers because of high rates. While the ERAM has certainly reduced debates in rate proceedings about sales forecasts, there have been negative side effects. The ERAM can be devastating to the normal incentive of the utility to keep its costs down in order to retain sales. In California, the ERAM removes virtually all utility concern over the loss of electric customers and their load; it simply does not matter if the customers leave for another state, ERAM will allow the utility to shift more of the fixed costs to the remaining customers. As long as there are fixed costs to be spread and generation reserves are more than adequate to meet load, the addition of load due to efficient use of energy for productive purposes is not necessarily an inherent evil. Furthermore, a death spiral caused by higher rates to remaining customers including those who can or must leave the system is not in anyone's interest.

Careful Development Of Alternatives Strategies

Large electricity customers may not have the degree of market power than some parties allege. However, a steady movement toward greater customer choice and competition over the next decade seems inevitable. This may happen in a managed way, by providing more customer choice, and avoiding non-economic bypass through recognition of customer opportunity costs when setting rates. It could also happen more abruptly, if, for example, stand-alone electric generation facilities become cost effective for individual customers as compared to tariff rates. (This could lead to stranded investment in a big way, virtually forcing a marking down of assets to allow major rate reductions and avoid a catastrophic loss of sales to customers.) Provisions of the Energy Policy Act of 1992 prevent the FERC from ordering retail wheeling. However, the FERC has authorized direct access to its pipelines by large customers seeking gas service. The FERC has permitted new or extended interstate pipelines to provide such service. These actions cannot realistically be seen as anomalies. The same applies to the introduction of competition in the long-distance telephone market and the gradual movement toward competition in the local telephone market as well. Increasing competition has been authorized in the telecommunications and natural gas industries because it made sense and because it offered the potential for downward pressure on utility costs and prices.

The fear of such changes is largely directed toward the fear of cream-skimming , i.e., that those customers who can most readily leave the system or negotiate with the utility will do so, and the rest will end up paying more. However, the extent to which this happens will very much be a function of the following factors: a) the price differential existing at the time between utility services and power purchased elsewhere and transported by the utility; b) the quality of service the utility provides at its price; c) the percentage of a customer's total costs that are represented by electricity and whether the transaction costs of buying power elsewhere are worth it; and d) the terms as well as the price of outside sources of power and their likelihood of longevity. It is not clear at this point that a substantial portion of possible commercial and industrial participants in an alternative market for electricity will decide it is worth the effort required. It is even possible that access to such an alternative market will enhance their ability to define an opportunity cost as a basis for negotiating a price to remain on the utility system. Utilities will negotiate either on an individual contract basis or for a subset of large electricity consumers who are particularly price sensitive, to reduce the risk to other ratepayers. After all, if price-sensitive customers leave the utility, these other customers face a greater risk, both in terms of higher electric rates and in terms of reduced economic viability.

The necessary concomitant of this is that customers who are more price-sensitive or who can afford to pursue alternatives will benefit more than customers who cannot. On the other hand, regulation that is sensitive to the dangers of non-economic bypass can spread costs among customer classes in such a way as to minimize the burden. Regulators can retain fixed cost contributions from those customers who can bypass by using creative rate design, including new methods of customer segmentation. Regulation that insists on loading unnecessary costs on price-sensitive customers will only stimulate ever-greater levels of bypass by increasing the gap between rates and costs. A continued and heightened focus on least-cost planning and investment on the part of regulators will minimize this gap between costs and rates.

Chapter Fifteen

CONSUMER PRINCIPLES FOR ELECTRIC UTILITY REFORM: "FIVE NOT-SO-EASY PIECES"

Michael E. Shames

As the electric utility industry restructuring accelerates, a not-so-silent majority of electric customers will become increasingly aware of the inexorable changes in the way electric utilities operate and are regulated. Small electric customers, including residential and small business will resist these changes. This chapter proposes five principles that, if applied by regulators and utilities, will improve small electric customers acceptance of the significant service and price changes being contemplated by the industry and its regulators.

The rate of evolution in the electric services industry is accelerating. This tradition-bound aristocracy of the business world has lost its divine right of governance over the electric consumer. The transition into a new electric services paradigm will create changes not only for the industry, but for its small consumers who, for many decades, have been insulated by regulators and, even consumer advocates, from the activities transforming the industry.

Proponents of industry restructure insist that greater consumer choice is an inevitability. Some claim that what small electric customers really want is choice. They hypothesize that if choice of services are offered, customers will gracefully accept the changes in service and cost. The discussion over the inevitability of increased choice is being argued throughout the country by regulators and industry alike. For the purposes of this discussion, we will assume that new service choices will be offered to small consumers.

Michael Shames is the Executive Director of Utility Consumers' Action Network.

This discussion focuses on another issue. If increased choice is to be offered to small electric customers, how can it be done effectively? The underlying premise of this discussion is that small electric customers, both residential and small business, place nominal importance upon choice as a right. Most electric customers gave up "choice" when they conferred monopoly franchises upon their local electric utility. There is little clamoring for choice from these same customers.

What electric services consumers want can be gleaned from history. When the landed aristocracies (also known as land barons of Britain) lost their "power franchises" as the British monarchy's monopoly powers faded, the inhabitants of the "manors" did not demand choice of new gentry to replace the old. Their primary concerns were economic. Will taxes rise? Is prosperity threatened? Will livelihoods be lost? Similarly, most small electric customers do not *demand* any change in electric service. If change occurs, their concerns are whether rates will rise and whether the new "regime" will affect their individual pursuit of prosperity.

Where does the fabled "choice" come into play? Is it the Holy Grail of the economist policymaker? Perhaps. From the economist policymaker's perspective, choice is an essential element, not only of a competitive marketplace, but of an increasingly unbundled electric services industry. Thus, on a theoretical level, choice is very important. However, economic perspective is not easily reconciled with the small consumers' hierarchy of needs, which places "choice" at much lower rung than does the economist policymakers. Given this reality, how do regulators acknowledge the realities of the changing marketplace while serving the customers' needs? Not easily.

I suggest that adherence to five proposed principles will increase the prospects of small electric customers accepting the service and price changes being contemplated by the industry and its regulators. These principles should guide regulatory agencies in the setting of their policies on change in the electric services industry.

First and foremost, the regulators should ensure that any changes are fair. Fairness may include reducing rates for all customers, not only those with bypass options. Without rate reductions, small consumers will not perceive the industry changes as being fair.

Second, and of no less importance, is that if regulators are committed to promoting "choice" for customers, then such choice must be *meaningful* choice for small consumers. "Meaningful" is defined as choice that includes:

➡ Phasing in of a few options;

➡ The options must be accessible, i.e., simple to understand;

➡ The choices should not be discriminatory, i.e., they should be available to most customers;

➡ Choices must offer real monetary differences for customers who choose the options.

Third, it is essential that regulators place a high priority upon protecting captive customers from cross-subsidies and stranded costs, including those costs attributable to the introduction of competition into other customer classes and industry restructuring as a whole.

Fourth, regulators should direct their efforts to use structural changes to encourage greater efficiencies in utilities' non-competitive utility activities.

Finally, regulators should also be actively promoting meaningful choice for utilities. In other words, the commission should offer choices to utilities of the roles that they wish to play in the "new world." Such choices must contain real risk and real reward for utilities who choose to compete.

Achieving Fairness

Utility consumer advocates place great weight upon rates. If rates go up, consumer advocates will be up in arms. Conversely, utilities are quick to argue that it is *total bills* and not rates that cause heartburn for the utility bill recipients. Both sides are right and both sides are wrong.

Utility customers are very rate sensitive. But rate acceptance is largely an indicator of whether a customer views a rate as fair. Small customers view rates and rate trends through "fairness" filters. If customers deem a rate to be "fair," then the level of that rate takes on less importance. Rate increases are less objectionable if the reason for the increase is deemed to be fair. And rate reductions can be objectionable, if the decrease is less than what customers view as "fair". So the concept of "fairness" takes on much greater importance than is desirable for the economist policymaker.[1] The issue of greatest controversy will be defining what is "fair". There is no definition, since fairness is situational, but it can be measured.

Rate decreases, where feasible, will make any structural changes more palatable to all consumers. If rate decreases are not feasible, and rate increases are more likely, consumers might be prepared to accept increases. However, the sacrifices must be reasonable, clearly explained and shared. If any one customer class suffers more than others, the proposed sacrifices will be viewed suspiciously. Thus, the policymaker must endeavor to secure broad buy-in by consumers and special interest groups.

In sum, if a broad range of stakeholder representatives accept the proposed changes, then "fairness" has been achieved. If consensus is not possible, fairness can be measured by the level of opposition to the proposal. Stakeholders' support will likely be secured if changes are accompanied by rate reductions, are consistent with basic principles of equity and comport with the other principles discussed below.

---

[1] Fairness is problematic for those who view the world economically, as it is almost impossible to quantify. But it is not impossible to measure. Most utilities conduct customer satisfaction surveys; these surveys are useful indicators of the fairness index.

Choice And Meaningful Choice

■ Death By Choice

As the redoubtable philosopher Woody Allen once suggested, choice is an opportunity to make a costly mistake, or worse, come face to face with your own utter confusion. To wit, more books and articles are published in one day than a person can read in a lifetime. Today there are 339 full-power TV stations and cable systems with up to 140 channels offering more than 72,000 shows per month, compared to the three networks that dominated only 20 years ago.

In 1978, the typical supermarket carried 11,767 items. Today, the average shopper chooses from among 30,000 items. And the volume of personal junk mail grew 13 times faster than the population during the last ten years.[2]

Mr. Allen's sentiments are reflective of the average American's plight; we have become the most time-presssed, distracted civilization in history. It is no small wonder, then, that most small utility customers do not seek out yet more choices when it comes to electric service.

For decades, utility customers were taught that when they turned on a switch, the lights would come on. Those same customers were also conditioned to believe that when they picked up an AT&T phone and made a call they would receive a bill from AT&T. The split up of AT&T and the consequential changes in the phone industry have left most customers pining for the days of the black phone and Ma Bell. Only larger customers have seen measurable benefits from the changes in the phone industry. Choice is not particularly desirable objective for customers who have long believed that they granted monopoly rights to utilities in exchange for the

---

[2] These, and other such facts, are found in *Breathing Space,* J. Davidson & T. Moore, MasterMedia Limited, 1993.

freedom from needing to make complicated choices about electric service. These customers will be resistant to having choice imposed upon them by regulators.

■ Meaningful Choice Defined

One of the consumer principles described above raises the concept of "meaningful choice". If regulators are committed to imposing more "choice" upon small utility customers then such choice must be *meaningful*.

Like beauty, "meaningful" is a difficult concept to define, let alone to gain consensus upon. I believe that meaningful choice includes the phasing in of the new options, that the options be limited, be simple to understand, be available to most, if not all, customers, and offer real monetary differences for customers who choose the options. Each of these elements are explained below.

New options must be few in number and must be introduced in a phased manner. Too many choices will discourage most consumers. Either consumers will rebel or they will simply ignore the options and retain the status quo. The fact that over 70 percent of telephone subscribers continue to use AT&T for their long-distance service is more of a testament to the resistance of utility customers to change than to superior service or pricing advantages offered by AT&T.

The deregulation of AT&T came rather quickly. The Federal Communications Commission opened the marketplace to all new comers offering long-distance service for large and small customers. In a short period of time, residential customers could choose from three major and twelve smaller long-distance service providers.[3] Small customers would have been better served by being introduced initially to no more than three alternative providers to

---

[3] Consumer Action News, Long Distance Survey, March/April 1988 by San Francisco Consumer Action.

AT&T. After resistance to alternatives was broken down, the market should have been opened up to other competitors. This phased approach would have more successfully changed the "consumer" culture that had been ingrained over one-half century of ubiquitous phone service.

The accessibility of options is an essential part of the formula. Those in the regulatory arena who have become fluent in our professional language and concepts do not readily relate to the language levels of the average ratepayer. Options must be simple to understand. This standard is not easily satisfied. For example, when inside telephone wiring was deregulated in California in 1986, small utility consumers were given a new choice for maintenance of their inside wiring. Instead of relying upon Pacific Bell, customers could use independent interconnect companies to handle inside wiring needs. From the regulators perspective, this was a fairly straightforward change; instead of being served by one company, consumers could draw from two or more companies.

The change may have appeared to be a modest one, but it was not. A 1993 study by the California Public Utilities Commission revealed that a significant portion of both residential and small business customers are not aware of their inside wiring options.[4] The study found that only 40 percent of Pacific Bell customers were aware of the six-year old inside wiring repair plan offered by the phone company. Sixty percent of those customers were not aware that they paid extra for these utility-sponsored plans. And only 3 percent of those customers who had problems with their inside wiring ever bothered contacting an independent interconnect company to fix it, even though such interconnects are generally less expensive than service by Pacific Bell.

---

[4] *Customer Awareness Study on Inside Wiring Policy,* May 29, 1993. Conducted by Freeman, Sullivan & Co.

There are many reasons for the failure of the inside wiring deregulation. One can reasonably conclude from the California commission's experience with small phone customers that changes in utility service are not readily embraced by these customers. Even though Pacific Bell spent considerable dollars educating small consumers about the inside wiring changes, the message was not grasped by many consumers because the changes were not phased and the company never fully explained the options to consumers. [5]

Another reason for the failure of the inside wire changes was that the amount of dollars at stake and the uncertainty surrounding this complicated service led customers to ignore less expensive options.

Does that mean that small customers are price insensitive? Not at all. Witness the thousands of protest letters and phone calls each time the California commission approves a major (5 percent or more) rate increase. It does mean that small customers are relatively price inelastic. Uncertainty will discourage them from pursuing less costly utility service options. Unless the cost differential is substantial, small consumers have little economic incentive to experiment with services that they don't fully understand.

---

[5] Utility Consumers Action Network (UCAN) conducted a 1991 study of California's telephone inside wire deregulation process. UCAN concluded that a competitive "interconnect" market that served small customers' inside wiring needs never developed. Those consumers who understood they had an option was unable to find a cost-effective provider. Pacific Bell recommended electricians to customers seeking alternatives to the phone company. UCAN determined that electricians were neither necessary nor cost-effective alternatives. Meanwhile, numerous ex-Bell repair persons or other qualified "interconnects" sought to mine the newly established inside wire service market, but consumers remained ignorant or skeptical of these alternative providers. The nascent competitors were never established and, as of 1992, were moribund.

Protection Of Captive Customers

It is essential that regulators place a high priority upon protecting captive customers from cross-subsidies and stranded costs, including those attributable to the introduction of competition into other customer classes and industry restructuring. This issue will attract the most attention from expert consumer advocacy groups, as the threat of imposing stranded costs upon consumers represents the most costly aspect of the industry's restructuring.

There is little controversy over the fact that as the industry changes, there will be increasing opportunity for cross-subsidies between customer classes. Those customers with options will exercise them (primarily large customers) and those with less compelling options will absorb the stranded costs or the hidden cross-subsidies.

For example, the cost of distribution and generation capacity is largely a fixed cost for utilities. As each large customer pursues self-generation or other generation alternatives, the fixed costs do not change significantly. Traditionally, regulators will assign those costs to remaining customers. Over time this burden will become so large as to trigger an overt objection by small customers to the shouldering of such stranded costs.

Hidden cross-subsidies are also likely to develop. When a utility divests itself or "spins off" an affiliate into unregulated status, consumer advocates will generally point out that the divested company has received a subsidy from the "mother" utility. At a minimum, trained personnel and goodwill established by the mother have been diverted into the newly unregulated affiliate. California has acknowledged these hidden subsidies or "intangible royalties".[6] There are an assortment of other such cross-subsidies, the intangible royalties being just one example.

---

[6] In Docket 86-03-090, the California PUC ordered San Diego Gas & Electric Company's (SDG&E) diversified affiliates to make royalty

The stranded costs pose a very serious and sizable threat to rates. Regulators must be very sensitive now to the potential for stranded costs that will materialize five or ten years from now. Thus, *any* sizable utility building proposal that comes before a regulatory commission must be viewed as likely stranded investment by the turn of the century. Commissions might be advised to begin structuring "de-evolution" funds similar to the "decommissioning trust funds" currently in place to address the costs of decommissioning nuclear power plants. A de-evolution fund could be a fund of money that will be used to offset the cost of future stranded costs.

Regulators must also be sensitive to the threat posed by existing utility infrastructure. Consumer activists are likely to call for the a widespread write down of utilities' non-cost effective infrastructure. Other previously regulated utilities, such as telephone and airline companies, used write downs and accelerated depreciation to enable their companies to compete. There is no reason for electric utilities and their shareholders to escape the same reality. In the long run, utility shareholders have been well served by the write downs.[7]

---

payments to the utility, which would then be transferred to ratepayer accounts. SDG&E rejected the ruling and withdrew its application to diversify. A subsequent order by the PUC in a later case reversed the requirement for royalty payments where spin-offs occur. More recently, in September 1993, a California PUC Administrative Law Judge ruled that Pacific Telesis' proposed divestment of its telephone affiliate, Pacific Bell, warranted further study to quantify that intangible royalties that would be reaped by Telesis. A Commission decision on the ALJ's recommendation was not issued at the time of writing.

[7] In particular, AT&T and the Regional Bell Operating Companies experienced sluggish returns due to large write downs taken in the 80s. However, over the past 10 years, their stock performance has more than doubled the NYSE average.

Encouraging Greater Efficiencies In Utilities' Noncompetitive Activities

An issue whose lower profile belies its relative importance involves the regulated utilities' noncompetitive activities. Regulators should use the industry's structural changes to promote greater efficiencies in utilities' competitive and noncompetitive utility activities. This involves no less than changing the utilities' entire corporate culture—an ambitious but essential agenda.

Much has been written about utilities undertaking the development of competitive generation abilities so that they could compete in a competitive generation marketplace. In some regions, discussions about competitive distribution (e.g., retail wheeling) have begun. In theory, utilities would have to hone their abilities and costs of constructing and maintaining distribution services. Federal Energy Regulatory Commission policymakers appear to have targeted transmission service as an area warranting changes. Utilities have begun to respond to these encroachments by preparing for competition in activities that previously were the exclusive province of the regulated utility.

However, it is not enough to encourage utilities to compete in these limited activities. The electric utility of the 21st Century will be, primarily, an energy service company. Their monopoly will lay with access to a broad base of consumers, primarily small consumers. These consumers will likely represent the utilities' major profit center. So there will be a natural proclivity for utilities to inflate prices for its service to these consumers as competitors court the utilities' larger customers.

For example, I expect that future utilities will offer education programs, energy efficiency consulting, customization of energy service via smart meters as well as continuing their general administrative activities. They may also explore energy service retailing and other similar activities that will exploit the access and goodwill they have developed with the broad spectrum of small consumers. They will likely be the only game in town. Or, if the phone companies inside wire experiences are an indicator, the only game that small consumers will accept.

It is imperative that regulators target these noncompetitive activities for greater efficiencies. Regulatory policies should be shaped to provide incentives for efficiency in all aspects of utility operations. This includes setting steep productivity goals with financial incentives if the goals are met.

Regulators might also develop benchmarking capabilities so that they can compare the costs of utilities' noncompetitive operations. This strategy may include encouraging benchmarking within the industry itself as a cost-assessment tool. Benchmarking of operations costs is a very common tool among businesses in competitive industries but is rarely used among electric utilities in different service areas.

Finally, regulators should also be actively promoting "meaningful choice" for the electric utilities. In other words, the commission should offer choices to utilities of the roles that they wish to play in the "new world." Such choices must contain *real* risk and *real* reward for utilities who choose to compete. As the utility employee begins to understand and integrate the concept of *real* risk, the corporate culture will inevitably change. So long as the utility views its business as oriented towards exploiting a regulatory process open to manipulation, the company's culture will remain unable to promote true efficiency.

Consumers will be justified in feeling betrayed if regulators and policymakers turn a blind eye to the noncompetitive activities of the electric utility. For it is the customer with fewer options that will pay most for these utility services. Unless the entire corporate culture of the electric utility is converted into one more akin to leaner cost-cutting private businesses, small consumers will pay more for less.

Conclusion

Increased choice of service may be an inevitability for small customers. Since increased choice is not a necessarily attractive prospect for most small customers, consumer resistance to choice can be expected. Adherence to five recommended principles will increase the prospects of small electric customers accepting the service and price changes being contemplated by the industry and its regulators. These principles should guide regulatory agencies in the setting of their policy on changes in the electric services industry.

First and foremost, the regulators should ensure that any changes are fair. Fairness may include reducing rates for *all* customers, not only those with bypass options. Without rate reductions, small consumers will not perceive the industry changes as being fair.

Second, and of no less importance, is that if regulators are committed to promoting "choice" for customers, then such choice must be *meaningful* choice for small consumers.

Third, it is essential that regulators place a high priority upon protecting captive customers from cross-subsidies and stranded costs, including those attributable to the introduction of competition into other customer classes and industry restructuring.

Fourth, regulators should direct their efforts to use the utility structural changes to encourage greater efficiencies in utilities' noncompetitive utility activities.

Finally, regulators should also be actively promoting meaningful choice for utilities. In other words, the regulatory commissions should offer choices to utilities of the roles that they wish to play in the "new world" and such choices must contain *real* risk and *real* reward for utilities who choose to compete.

Chapter Sixteen

ASSESSING FUTURE ENVIRONMENTAL ISSUES FOR ELECTRIC UTILITIES

Stephen G. Brick

For more than two decades, utilities have been subject to more and increasingly complex environmental restrictions. Companies have spent billions of dollars bringing their systems into compliance with state and federal laws that run the gamut from air quality to nuclear waste disposal. A utility without a fully staffed environmental department is a rarity. The importance of environmental issues in day-to-day utility operations is evidenced by the proliferation of environmental sections in the numerous trade press publications, including a number devoted exclusively to utility environmental affairs.

At present, utilities grapple with the costs and implications of environmental compliance in a variety of areas. Air quality is today perhaps the most prominent. Around the country, utilities are developing plans for complying with the various requirements of the Clean Air Act Amendments of 1990 (CAAA). The provisions of this legislation concern the control of sulfur dioxide and nitrogen oxides that contribute to acid rain, ozone control, toxic air pollutants, and a new operating permit law. Water quality laws also affect utilities. Power plant waste water must be treated properly before discharge; water used for cooling thermal power plants cannot exceed specified discharge temperatures. Utilities face a variety of waste-disposal and hazardous waste regulations. These rules govern everything from coal ash and scrubber sludge to procedures dealing with hazardous substances, such as polychlorinated biphenyls (PCBs) from transformers. Virtually every aspect of nuclear power plant operation is affected by one sort of environmental regulation or another, from transport of nuclear fuel to the plant to removal and storage of spent fuel from the plant.

Stephen G. Brick is Vice President of MSB Energy Associates, Inc.

Considering the wide range of existing environmental laws and the cost and complexity of compliance, it may be difficult to entertain seriously the possibility of yet additional regulation. But, regulation of the various by-products of electric power generation will continue to increase in the future.

Considering the extent to which utilities have already cleaned up, it may be difficult to entertain the notion that utilities will be subject to yet more environmental laws. But, utility operations will continue to be closely scrutinized by environmental regulators and utilities will be subject to a high degree of new regulation.

Considering the already high level of utility expenditures for environmental compliance, it may be difficult to believe that future regulations could impose additional significant costs. But, future regulations will be more costly for utilities, both in terms of their cost and in terms of the restrictions they will impose on utility planning and operations.

In the past, the utility industry has, for the most part, focussed its energy on attempts to minimize new regulations; once passed, utilities have focussed on minimizing compliance costs. This strategy will prove increasingly flawed as we move into the 21st century. Successful utilities will replace the "resist-then-comply" mentality with one that focuses on anticipation and risk reduction.

Historic Strategy Toward Environmental Regulation

The electric utility industry has tended to treat existing laws as if they were a fixed aspect of the regulatory landscape. Since the 1970s, however, federal, state and local environmental laws have been amended and created with some frequency. Actions taken by the industry between these changes, however, have almost always assumed that the existing regulations were a terminal state. This practice appears to have led to higher compliance costs than would have occurred if the pending regulations had been anticipated rather than ignored. While it is inherently impossible to predict with certainty the future course of regulation, it is possible to look at recent scientific, political and legal activity to gain a sense of what is likely to evolve in the future.

As an example, the first serious federal legislative proposal to control acid rain precursors (sulfur dioxide [SO_2] and oxides of nitrogen [NO_x]) was drafted in 1979. While it would have been hard to predict that it would take until 1990 to amend the federal Clean Air Act, at some point in the early 1980s, it became clear that acid rain legislation had become a matter of "when" as opposed to "if". This could have been factored into utility planning at that time.

Most utilities with responsibilities under the acid rain title of CAAA now find themselves having to make significant pollution control investment (scrubbers or fuel switching). For a variety of reasons, the timing of these investments is not optimal. Bond-rating agencies and Wall Street analysts look nervously at utilities that must invest billions of dollars in pollution clean-up. The industry is in the early stages of restructuring, and any expenditures must be weighed in the balance of competition and deregulation.

Some utilities, however, find themselves well-positioned to respond to and even profit from the acid rain provisions. These are the utilities that, for a variety of reasons, reduced their SO_2 emissions between the baseline period (1985-1987) and the present. These utilities' emissions came down because prices for western, low-sulfur coal were decreasing or because states had acted independently to reduce the effects of acid rain (Wisconsin, Massachusetts, New York). For whatever reason, these utilities now find themselves "ahead of the curve", and are better positioned to respond to a changing industry. Is there a lesson to be learned from this experience? If these utilities constitute any sort of sample, the lesson is clearly that anticipation is better than reaction.

Future Regulations

It is clear that we have not seen the end of new environmental regulation. Although most companies have their hands full just complying with the existing laws, it is none too soon to look ahead and assess how a variety of future regulations will affect utilities. Air quality regulations will continue to have a significant effect on electric utilities. A detailed look at this one aspect of environmental regulation provides a useful perspective from which to examine the future of environmental regulation. Potential air quality regulations are discussed below along with a brief description of the probable effects, and a description of the resources that present less risk when considering the regulation.

➠ Stricter regulation of utility emissions of oxides of nitrogen (NOx), sulfur dioxide (SO2) and toxic air pollutants (particularly mercury) are likely in the future.

For a variety of reasons, environmental groups, health advocacy groups and segments of the scientific community support lower standards for various pollutants and the imposition of standards for currently unregulated pollutants. These reasons concern both human health and environmental resources.

➠ Support exists to lower the ambient standard for ozone from .12 ppm to .08 ppm.

The US Environmental Protection Agency (EPA) is in the process of reviewing recent studies on the effects of ozone on human health. EPA Administrator Carol Browner recently announced that the ambient ozone standard would not be revised until this study is complete. The American Lung Association along with a coalition of environmental groups have sued the EPA, arguing that the present standard is insufficient to protect human health.

In addition to its adverse affects on human health, ozone is implicated in forest decline, and its NOx precursors contribute to acidic deposition. A lowered ozone standard would most likely call for greater levels of utility NOx reduction to meet attainment than now appear necessary, perhaps necessitating widespread retrofitting of selective catalytic reduction. Many areas of the country currently meeting the present ozone standard, would find themselves out of attainment.

➠ Support exists for establishing a one-hour SO_2 standard.

The American Lung Association, the Environmental Defense Fund and other groups have charged that the present standard does not adequately protect human health, and support imposition of a one-hour standard. EPA is currently negotiating a settlement agreement with these parties.

A tighter standard may require shifting to lower-sulfur fuels, including lower sulfur coal or oil or natural gas. Post-combustion controls, such as flue-gas desulfurization systems, may be needed where coal is to be used as a primary fuel.

➠ In the 1990 Clean Air Act Amendments, Congress directed the US EPA to study the effects of utility emissions of toxic air pollutants and mercury on human health and welfare.

Congress authorized the EPA to promulgate standards if the study suggested that they were needed to protect human health and welfare. It appears that utility emissions of mercury are a likely target for future regulation.

♦ Bioaccumulation of mercury in fish and associated game animals can have substantial health effects on humans that ingest the meat of these animals. Health advisories have already been posted in many states concerning consumption of mercury-contaminated fish.

♦ Documented health affects include human neurological and kidney damage and adverse impacts on fetal development.

♦ Fossil fuel combustion now accounts for about 20 to 30 percent of U.S. anthropogenic mercury emissions; utilities account for a substantial fraction of that 20 to 30 percent.

♦ As federal regulations come into force that eliminate mercury from many sources (the most important being latex paint and batteries), utilities will account for a growing share of the remainder.

♦ The Center for Clean Air Policy estimates that by the year 2000, utilities will be responsible for about half of the remaining mercury emissions and that by 2010, this will have risen to 60 percent.

➡ Recent epidemiological studies suggest that very fine particles (particles less than 2.5 microns in diameter) have an adverse impact on human health.

Although these studies have not yet been published, the general results were described at the 1993 annual meeting of the American Lung Association. If the results are borne out by subsequent research, it is likely that utility emissions of very fine particles will be regulated. These particles consist of sulfate and nitrate aerosols (emitted from power plans in gaseous form) and the very smallest fraction of typical particulate emissions.

➡ Concern over the possible effects of global climate change have led to international calls for action to reduce emissions of greenhouse gasses (GHGs).

Because of their dependence upon fossil fuels, utilities emit substantial amounts of carbon dioxide (CO_2) and smaller amounts of other GHGs. Regulations to stabilize or reduce GHGs have been introduced in the US Congress. The Clinton Administration recently issued its Joint Action Plan to stabilize emissions. For the time being, the plan entails only voluntary actions on the part of utilities. Any mandate would clearly affect electric utilities.

Considering the standard palate of utility resource options, demand side management and renewable resources, coal-gasification and natural gas burning will be favored over traditional coal- or oil-fired generation under any of the potential regulatory scenarios. While a single new regulation might result in only small incremental costs to a utility, multiple new regulations would have potentially substantial impact and are the biggest threat.

Anticipating Risk

Each of the regulatory scenarios just described has some probability of occurring. How should utilities factor these risks into resource planning decisions now, in a reasonable way?

The first action all utilities should take is to account for these risks as new resource options are considered. In addition to factoring the costs of meeting existing standards into the cost of new resources, utilities should undertake an analysis of how potential options fare under various future regulatory scenarios. Options that appear to be cost-effective considering only known regulations, may not fare as well when the host of potential future laws are considered. Often the cost difference between two resource options is fairly narrow. Consideration of these potential regulations may swing a resource decision in favor of a more costly option in the belief that the added cost is good insurance against tighter restrictions.

Second, utilities should also begin to develop an array of more benign resources, both on the supply and demand side. Many companies find themselves with excess capacity at this time. In this situation, companies can experiment with small increments of clean resources at relatively low risk. Utilities clearly need more experience with renewable resources—wind, biomass and photovoltaics, among others. Advanced biogasification is a promising technology for making use of waste biomass.

Energy efficiency—both on the customer side of the meter and within a utility's own system—also needs increased emphasis. Because of excess capacity and a slack economy, many utilities are backing away from investment in efficiency. Considering the future risk posed by environmental regulations, this is an inappropriate strategy. Improved customer end-use efficiency reduces all of the pollutants described. Efficiency is clearly the best means of reducing greenhouse gasses. Improved efficiency on the utility side of the meter also has potent benefits. Overall heat-rate improvement and reduction of transmission and distribution losses should be part of the planning portfolio. Improved efficiency of existing hydroelectric facilities can increase the capacity and output of existing dams without adversely affecting the environment.

Third, utilities should explore options that provide collateral benefits and reduce overall environmental impact. For example, utility-industry partnerships can lead to the replacement of aging, inefficient industrial boilers with new utility-owned cogeneration units. In addition to reducing environmental impact, the utility can provide tangible economic development within its service territory. Economic development efforts of this sort are much more likely to retain customers than those aimed at merely providing lower rates. The trend towards market-based pollution trading systems, as evidenced by the 1990 acid rain law and by the emerging market-based approaches to ozone control, makes it likely that utilities will be able to take credit for pollution reductions undertaken in this way. Additional collateral benefits are possible as well. Advanced biogasification, mentioned previously, in addition to producing gas that can be burned in a boiler, can also produce various valuable by-products. For example, a Michigan cherry-growing cooperative was faced with rising disposal costs for waste cherry pits. Working with a regional biotechnology center, a biogasifier was designed in which a light, high quality lubricating oil, natural cherry flavoring, and activated charcoal were produced in addition to burnable gas. The gas was used to produce both electricity and steam for the cooperative, in addition to producing a small amount of electricity for sale back to the grid. A waste disposal problem was turned into a potential economic benefit, while lowering overall environmental impacts. The project foundered due to lack of financing—in spite of a relatively short payback period. In this situation, a local utility could have gained a clean resource and provided regional economic development as well. Virtually every sort of organic waste can be gasified; utilities should take a major role in advancing this technology.

A number of utilities have adopted explicit policies towards the threat of various types of future regulation. For example, the New England Electric System and Southern California Edison Company have adopted explicit goals for reducing greenhouse gas emissions. The Sacramento Municipal Utility District is advancing the use of renewable energy and efficiency in a dramatic way. Recognition of future environmental risks and development of specific policies to address the risks should become standard operating procedure. The exercises involved in analyzing these risks can be equated to calculating the cost of insurance. Without knowing the cost of insurance and its alternatives, intelligent planning decisions cannot be made. But, in fact, this is how most utility planning is now done. As we move into the 21st century, this will become a central focus of every successful utility's planning staff.

Chapter Seventeen

WHAT THE FINANCIAL MARKETS EXPECT OF ELECTRIC UTILITIES: AN INVESTOR'S PERSPECTIVE

Julie M. Cannell

The past few years have seen remarkable changes underway in the electric utility industry. Certainly the external dynamics have evolved markedly. But perhaps of equal importance is the fact that there has also been a distinct increase in utility management's awareness of investor expectations. With the days of utility securities as investments for widows and orphans gone forever, this heightened responsiveness is critical to insure a continuing supply of new funds to meet the industry's capital requirements.

Solid communication with management is of great importance from my own perspective as a value investor. This particular investment discipline involves seeking out industries and companies that represent intrinsic value (usually as measured by above-average dividend yield, lower price-earnings ratios, and/or low price-to-book value relationships) which is as yet unrecognized by the markets. This strategy is a very deliberate and disciplined approach, one which takes a somewhat far-sighted view of a company's and industry's fundamentals, and one which, obviously, is a significant contrast to the investor who looks for momentum in a stock's price or the risk arbitrage investor's focus on near term events. Because value investing generally means buying stocks early—far ahead of general investor recognition and often before a trend in price decline has fully run its course—substantive communication with management can be of critical import.

But value is only one of several investment disciplines employed by financial institutions today. Despite the differences in style,

Julie M. Connell is a securities analyst at Lord, Abbett & Co. and the portfolio manager of America's Utility Fund.

focus, or orientation of the different approaches comprising the institutional segment of the market, all investment managers share a common goal: to provide clients and shareholders the highest return possible within our stated investment style. We must correctly and consistently select portfolios of stocks that will outperform the respective market or industry bogies, and these choices must be made from a huge universe of available opportunities. It should be emphasized that our need to realize positive performance emanates not simply from the professional desire to do a good job, but probably more importantly from the fact that we have a fiduciary obligation and responsibility to provide competitive returns for clients. The simple truth is, if we fail to produce results, we are at risk of losing clients to other managers. We need to select stocks that will outperform. For the same reason, when an investment is not performing, we have a fiduciary responsibility to acknowledge the fact, and sell the stock.

In 1993, the fundamental investment landscape for electric utilities is particularly murky. Certainly over the next three to five to ten years there will be increased competition, a heightened focus on more efficiently managed operations, and mergers are likely. The point is, to use a hackneyed phrase, it really no longer is "business as usual" in the utility world. Corporate managements have to make decisions daily in the face of uncertainty: difficult decisions, decisions with far-reaching, long-lasting implications. At the same time, investors must make daily decisions as to which stocks to buy or sell, in the same uncertain environment managements face.

In tackling our respective decisions, investors and managements ironically have a symbiotic relationship. A mutual need exists, and we can provide each other with powerful assistance. Within the context of our own respective views of the future, managements can supply investors the accurate information needed about their companies and industry. Investors can then accord the stocks their appropriate value in the marketplace. To really assist each other, management and investors must be utterly candid: management in conveying what they really see transpiring and the obstacles they are facing, and the financial markets in making valuation decisions as they truly see them.

This leads to the issue of expectations, and just what it is that the financial markets desire from utility management. Responding from my own perspective of a value investor, first, let me mention what I do not expect:

⟶ For managements to have all the answers. Nobody does. Do not pretend to. Any analyst worth his or her salt can see through the smoke screen of pretension.

⟶ For a company's fortunes to move upward in straight line progression indefinitely. A rare company can excel for a long time, but something will slow or halt the ascent eventually. Trying to keep the momentum going artificially is eventually going to be viewed with derision by the markets. The stock's price will suffer more than had the slowdown been allowed to occur in its own natural time.

⟶ For managements to tell investors anything and everything under contemplation. Some prospects do not need to and should not be shared with the financial community. Wall Street can, at times, blow things out of proportion and do more harm than good with unnecessary information.

Turning now to what I do expect:

⟶ First and foremost, absolute candor. The worst approach a management can take—and I mean the worst—is to lie to the financial community, or not disclose enough information. Admittedly, the line between what is not enough, too much, or just right can be very fine and require considerable judgment. Investment history is replete with examples of stocks that lost a significant portion of their market value in a single day's time after management revealed some unorthodox practices or critical facts which had previously been kept hidden from investors.

When in doubt as to what reaction a potential action or disclosure might evoke, management might simply seek advice. Certainly an analyst with a brokerage firm who knows the company well and whose opinion is respected would offer counsel. Institutional owners can prove valuable in this regard as well. In fact, their credibility with management may be reinforced by their ownership position in the company.

➡ Have an appropriate and accurate corporate strategy, clearly articulate and communicate it, then follow it. Investors want to know how electric utility managements view their world— particularly in light of the challenges posed by growing and frequently conflicting competitive, regulatory, environmental, and financial pressures. Plans for enhancing the company's prospects are also of interest.

The heightened responsiveness to investors' requirements has recently been evident in the letters to shareholders in annual reports. A representative sampling of these texts in utility annual reports only a few years back revealed only a sprinkling of letters that contained any message of corporate strategy. Much emphasis was placed on growing competition and poor regulatory treatment, but little indication was given of how progress would be made. By contrast, the majority of current letters address the strategy issue right up front. Admittedly, no guarantee exists that rhetoric will be translated into decisive action, but clear signs show that the issue of corporate strategy is at least receiving the attention it needs.

➡ Convey that the right questions are being asked, both internally and externally. Having the right answers is not what counts. Posing the appropriate questions matters far more. The topics of serious concerns will change with the times. Answers often do not exist when questions need to be raised about the difficult issues, both industry-wide and company-specific. These issues may—and often do—eventually become ones which will require major corporate resources. With management communicating what those questions are, investors in turn can pose the appropriate queries of both the companies and themselves.

➟ Control the company's corporate destiny. Make the tough decisions. Armed with their own vision of the world, management should act decisively in whatever ways are required. Let investors see that management is not waiting for events to happen to them; rather, they are shaping what will transpire. If costs need to be cut, slash them. If ways are needed to add revenue sources, locate them. If improved communications with the all-important regulators are needed, management should swallow its pride, stop complaining and blaming, and find a new avenue for agreement.

On the expense side, the companies that understand precisely how their costs drive their business, and can analyze them in such a way as to know what really is unnecessary so they know what can safely be eliminated, are the utilities that will become the more competitive outfits and more desirable for investors.

On the revenue side, numerous approaches have been taken by different companies. Some have sold off businesses that no longer fit their corporate strategy. Others have clarified their territorial business, both enhancing revenues and expense control. Many have either started from scratch or made imaginative purchases of diversified, but utility-related enterprises.

With regard to regulatory relations, the most notable examples of responsiveness which come to mind are companies that received nasty surprises from their commissions, then worked assiduously to rebuild broken relationships. No matter how much deregulation continues to be discussed, the simple fact is that there is little likelihood of utility regulators disappearing altogether. So, management has a lot to gain from learning to work with, and not against, their commissions.

➟ Help investors, both existing and potential, understand a company. From a simply practical standpoint, with an available universe of almost 200 electric utility and telephone stocks from which to select, the companies investors can understand the quickest and easiest are the ones they are most likely to consider.

Utilities that communicate frequently and effectively via written communications, telephone, and fax, particularly if they have a good story to tell, will receive attention. Summary presentation of information helps. For example, profile key rate case filings or decision statistics in a single page, all-in-one-glance format. Companies should use the same format for quarterly earnings, emphasizing the earnings per share impact of certain items. An added benefit of presenting information in earnings per share terms is that it definitely translates into a time-saver both for the investor and the management being asked questions.

➠ Understand and know who owns—or can potentially own—a company. "Enhancing shareholder value" has become another hackneyed phrase in today's financial markets, but it pays to venture beyond the rhetoric. The results that a management team will be producing will directly benefit—or hurt—those individuals and institutions (which of course represent the interests of individuals) who own a stock.

First, most companies typically know the composition of their ownership—a certain percent is represented by individuals, another by institutions, and so on. Few companies have acquainted themselves with the profile of institutions, in particular. For example, the information needs and timing horizons of a value manager and a momentum investor are obviously different. Few utilities have initiated contact with me on a one-to-one basis, when they didn't yet have a great story to tell but would soon—obviously precisely the time to approach a value investor. An opportune contact can result in a beneficial outcome for both the investor and the company.

Second, consider what impact some decisions will have on investors. Some companies, for example, discuss within their management ranks what reaction potential actions might evoke from the financial community. They don't let Wall Street dictate decisions, but are obviously sensitive to the impact the market can have. The vast ranks of individual owners have needs which may occasionally conflict with the institutional owners' desires. There are times when one must be given priority over the other, and only management can know what is the appropriate decision.

And finally, I offer an editorial comment. Every proxy season presents an interesting opportunity to see just how much of a stake managements hold in their own companies, and how much of their respective compensations are tied to performance. Over many years of reviewing these documents, it is astonishing just how little some utility managements, and certainly many directors, are apparently willing to invest in their own efforts. But even if management are not owners, other people are, and it is to those investors that fealty in the form of good returns are owed, and yes, expected.

➠ Understand that no company is constantly in investment favor. It must be that way, if a company is to be managed with integrity, for there are times that corporate actions will be at odds with the market's desires, or occasions when the market does not fully understand the ramifications of a decision. But the worst thing a management can do is to disappear during the tough times. Rather, the smart tact is to remain accessible, open, and to continue to communicate proactively. Informing investors how a problem or issue is being handled, describing what the strategy is for getting through it, and what the ultimate outcome might be, should eventually pay off in the form of continued investor good faith. And that, in fact, is what has occurred during protracted ordeals endured by several utilities over the past decade.

There has been much negativism about the electric utility industry for so many years—about nuclear safety, acid rain, capacity planning, financial integrity, regulatory fairness, caliber of management, and on and on—that it is now almost second nature for analysts and investors to echo that pessimism. But reasons for optimism exist. Without attempting to don the mantle of a Pollyanna—for one must be fully cognizant of the present and future challenges facing utilities—it is appropriate to reconsider the many positives this industry has to offer investors.

For starters, in this era of increasing nationalism, electric utilities are one of the few totally domestically-owned industries, and one that is likely to remain so. In these times of certificates of deposit and money market rates in the 2 to 3 percent range, utility stocks still generally offer a safe, reasonably high yield with the prospect for some growth, particularly attractive to the individual investor. Further, in a period when economic uncertainty may spell murky prospects for corporate earning power, these companies enjoy relatively stable, predictable returns. Because the dividend yield is often the greater component of the stocks' total return, the compounding effect of a utility investment provides very competitive returns over time. In fact, over the last 35 years, utilities (as measured by Moody's Electric Utility Average) have matched the market (proxied by the S&P400) on a total return basis 50 percent of the time—a pretty competitive track record for a so-called lackluster industry.

America's Utility Fund was established to provide this overall stability of returns that so many individual investors want and need today, rather than the high-flying volatility that characterizes numerous other investment vehicles available. The truth is, the U.S. electric utility industry is one of the few remaining reliable avenues available for accomplishing something direly needed in this country today: more investment in America.

Admittedly, encroaching competition will no doubt alter utilities' complexions, but this should not negate the entire industry outlook across the board. Rather, managements and companies will continue the process already underway of distinguishing themselves as excellent, average, or poor according to their respective responses to the changing industry circumstances. One important component in this process of differentiation will be how well companies individually are able to meet the financial markets' expectations. Investors want this industry to remain strong and healthy in the years ahead. They want utilities to succeed. Management needs to help investors recognize that success is possible, by meeting expectations for complete candor, solid strategic thinking, incisive questioning, firm action, and demonstrable knowledge of the existing or potential ownership base. By showing investors the tremendous inherent value contained in utilities, managements can be assured that investors in turn will provide the financial support the industry will require in the years ahead.

Chapter Eighteen

VALUING ELECTRIC UTILITIES IN A COMPETITIVE ENVIRONMENT

Gregory A. Wagener

Introduction

There is general agreement among utility managers, industry analysts, regulators and other industry specialists that the electric utility industry is in the midst of a transition to a more competitive environment. Moreover, it is widely recognized that this transition will dramatically alter the structure of the industry as it exists today. The only issues open to debate are the length of the transition period and the extent of the structural transformation. The uncertainty surrounding these finer points hardly diminishes the need for investors to prepare for this new environment. Such preparation involves the consideration of new analytic tools to be used in the valuation of utility securities as well as the myriad of industry and company specific factors that will impact the inputs into these new valuation methods. There is nothing mysterious about the appropriate methods for valuing electric utilities in a competitive environment—they are the same ones used to value the securities of firms in other industries. Similarly, it is not too early for investors to anticipate the impact that the industry restructuring will have on the value of electric utility securities and to take appropriate action. Competitive forces in the industry have been building momentum for the past twenty years. These forces are already beginning to exert pressure on profits.

Because the next set of competitive initiatives are likely to occur at the state jurisdictional level, the path to competition may not be well marked nor the milestones all that visible. Investors need to

Gregory A. Wagner is a Partner and senior investment analyst with Brinson Partners Inc.

be ever alert for signs that indicate both the rapidity of the pace toward competition and the magnitude of its impact. Those investors taken by surprise by some "watershed" event are likely to suffer financial losses.

The primary purpose of this chapter is to consider how the restructuring of the industry is likely to impact both the manner in which utility equity securities are valued and the value placed on them relative to current levels. During the course of the restructuring, utility management will be presented with strategic options, both operational and financial, which have the potential to dramatically impact common stock valuation. These strategic options will also be discussed.

Electric Utility Equity Valuation: A Historical Perspective

The methods employed by investment analysts in valuing electric utility equities range from rather sophisticated multi-stage dividend discount models to more simplistic comparative models. Over the past two decades, models in this latter group have enjoyed increased popularity among investment analysts.

Some of the comparative models are aimed at determining the value of utility equity securities as a group relative to other investment alternatives such as industrial stocks or government bonds. For instance, one industry valuation approach compares the current spread between the average utility dividend yield and the long term government bond yield to the historic spread. Another approach compares the price-earnings (P/E) ratio of utility stocks to the price-earnings ratio of industrial stocks.

In conjunction with such comparative assessments of industry value, investment professionals often apply additional analysis aimed at distinguishing relative value among individual utility stocks. As an example, one approach uses either the current or a hypothetical authorized rate of return on equity (ROE) as a proxy for normal profitability. This ROE is applied to the company's current book value or some future estimate of book value in determining earnings per share. Relative value is then distinguished by dividing this earnings level into the current stock price and comparing resulting price-earnings ratios. This analysis can be taken a step further and the growth in earnings or dividends can be estimated by applying an assumed retention rate to the ROE used to develop "normal" earnings. The total expected annual return then is the product of the growth rate and the current dividend yield. The annualized total return estimates are compared as a way to distinguish relative value among utilities.

The ability of the comparative models to accurately value utility common equity is dependent upon the legitimacy of a number of assumptions inherent in the models themselves. These assumptions are borne out by the lack of explicit inputs required. For instance, the bond yield/dividend yield spread analysis assumes that there is some appropriate yield differential that accounts for dividend growth. Moreover, this approach assumes that the appropriate spread is somehow approximated by the historical spread. Similarly, the one comparative method aimed at distinguishing relative value among utility stocks implicitly assumes that book value approximates the common equity financed portion of earning assets on a per share basis. In addition, it is assumed that the authorized rate of return or some hypothetical rate of return is equivalent to the companies future cost of equity.

The application of these rather assuming and generic valuation models on the part of the investment community is related to its perceptions of the industry. As the industry has matured, the level of dividend income, as opposed to its expected growth, has become the more dominant determinant of total return. As a result, the investment community has come to view equity securities as bond surrogates. Additionally, the regulation of the industry on a rate of return basis has fostered the belief that: ROEs are relatively stable over time; ROEs are sufficiently upwardly flexible to provide limited downside risk during prolonged periods of higher interest rates; and disparities in ROEs among individual companies tend to dissipate over time. These perceptions have more or less served as the basis for valuation over the past decades and are responsible for the characterization of electric utility equities as defensive investments.

Clearly, the market's perception of utility equities as investment vehicles is highly dependent upon the continuity of the current regulatory regime, the tenets of which were articulated in the Hope and Bluefield U.S. Supreme Court decisions. Investors' reliance on the regulatory compact is somewhat surprising given some of the decisions handed down during the past several years. For example, in the mid 1980s public utility commissions began disallowing significant portions of utility investments in facilities that were not immediately "used and useful" in providing electric service or that were not efficiently constructed. Investors were substantially harmed by these decisions since for years they received risk adjusted returns that reflected the "protection and safety" provided by the regulatory system. Ironically, it was this same regulatory system that abruptly wiped out substantial portions of utility asset values that provide the basic support for investment value.

Another premise important to the comparative valuation techniques relates to the utility's degree of exposure to the core utility operations. As with the "regulatory compact" premise, the legitimacy of this premise was called into question in the 1980s when a number of utilities began investing excess cash in businesses unrelated to the electric utility business. These diversification efforts more often than not proved woefully unsuccessful and caused many of the utilities engaged in these activities to report very poor operating results—even though the core regulated business continued more or less unhampered.

In both instances the investment community, however, merely looked upon these cases as anomalies and even used the phrase "special situation" to describe those utilities adversely impacted by regulatory decisions or diversification. The application of the generic and comparative valuation methods continues despite their inability to accurately value those utility that fall into the "special situation" category.

The Consequences Of Competition

■ Impact on Industry Structure

Competition will undoubtedly have a dramatic impact on the industry, the repercussions of which will be felt by the U.S. economy and global financial markets. Its most obvious impact will be the establishment of electric power generation as a separate industry with new low cost entrants seeking to earn fair or excess returns. The power transmission and distribution segments will likely retain their exclusive franchise due to the barriers to entry created by the increasing inability to site new facilities. Competition will have the effect of forcing electric rates down towards the cost of the most efficient producer in a particular geographic region. In many cases the "most efficient producer" may only exist on paper, i.e., rates would gravitate towards the cost at which electricity could theoretically be supplied by a new competitor.

■ Impact on Utility Financial Condition and Performance

The higher a utility's cost of power generation, the more severe the financial consequences. This is true for two reasons. First, if a utility is uncompetitive in power generation it will be difficult to offset those costs by reducing overhead expense or by reducing expense in the distribution and transmission segments. Second, the higher a utility's cost—and therefore rates—the more likely it is to attract competition. Because the most efficient producer of power is unlikely to be the established utility, most utilities will be adversely impacted by the development of a fully competitive power generation market.

Those utilities with especially high costs will experience significant reductions in revenues and so too earnings and cash flow. These utilities will be forced into drastic cash conservation measures including dividend omissions. If after such actions, interest coverage is still not sufficient and short term credit is not accessible, the consequence will be bankruptcy. Absent a financial and

295

operational restructuring, the uncertainty created by the new competitive environment is likely to keep a utility from raising its common dividend in order to avoid an unreasonable payout ratio.

■ Implications for the Financial Markets

Competition will significantly increase the risk in the most capital intensive segment of the electric utility industry. Public utility bonds and common stocks currently viewed as safe havens and renowned as defensive investments will lose those attributes. As a result, capital will flow out of the industry. When this occurs it will be interesting to see what premium investors will pay for "safe yields". The holders of the securities of natural gas distribution companies may initially benefit from the capital flows out of the electric utility industry.

Utility Equity Valuation In A Competitive Environment

■ A Return to Fundamentals

If the assumptions inherent in the comparative approaches to valuation seem suspect now, they certainly will be invalid in a competitive environment. Based on the impacts resulting from competition as outlined above virtually all utilities are likely to become "special situations". Authorized ROEs will have little bearing on utilities financial performance. For higher cost utilities, the uncertainty surrounding book value will render it useless as a valuation parameter. Similarly, the uncertainty surrounding dividend payout and growth under competition is likely to make any valuation approach dependent on dividend yield of little use. Asset values and non-cash earnings associated with traditional generating assets that are solely the result of regulatory accounting are likely to be ignored by investors. Investment analysts will be forced to take a more fundamental approach to valuation—one that emphasizes the amount of free cash available over time. Also, because industry restructuring is likely to occur over several years, the proper valuation paradigm will necessarily require a longer term outlook. Assigning a P/E on next year's earnings estimate will be meaningless for a company in the midst of an industry restructuring. These factors all suggest that multi-stage, discounted cash flow models applied on a company by company basis is likely to become the most appropriate methodology for valuing electric utility equities under a competitive environment.

■ Competitive Analysis

In applying a more fundamental, company specific approach to the valuation of utility equities, investors will need to consider the myriad of factors that are likely to impact a utility's profitability and need for financial capital going forward. In an operating environment marked by competition, utility analysts will be faced with the ardent task of assessing each individual utility's vulnerability to competition and the probable revenue short fall created by it. In order to perform such an assessment, analysts will need to consider such things as:

➡ the utility's embedded and marginal cost of power generation compared with that of neighboring utilities and potential new suppliers;

➡ the utility's cost exclusive of power generation;

➡ the utility's reserve margin;

➡ the accessibility of and the cost to access the utility's distribution system;

➡ the utility's current rate design and the flexibility it has in pricing power to industrial and wholesale customers;

➡ the level of load concentration among industrial customers;

➡ whether the utility provides electricity exclusively or in combination with natural gas;

➡ and the willingness on the part of the utility's regulators to let it recoup through transmission charges the cost associated with being the provider of last resort.

Management Strategies and Valuation

In addition to analyzing the impact that competition has on a utility's continuing operations, there are a number of strategic options available to utility managements that have the potential to dramatically affect valuation. While competition overall has negative implications for the industry, it will also create some offsetting opportunities. A thorough assessment of value requires investors to consider the appropriateness of such strategies for the specific utility being analyzed. Some of these strategies are briefly discussed below:

■ Mergers and Acquisitions

There undoubtedly will be a number of instances where utilities combine operations in an effort to improve efficiency. Such combinations can reduce costs by improving plant utilization and reducing corporate overhead. Mergers can also alter the transmission network to improve access to lower cost power or make it more difficult for competitors to provide lower cost power. Thus, utility combinations have the potential to mitigate the adverse consequences of competition.

There are a number of reasons, however, why investors should not expect to realize extraordinary profit through utility mergers and acquisitions. First, there are probably a limited number of combination that truly make economic sense. Second, of the mergers that make sense, not all will occur due to reluctance on the part of management and regulators. Third, and perhaps most importantly, the idea that an acquiring utility would offer a substantial premium above book value for the utility being acquired is counter to the rationale for the merger.

■ Corporate Restructuring

Utilities faced with uncompetitive generating assets may seek to sever those assets from the transmission and distribution segment through a corporate restructuring. Such a restructuring could involve spinning off the generating assets to shareholders. There are a number of potential benefits associated with such a transaction. First, it may be appropriate for the generating segment to be more highly leveraged than the transmission and distribution segments. A restructuring would allow for such differences in capitalization. Moreover, if for competitive purposes it was necessary for certain assets in the generating segment to be written down, such a write-down could be accomplished without damaging the financial condition of the entire entity. Second, placing the power generation segment in a separate entity would allow the transmission and distribution segments to engage in arms length transactions for power supplies that are in the best interest of customers and thus may be important to the ability of these segments to prosper. Third, it may be possible to restructure the firm in such a way that one of the pieces qualifies as a return of capital to shareholders and thus, the taxes on shareholders' realized gains, in the events there is one, could be minimized. Fourth, in order to maximize shareholder value, it may be necessary for a utility to cater to the differences in investors' risk tolerance by separating the competitive portion of its operations from the portion that remains a regulated monopoly. Risk-averse investors may not care to hold the securities of a utility that faces intense competition in one aspect of its business. Similarly, more risk-tolerant investors may not be attracted to the relatively low total return potential offered by an entity engaged strictly in the transmission and distribution of electricity.

■ Opportunities For Greater Regulatory Flexibility

The restructuring of the industry will provide an excellent opportunity for utilities to lobby for ratemaking reforms and for the freedom to pursue certain operational strategies. The financial distress inflicted upon the industry during the process of its restructuring is likely to facilitate a more constructive attitude on the part of regulators. In particular, it is widely understood that traditional cost-plus, rate of return regulatory model provides little incentive for efficiency. Efficiency improvements motivated through the award of excess profits can be mutually beneficial to utility shareholders and ratepayers. Perhaps more realistically, investors should consider the fact that utilities will be better positioned to argue for incentives and, in the event they are granted, financial performance is likely to be better than it otherwise would have been.

■ Opportunities in Telecommunications

The exclusivity of the distribution franchise is likely to survive the industry's transition to competition, despite the fact that retail wheeling has the potential to relegate it to a "common carriage" function. In an era marked by accelerating advances in telecommunications technologies, investors should not underestimate the value of providing connectivity among every household, commercial establishment, office building and industrial site in a given geographic area.

Many electric utilities have deployed fiber optic based telecommunications networks for their own internal communication needs. These fiber optic communications systems have so much capacity that it is not uncommon for electric utilities to serve as links in local, regional and nationwide telecommunication networks. Some utilities are beginning to expand the use of their telecommunications network by deploying new technology and additional infrastructure that allows the utility to interactively communicate with the customer. The impetus for developing such capability is demand side management. Two-way communication between the utility and its customers provides the utility with the ability to cycle down customer equipment and appliances during peak load time but also provide the customer with override capability. The process is iterative until the utility has achieved its load shedding objectives by reaching enough customers who choose not to override. It also enables utilities to manage load through less drastic actions, namely through the communication on a real time basis of short duration tariffs designed to encourage load shifting.

This communications based demand side management system is still in the trial stages but clearly holds great promise. Early studies indicate that the savings stemming from avoided cost greatly outweigh the cost of implementing such a system. Importantly, the system deployed by the electric utility would be capable of providing bandwidth capacity into each customer comparable to that provided by cable television companies and superior to that currently provided by the local phone companies. With the franchise protection once afforded telephone and cable monopolies now crumbling, electric utilities could potentially become the third provider of video, data and voice communications. This opportunity has the potential to significantly enhance both the level of profitability and earnings growth for the electric transmission and distribution industry.

Conclusion

The assumptions inherent in many of the models currently used to value electric utility common stock will be invalid in a competitive environment. As a result, those methods will be of little use in assessing the value of electric utility equities. The competitive challenges faced by electric utilities and the industry restructuring that follows from competition requires that investment analysts take a more fundamental approach to estimating value. Such an approach emphasizes the free cash flow available to shareholders over the long term. Because each utility will be impacted differently by competition, valuation analysis must proceed on a company by company basis. In employing a long-term, discounted cash flow approach to valuation, the investment analyst will need to predict profitability and the cash needs of the utility in a more stable operating environment. Importantly, due to the length of the transition created by competition, it is necessary for investment analysts to extend their analyses several years into the future.

In developing estimates of future profitability and cash needs for utilities, investment analysts should also be alert to the impact that certain strategic initiatives or regulatory developments can have on these variables.

Chapter Nineteen

ELECTRIC UTILITIES IN THE 21ST CENTURY

Gregory B. Enholm and J. Robert Malko

Forecasting the future involves looking at the past, assessing the present and making an educated guess about what could happen next. It is our belief that the dramatic change which has been predicted for years has begun to truly appear in the U.S. electric utility industry. The preceding chapers of this book have provided many assessments of what has happened and what could happen. In this chapter, we attempt to present the key issues affecting this industry in the 1990s. As we consider these issues, we also try to develop a projection of how these issues will change the industry. Finally, we present our best educated guess as to the industry's structure in the 21st Century.

Business Risk Is Increasing

We see increasing business risk for U.S. electric utilities as a primary consideration. We define business risk as the variability in earnings before taxes when no debt is outstanding. Financial risk measures the effect of making interest payments. Standard & Poor's explicitly stated that, "more stringent financial risk standards are needed to counter mounting business risk . . . " when it tightened its criteria for rating electric utility bonds in October 1993. All the factors causing change really converge on business risk, either increasing or sometimes reducing it. How the various participants respond to this increased business risk will affect the industry's new structure. Utility management is reorganizing the work force and requesting more competitive tariffs. NUGs are pressing for more market share. Large electricity users want their rates based solely on the utility's costs to serve them. They are

Gregory B. Enholm is President of Electric Utility Research Inc and J. Robert Malko is Professor of Finance at Utah State University.

They are quite willing to consider offers from sources other than their local utility. Residential ratepayers seem to be uninterested in change, even resisting it. Environmentalists worry that control over utility actions that affect the environment may be diminished. Regulators are aware that they are still in control of the process but wonder about just how to proceed and whether that control will be lost as competitive pressures rise.

Utilities As Businesses

Before delving into a forecast of what how the U.S. electric utility industry will look like in the future, the current business should be examined. Utilities now generate and distribute most electricity for residential use, for use as an input for creating goods and services by businesses, and to be sold in a wholesale transaction for ultimate delivery either to a residence or a business. Despite the emphasis on rate base, a utility's earnings in reality are the difference between its revenues and its costs. A utility cannot readily adjust the price it charges except for wholesale sales. Regulators set most prices for electricity thus these prices are called rates. Although many utilities insist on referring to their ratepayers as "customers," only a few are truly free to choose where they buy their electricity. In general, the regulatory compact can be defined as a legally-sanctioned monopoly with prices set, in theory, to allow an opportunity for the utility to provide reliable service and to earn a fair return on its investment.

What factors are causing change in the U.S. electric utility industry?[1] We believe that the many factors can be grouped under two broad categories: increasing competitive pressures and a need to assure an adequate financial condition. The competitive pressures arise primarily from the ability of nonutility generators (NUGs) sell power to utilities, thus creating an alternative to the utility monopoly, at least for wholesale purposes. Many regulated electric utilities have entered the NUG business by forming subsidiaries.

---

[1] See Chapter 2 for a review of these factors.

Thus much of this competitive pressure is caused by utilities themselves. NUGs developed as a result of the turmoil in the electric utility industry caused by the sharp oil price increases of the 1970s, a persistent imbalance of excess generation capacity versus demand for electricity, and, most importantly, the exhaustion of decreasing costs from ever larger power stations. In authorizing qualifying facilities and small power producers, the Public Utility Regulatory Policies Act of 1978 (PURPA) merely ratified—and gave official encouragement to—a trend already underway.

Initially, concerns about utilities' financial conditions arose from the stress created by building power plants which were not needed. Regulators' actions to protect ratepayers from the risks associated with these plants included cost disallowances, rate increases phased-in over time, and other innovative actions.

Now, in the 1990s, two major concerns regarding electric utility financial conditions exist. With interest rates declining sharply from their 1980s levels and with most utility construction programs nearly complete, regulators are making dramatic reductions in allowed returns on utility common equity. Such actions threaten not only the ability to pay common dividends but also raise bondholder concerns regarding interest coverage ratios and other financial measures. The other major financial concern is the likelihood of major write offs and operating losses as competitive pressures evolve into workable competition and utilities lose customers either to other utilities, NUGs or self-generation.

Standard & Poor's (S&P) recognized these—and other looming problems—in October 1993 when it raised the benchmarks it uses in assigning bond ratings.[2] In addition to making it more difficult to achieve a rating, the ratings outlooks for 48 electric utilities were revised from stable to negative. S&P also established three categories to assess the business positions of utilities. Only 24 utilities have above average business positions; 78 are rated average; and 22

---

[2] Standard & Poor's Creditweek for October 27, 1993 has the announcement of the revision and lists the companies affected.

fall below average. In so doing, S&P is warning bond investors that significant problems are likely to be encountered by this industry.

Adjusting to Change

Actions by industry participants to adjust to these factors seem certain to change the industry structure in several significant ways. The utility's monopoly on owning generation has clearly ended. Actually, generation seems to be where most, if not all, of the increase in business risk is occurring. Decreasing costs of electricity production previously made possible by increasing returns to scale are not achievable now. Large power stations (1000 MW or higher) are just not cost competitive with the now typical 100 MW to 300 MW station. With the end of the utility's generation monopoly, access to the transmission system and priority in dispatching have become major contentious issues. NUGs want to be able to supply any entity that will buy their power. Utilities which need— or prefer—to buy power, including municipal, cooperative and government utilities, want to be able to buy from the lowest priced source. New players, electricity brokers and marketers, are trying to establish a role for themselves similar to that which has developed in the natural gas industry.

Utilities are increasingly aware that to keep their market share and avoid dramatic financial deterioration, they must reduce their costs. Utilities are reducing their work forces and adopting more flexible management structures to prepare for competition. In November 1993, LG&E Energy Corp., the holding company for Louisville Gas and Electric Company, announced that it was combining its NUG power plants with its utility plants under the same management structure and placing one executive in charge.[3] Effective December 1993, Central and South West Corporation, a

---

[3] For additional information on LG&E Energy's action, see the November 26, 1993 issue of Upcoming Electric Utility Events, edited by Gregory B. Enholm and published by Electric Utility Research Inc, Oakland, California. More information on the activities of other electric utilities mentioned in this chapter can be found in this and other issues of the newsletter.

holding company with four operating subsidiaries, set up a unified management for those subsidiaries' power plant operations. Southern Company and Entergy Corporation have been consolidating operations of their nuclear plants under one management. Some utilities are either merging with others or considering mergers to be better able to survive in the future. Indeed, that was one reason given for the merger between Cincinnati Gas and Electric Company and PSI Resources, Inc. into a new registered holding company to be called CINergy, Inc.

We believe that these innovative utilities are establishing holding companies for a very clear reason. A parent holding company provides more financing flexibility, allows for rapid growth especially for nonutility operations, and lowers regulatory oversight when compared with a stand-alone utility structure. The holding company may become the dominant corporate structure as managements seek to respond[4] to increasing competitive pressures.

Regulation is Accommodating Change

Regulators have been accommodating—and some times encouraging—change in the industry. Settlements—where the participants in a proceeding agree among themselves to an outcome—became a method used in the 1980s to avoid contentious traditional rate case proceedings. New regulatory concepts, such as cost savings sharing and splitting of excess earned equity returns between ratepayers and shareholders, were also introduced.

Incentive regulation was adopted in a move away from the idea that utilities could only earn on their physical assets, rather than on their ability to run their operations efficiently. Incentive regulation established rewards and penalties based on how a utility meet criteria such as price, user satisfaction, plant operations and safety.

---

[4] For an extended discussion of issues regarding deregulation, see Utilities Policy, Volume 3 Number 4, October 1993 published by Butterworth-Heinemann Ltd, Oxford UK. For the holding company matters, see pages 283-284 by J. Robert Malko.

Incentives set on an absolute basis are being supplanted with rewards based on meeting or exceeding benchmarks determined on a relative basis. Often individual performance is compared to an index or a how a group of other utilities performed.

California regulators have approved an experiment for San Diego Gas & Electric Company that will provide rewards or penalties based on natural gas procurement and electric generation dispatch. A comprehensive base rate incentive program intended to replace traditional rate base regulation is likely to be approved for this utility in 1994.

Regulators have also been active in reshaping the rules governing utility behavior. Consumer and environmental activists encouraged the use of regulatory controls that have culminated in integrated resource planning (IRP). IRP is an attempt to impose an overall rationality to utility actions on providing electricity.[5]

Demand side management and conservation were a response to the recognition that not producing electricity at times was far cheaper and had less negative environmental impacts than producing more electricity. Previously, utilities did not care what happened once the electricity reached its destination—just as long the bill was paid.

Environmental concerns led to the encouragement of generating sources other than oil, coal and uranium. Major subsidies, either explicit or implicit, were given to solar, wind, geothermal and other renewable power sources. The development of NUGs was encouraged through generous contract terms which often passed the point of being economic in either the short or long term. All these changes led to the passage of the Energy Policy Act of 1992 which, as with PURPA before it, primarily provided a legal framework for an existing economic reality. Regulatory commissions are now increasingly focusing their efforts on the transition from regulation to competition.

---

[5] For a discussion of the future of IRP, see Chapter 9.

In reality, regulators and legislators have been responding rather than initiating. The initiators of change have been the active industry players, especially farsighted utility managements, consumers, environmental groups and other intervenors, the large electricity users and NUGs.

An increasing number of utilities have been encouraging their employees to drop the cost-of-service mentality and replace it with a focus on the user. Pacific Gas and Electric Company has adopted an incentive compensation plan under which a worker's pay depends upon achieving a a target earnings per share. Utility workers are learning about their users' needs and are beginning to assess the best way to meet those needs. Any utility that does not do so is likely to face opposition from large users and consumer advocates at the regulatory commission.

Large users of power are willing to seek alternative sources for electricity.[6] NUGs and other utilities are willing to court dissatisfied users. Large users are demanding that their electricity be priced at the utility's costs, without being burdened with subsidizing other groups, especially residential users. It is interesting that, with the end of large construction programs which had been pushing rates up, residential users seem far more satisfied with their electric utility service than they have been in the past. These users do not seem to be demanding change or more choice in electricity.

Environmentalists appear to have seized the initiative to impose more controls on utility activities that affect the environment. The successful passage of the Clean Air Act Amendments of 1990 is causing utilities to expend funds to reduce emissions of sulfur dioxide, nitrogen oxides and other pollutants. These expenses are being used to justify rate increases. While the goal of a better environment is laudable, the utility that is spending to reduce that pollution is becoming less competitive in pricing its electricity. Investment in the environment may be a good idea from the standpoint of society, but may not be appreciated by the utility's rate-

---

[6] The perspectives of large users are presented in Chapters 13 and 14.

payers who pay higher bills and the utility's investors who face higher risk. Given this history and the new Clinton Administration's attitudes on the environment, utilities need to reconsider their strategies in this area.[7]

Yes, Utilities Are Businesses, Not Government Agencies

Many participants in the utility community do not view investor-owned utilities as businesses, but they are. That raises some important considerations. A product is created by the utility. Users receive that product. They send cash to the utility. The utility uses that cash to pay its suppliers for their products. The utility pays its bondholders cash as interest payments and eventually principal repayment. Preferred stockholders are paid their dividends in cash. Common shareholders receive cash dividends, although many reinvest those dividends into more shares. Common shareholders will see the price of their stock rise if management can increase earnings over time.

Unfortunately, many participants view electric utilities as a kind of quasi-governmental agency. They are not government agencies. No utility can raise funds by levying a tax. As a monopoly, however, a utility can operate like a government agency, providing discounted service to low income families or placing wires underground in new residential developments, with the costs collected from all ratepayers.[8]

How does a utility differ from other unregulated businesses? Basically, regulation is a substitute for competition. A utility's monopoly power is mitigated by the regulators. To be financially sound, however, the utility must eventually recover its costs. Therein lies the problem. As long as the monopoly is intact, the utility can recover its costs from its captive ratepayers. When the

---

[7] An assessment utility activities from the environmentalist's perspective is contained in Chapter 16.

[8] Utilities are viewed from a broader, societal perspective in Chapter 3.

ratepayers begin to become customers who can choose not to buy from the regulated utility, recovery of costs is threatened.[9] If a utility's rates are sufficiently low relative to the customers' alternatives, however, the utility should be able to continue to recover its costs and remain financially sound.

However, even a highly efficient utility may find that its rates are too high to be competitive. This can happen when regulators have chosen to have one class of ratepayers subsidized by another, distorting the link between rates and costs for the ratepayers providing the subsidy. Uneconomic contractual arrangements may have been imposed for the purchase of NUG power. Uneconomic demand side management expenditures may have been made. Recovery of costs from previously abandoned assets could be distorting current rates. Thus, many utilities are at risk of losing sales to customers who have lower priced alternatives that are not burdened with the same kind of uneconomic items boosting their costs. This is one area where the NUG could be considered to have an unfair advantage over a utility in competing for a large load. The NUG will not have subsidies for low income customers, demand side management costs, and other similar burdens. Of course, the NUG may counter argue that the utility can cross-subsidize its large power sales if regulators will allow reallocation of expenses from the large user who has competitive options to users who do not have such options.

Making the Transition to Competition

Competition is a relatively straight forward concept. The business that can supply the product to the customer at a price the customer accepts will succeed if that price allows the business to recover all its costs. Elementary demand and supply concepts apply. If all businesses face exactly the same costs in production, the price for

---

[9] A new regulatory framework is proposed in Chapter 8 by three individuals who have been involved in regulating utilities. Their approach emphasizes letting customers choose with regulation maintained.

the product should eventually reflect the minimum achievable cost of producing the product. Of course, herein lies the reason for regulating a monopoly. A monopoly can have a much higher profit if it restricts output and keeps price above average cost. In theory, profit would be maximized by setting the marginal revenue from selling more of the product equal to the marginal cost of producing more of the product. In a competitive market, with many buyers and many sellers, the price will equal marginal revenue for each firm. Competitive firms will produce product until their marginal costs rise to equal the price received.

Can competition work for U.S. electric utilities?[10] Not without major changes in how utilities operate and how prices for electricity are set. Competition is likely to arrive in stages rather than all at once. A process of change will occur involving the utility, its customers and its regulators at the center, with other participants such as consumer advocates, environmentalists and investors being one or more steps removed.

How Does Change Occur?

How will that process of change work? It should be driven primarily by economic considerations. Is there a less expensive or less risky alternative? Who will benefit from the change and will anyone be made worse off? Will the courts block or back change? Will investors flee utilities causing the sort of financial crises faced by many financially weak utilities in the 1970s?

Change is most likely to occur when it begins with a well-thought out idea. The previous chapters in this book have presented numerous ideas—many of which could become the catalyst for change in the U.S. electric utility industry.[11] Change also must be accepted to

---

[10] Two chief executives present their views on competition and electric utilities in Chapters 4 and 5.

[11] In Chapter 12, a survey of utility managers shows their attitudes on change and provides an analysis of what these attitudes mean in terms of how the industry is evolving.

succeed. Here, some of the industry's strengths—the stability of the monopoly relationship and long-lived assets—could work to make change a far more disruptive force than necessary.

If gradual change can occur, the participants have an opportunity to adjust. If all change is resisted, particularly on an irrational basis (e.g., "We've never done it that way before"), major disruptions can occur as many changes happen at once, overwhelming the prior resistance. Perhaps the best examples of such major disruptions from blocking change can be seen in Eastern Europe and the Soviet Union as communism collapsed. Decades of opposing technological and social changes helped to undermine government authority leading to its dissolution.

Nuclear Power Remains a Challenge

Fortunately, U.S. electric utilities have been willing to change, although often with caution in the face of risk and uncertainty. Perhaps the best example of being willing to change quickly was the industry's reaction to the accident at the Three Mile Island nuclear unit 2. This unit was in its initial stages of operation in March 1979 when a series of equipment malfunctions and operator errors led to a partial fusing of the nuclear fuel in the reactor vessel, causing the unit to become inoperable. The industry's response, prodded by public opinion and governmental directives, was to organize a national organization called the Institute of Nuclear Power Operations to evaluate nuclear plant operations. Each utility operating a nuclear plant also worked to upgrade its training and other operations. As a result, no similar accident has occurred in the U.S. While many nuclear plants have experienced problems, these problems can usually be detected and corrected before becoming threats to public health and safety.

With the rise of competitive pressures, a new dimension has been added to a nuclear utility's business risk—the premature closing because of a nuclear plant is no longer cost-effective. In recent years, unit 1 at the San Onofre Nuclear Generating Station in California and the Trojan nuclear plant in Oregon were closed because less

less costly alternative sources of electricity were available. In the former case, regulators approved a settlement allowing recovery of the unamortized investment. That recovery though has artificially raised the rates of San Diego Gas and Electric Company and Southern California Edison Company, adding to customer complaints that their rates are too high.

A FERC administrative law judge proposed that the owners of the Yankee Rowe nuclear plant, also closed prematurely, be allowed to recover only 82 percent of their remaining investment. Many complaints were raised by utility and government officials that such a precedent would discourage utilities from acting in the best long-term interests of their users by closing uneconomic units. Nuclear decommissioning costs present a difficult situation in an increasingly competitive environment. Can funds to be spent decades later be collected in a competitive market?

Additionally, significant problems could arise in the U.S. Department of Energy's program to find permanent storage for spent nuclear fuel. A surcharge of one mill per kilowatthour generated at every nuclear plant has been collected to finance permanent storage by 1998, a deadline that certainly will be missed. Could additional costs be collected from users in a competitive market? When the British government decided to privatize their electric utilities, the nuclear plants remained as government-owned operations in part because of decommissioning cost concerns. It will be interesting to see the arrangements under which a new nuclear plant is ordered in the United States.

Change from Ideas or Disasters?

Change usually is initiated either by reactions to disasters or by the ideas of leaders. It should be easier to implement change based on well thought out ideas, but disaster usually speeds the process of change more quickly. Change in the electric utility industry now seems more likely to arise from ideas than disasters which have not yet occurred. Financial disasters at some utilities, however, could speed the adoption of change for all utilities. Where are ideas likely to be generated and refined? Where can disasters occur?

A review of the preceding chapters in this book reveals that ideas for change in the electric utility industry are arising from many sectors, including the utilities themselves.[12] Industrial users have their own agendas. Consumer advocates are defining what consumers' interests need protecting. Academicians and financial analysts present a mixture of theoretical and practical suggestions. Regulators, however, seem to hold the center position.

Role of Regulation in Change

Most change is likely to need either regulatory approval, or at least acquiescence. Thus, the state and federal regulatory commissions are likely to continue to be the locales for debate and refinement of how the industry will evolve. With more than 50 state commissions and a handful of federal agencies, the likelihood is that a few will lead and most will follow. What will the few leading regulators be like? They probably will be the decision-makers most pressured by the participants to "do something." Federal and state commissions are likely to be in opposition on many issues. Some will urge that joint boards of federal and state regulators be created to address issues but others will argue that these boards have not worked in other regulated industries. We expect to see changes happening first in California, Michigan, New England and New York, but see the potential for leadership from Texas, Wisconsin and others as well.

What are the factors that will force commissions to "do something"? Higher than average rates for electricity are a clear motivating factor. Recognition that prior decisions are not working out well—such as NUG contracts—will also be important. Regulators will recognize a need to adjust to new circumstances, such as the Clean Air Act Amendment standards for emissions or the economic

---

[12] Two utility managers present contrasting views of how utilities are responding to change and what could happen at these companies in Chapters 6 and 7.

turmoil created when an area's economy is losing an established industry or gaining a new one. Each of these factors, and others will likely cause the electric utility to need regulatory approvals for change. Herein lies the highest likelihood for change.

Change is likely to be a step-by-step process. What is easiest to change will be changed first. The most difficult changes are likely to take longer unless they overwhelm opposition. One other factor is whether the individuals involved in the process of change have a strong attachment to the status quo. The longer an individual has lived under the status quo, the more likely that the resistance to change could be high. As a result, turnover in regulatory and utility personnel could substantially speed the process of change.

The ability to forecast future circumstances with reasonable accuracy will be increasingly important as change—and the associated uncertainty—occurs in the industry. Strategic planning both by utility managements and by regulatory commissions can help prepare for that uncertain future. It is likely that solving pressing problems will be the focus of attention, at least initially. Three key problems facing the industry now are (1) increasing competitive pressures which will lead to some kind of competition eventually; (2) increasing pressure on regulated earnings from commission decisions that lower allowed equity returns based on lower interest rates; and (3) increasing recognition by utility management that costs must be reduced both to keep rate levels competitive and to increase earnings. Attempting to solve these problems is likely to require regulatory action and will also require that the utility change the way that it runs its business. Questions will also be raised regarding the obligation to assure reliability of service.

Will the Transition be Long?

It seems inevitable that a relatively long transition period will be needed to allow such a large industry (over 100 companies) to make the adjustments needed. The omnipresent nature of state utility regulation is likely to lengthen rather than shorten the transition period. Appeals to the courts by dissatisfied participants—

including utilities—could also extend that period. It seems likely that, while the focus of change must rest with the utility and its management, the regulators, their staffs and intervenors will be active shapers of the transition.

What will be the key features of the transition? Farsighted utility managements will try to control the transition by proposing and implementing changes that will prepare the company and its emplyees for the future. These managements will take specific actions, including cost reductions and management restructurings.

Managements will also work with their commissions to try to reduce the negative aspects of traditional rate base regulation. Limiting a utility's earnings based on the amount of equity capital invested to serve consumers is the primary drawback of this regulation. That limitation can lead to perverse incentives—such as building power plants when buying power from others would be cheaper—which are bad in the long term for both ratepayers and investors. Another major negative feature of rate base regulation is the concept that all cost savings must be passed through to ratepayers. That leads utilities to err on the side of being excessively prepared rather than be caught unprepared. What incentive is there to reduce costs if all savings are passed on with no reward for efficiency or penalty for inefficiency? Thus, a key focus for the future will be proposing new regulatory policies to better align customer and investor interests so that actions taken will benefit both.

During the transition, utilities that are not able to adjust as necessary are likely to be faced with major difficulties. The failure to make adequate reductions in costs to improve the relative competitiveness of rates will have risks. Neglecting active communication with large users will also have risks. The main risk will be losing major customers with large loads, causing a significant revenue loss. Failure to convince regulators to adjust the regulatory process could result in low earnings potential. Missing opportunities to avoid or minimize potential negatives—such as mandated purchases of NUG power, environmental compliance costs and ineffective demand side management programs—will disadvantage the utility.

All utilities will need to carefully assess whether they want to create more regulatory assets such as cost deferrals that may not be recoverable and could be written down in the future. Current regulatory assets may need to be re-evaluated to determine whether full recovery is possible. Nuclear utilities must carefully review their nuclear operations. Every reasonable effort must be made to assure that a nuclear plant will be producing power with a minimum of outage. Current costs, however, must be kept to the minimum necessary to achieve that minimum outage rate. A major management challenge, as we discussed above, arises regarding whether premature closure of a nuclear plant is likely. Full cost recovery could be impossible leading to write downs.

What Will Happened to the Unprepared?

What could happen to a utility that is not fully prepared for the transition? What will happen if a utility's customers switch to competitors, if regulators set low allowed equity returns, and if the utility cannot keep some of its cost savings for earnings? It seems certain that earnings will decline sharply, leading to the reduction or omission of the common dividend and possibly omission of preferred dividends. This earnings reduction will likely lead to bond rating downgrades to minimum investment grade for secured debt and below investment grade for unsecured debt. What will happen at the unprepared utility? First, management will need to take decisive action to improve the company's prospects. Cost reductions, proposals for new regulatory incentives and efforts to retain customers must be made. If those actions are not successful, the utility may volunteer to merge with a stronger utility or find that it remains in a weak financial condition indefinitely.

Reviewing the predicament of Public Service Company of New Mexico shows how quickly a utility's economic and financial condition can deteriorate. At the end of 1986, the company's stock was trading at $33 per share with $3.29 per share in earnings. In 1986, its average revenue per industrial kilowatthour was 7.1 cents compared with 9.3 cents for residential sales. The warning sign was that the company's reserve margin was 70 percent; the company built for demand that did not appear. By the end of 1988, the company had failed to secure an adequate rate increase for that added capacity. Its efforts to diversify into fiberboard manufacturing, real estate, coal mining and financial services had failed as well, requiring an $8 per share write down. By the end of 1988, the common dividend had been reduced by 48 percent and it was omitted in 1989. In 1990, earnings per share fell to $0.31 on a continuing basis. The stock ended 1990 at $8 per share. It is interesting that the company has been able to maintain a BBB-, minimum investment grade bond rating, despite these difficulties.

The strategy pursued by Public Service Company of New Mexico has been to reduce costs, especially through personnel reductions, and to sell off assets—especially unneeded generating capacity. The chief executive during this period has retired and his first successor came from within the company. The current chief executive was hired from Pacific Gas & Electric Company. A new regulatory framework is likely to be proposed in 1994. The company's main challenges are to lower its rates and retain service to the Albuquerque area even though its franchise has expired. Many politicians are adamant that another supplier be found.

For the 1988-92 period, the common stock of Public Service Company of New Mexico had an average annual return of negative 5 percent compared with a positive 16 percent for the average electric utility. Despite progress in selling assets, the company's earnings remain weak. For the first eleven months of 1993, the company's share price had declined by 20 percent. Investors reacted negatively to proposals by New Mexico state legislators to allow retail access to transmission lines. This company's problems could become common in the industry if managements fail to act properly in positioning for the future.

Will Regulators Retain Control?

This example regarding Public Service Company of New Mexico demonstrates a potentially major shift in how investors and others view electric utilities as business risk rises. In the past especially and even today, investors accepted utility managements who were not as farsighted and aggressive as they could be.[13] Regulatory commissions controlled the setting of rates and the opportunity to earn a return. Thus, if a utility management erred, the regulators had the potential to—and often did—compensate for the error through the rate process.

A stark contrast exists in two adjacent states on the treatment of proposed nuclear plant construction. In Wisconsin, three nuclear plants proposed for reconstruction in the late 1970s by the state's utilities were actively opposed at the state's public service commission. Major expenditures had been made by the utilities but the commission offered full recovery if the plants were abandoned. That offer was accepted and the utilities canceled the plants, keeping their high bond ratings. In Michigan, Consumers Power Company and The Detroit Edison Company went ahead with one nuclear plant each and saw their financial conditions deteriorate markedly in the mid 1980s. Both plants had dramatic cost increases but Consumers Power's Midland plant also had major construction difficulties, causing it to be canceled after $4 billion had been spent. Consumers Power nearly had to file for bankruptcy law protection. An emergency rate increase granted by the state's public service commission prevented that from occurring. Detroit Edison's Fermi nuclear plant was completed but had significant cost disallowances and still needed large rate increases phased in over several years. Similar scenarios could occur as the industry moves into the 21st Century. However, regulators will have less ability to set rates and influence return as competitive pressures evolve into true competition.

---

[13] For a discussion of what investors are seeking from electric utilities, see Chapter 17. For a forecast of how investors could change the way they value utility stock, see Chapter 18.

After the transition, what will be the new structure for U.S. electric utility industry? It is useful to consider the economics that seem likely to prevail. Generation will become a truly competitive business with prices set in a market with many sellers and many buyers. In most parts of the country now, the wholesale market for transactions among utilities with interconnected systems certainly looks and performs like a competitive market. The FERC has recognized this reality by essentially ending its oversight of this spot or "economy power" market.

What About Bypass?

The active efforts of NUGs to provide power to any user—not just utilities—is raising fears that large users could bypass their local utility. Large users are also interested in buying electricity from another utility if the price is right. The Energy Policy Act of 1992 prohibited the FERC from ordering that bypass (called "retail wheeling" or "retail access").[14] However, the Act assures that wheeling cannot be denied for wholesale transactions between utilities. The concern is that widespread bypass would create "stranded investment" (that is, facilities that are no longer providing service to a user who has switched to another electricity supplier and the facilities cannot serve other users). The costs of that stranded investment would either be shifted to the utility's remaining ratepayers or be absorbed by the investors as a write down.

How can this bypass be avoided? First, only uneconomic bypass needs to be avoided. A user's desire to bypass a utility is almost always caused by being charged a rate higher than the cost of an alternative source. If a utility can shift the resources serving that user to serve other ratepayers, it may make sense to allow bypass to occur. A good example is provided by Arizona Public Service Company which provides about 100 MW to mining companies. The margin earned on these sales is low and the contracts can be

---

[14] Chapter 10 has a review of what preceded the Energy Policy Act of 1992 to cause its passage and what changes it mandates. Chapter 11 has an assessment of the Act's significance.

canceled with proper notice. This utility is still experiencing significant demand growth in its residential class. If the mine load were lost because of price or other reasons, management is considering reducing its capital expenditures for new plant or scaling back purchased power to effectively meet demand growth in part by redeploying the generating capacity from the mines. Thus, the loss of the mine load could increase earnings for Arizona Public Service because residential sales have a higher margin.

To avoid uneconomic bypass, the utility usually must have a special rate for each large user with realistic alternatives that are lower than the assigned tariff rate. A long-term contract would also make sense to justify the loss of revenue from the lower rate. Under most circumstances, there will be a net loss of revenue for the utility. The effect will be either to lower earnings or push up the rates of other ratepayers. Here, the commissions have usually required that shareholders absorb part of the revenue loss (usually around 25 percent), in part to provide an incentive for the utility to bargain aggressively.

Will Electricity Pricing Change?

Does a generic solution to bypass exist without having retail access? If pricing is the problem, a solution to bypass could push the industry into a new organizational structure. Economists posit that prices should reflect cost of production to assure that resources are being allocated to their best use. Most regulatory commissions set rates on the principles that rates should be based on costs (not set equal to cost necessarily) and the party causing the cost to be incurred should pay that cost. Most electric rates in the U.S. today reflect cost of production only in the sense that the revenue likely to be collected by the utility over a year will be about equal to operating and capital costs over that year.

However, the cost of producing a kilowatt and a kilowatthour of electricity vary significantly depending on the time of use. Most utilities operate, or "dispatch," their generating units under the concept that the least costly units are operated first with more costly units added as demand rises. Thus, at night, most utilities are using base load coal and nuclear plants which cost about one to three cents per kilowatthour to operate. During the day, and especially during periods of extreme hot or cold weather, the utility will also run its most expensive plants, often at costs of eight cents or more per kilowatthour. If the utility charges the same rate every hour, sales are far more profitable at night and losses could actually be experienced at peak times during the day. Time-of-use rates are intended to pass that cost information on to ratepayers.[15] Most time-of-use rates have only a few different periods (day, evening, night and weekends) which only approximately reflect costs being incurred.

The only readily apparent way to have rates reflect costs on a continuous basis would be to have rates change throughout the 24-hour day. That is how electricity generated is priced in England and Wales as a result of the privatization of the British electric utilities. Two investor-owned companies—National Power and PowerGen and the government-owned nuclear utility—provide power to 12 investor-owned regional distribution companies (which also can produce their own power). Power is priced in an exchange where producers provide half-hour quotes on their willingness to supply and buyers place orders on what they are willing to purchase. This exchange works in a manner similar to the spot or "economy power" sales in the U.S. discussed above.

While the United Kingdom has only one electricity generation market, it is likely that the U.S. would have many regional markets. Actually, many U.S. electric utilities have made the first step toward such markets by using competitive bidding in securing new generating resources. It would be a relatively simple step to have an electric utility conduct its own auction provided that it could not exercise monopsony (single buyer) power to disadvantage the suppliers.

---

[15] A consumer advocate argues in Chapter 15 that small users seem relatively satisfied now and would resist change especially if it does not present them with meaningful choices.

Why would continuous pricing of electricity be helpful? If a true market could be developed, it would lessen the need for regulatory control of rate setting for generating assets. Direct regulation would be replaced by competition, which is used in most other sectors of the economy to set prices. It would also place a premium on having a good management with an ability to compete in that market.

Should T&D be Spun Off?

What would happen with transmission and distribution in this newly structured industry? While business risk seems to be increasing significantly for the generation sector, business risk for transmission and distribution does not seem to have changed materially. These operations still seem to exhibit decreasing costs and therefore would have monopolistic characteristics that require continued regulation. Thus, an intermediate structure for the industry could be a small, but significant, modification of the current structure.

Instead of signing long-term contracts for NUG power, a utility would conduct competitive bidding auctions to have NUGs provide electricity (perhaps both a kilowatt capacity and kilowatthour components) for a limited period—perhaps for several months initially with the eventual goal of hourly auctions. That change would significantly reduce the risk to the utility and its ratepayers of having unneeded NUG power. That risk would be transferred to the NUG and its investors. Most NUG projects rely on a long-term contract with a utility to obtain reasonable cost financing. The banks and investors would likely adamantly oppose switching from a long-term contract to a bidding process. Thus, a transition period would be needed to have new contracts be continuously bid, a process that could take decades unless a combination of incentives and coercion is used (as happened with take-or-pay natural gas contracts).

In the 1980s, gas utilities—with the assistance of regulators and the courts—terminated their contractual obligations to buy extraordinarily high-priced natural gas from producers. All parties got less than full recovery, with ratepayers and shareholders absorbing the payments to producers. While most utilities were able to reach satisfactory contract resolutions, one major gas utility, The Columbia Gas System, had to file for bankruptcy protection because it could not satisfactorily end its obligations under its take-or-pay contracts.

The risks of being exposed to price fluctuations in an electricity market can be significantly reduced. Commodity exchanges have expressed strong interest in making markets for electricity futures and options as exist now for natural gas and other more traditional commodities. Utilities and NUGs could hedge their risk by using futures and options. They could also work with the emerging corps of brokers and marketers of electricity. In addition to combining its NUG and utility power plants under one management, LG&E Energy Corp. also wants to be active in electricity brokering and marketing. An electricity user who wanted fixed rates rather than varying prices could be accommodated by having the utility hedge the user's risk for a fee. Risk averse users may discover that the savings from shifting usage to low priced periods are worth the effort and actually prefer varying prices. Such an attitude would delight the economist seeking optimal resource allocation, especially since theory assumes that behavior.

If a utility's additional need for electricity can be priced competitively in a market, there would be pressure to have the utility's existing generation compete as well. A new industry structure with NUG power being competitively priced but utility power being regulated to reflect cost, would be under stress. If the utility's power cost were below the market price, the utility's investors would ask why the higher market price should not be received for the utility's electricity. If the utility's power cost were above the market price, ratepayers would ask regulators to only allow the market price to be paid. That problem has arisen with utilities that buy coal from affiliated companies. The usual result is that the utility is limited to recovery of the lower of its cost or the market price—a formula which clearly suppresses the utility's earnings ability on any transactions.

At some point, one or more utility managements are likely to recognize that they would have more flexibility to maximize earnings if the utility's generating assets could compete directly in a market with NUG power. These executives would also recognize that prudence reviews by regulators are inherently unfair to investors because poor performance results in having costs disallowed from recovery but outstanding performance receives no more than the standard utility return. It is likely that these executives will have a significant part of their compensation affected by how their stock price performs on a relative basis—a rare, but increasing, occurrence for today's electric utility executive. Such a management could propose that the utility's transmission and distribution (T&D) operations be spun off as a regulated entity.

That T&D entity would continue to have competitive bidding for NUG power and would phase in competitive bidding for the now-separated previously utility-owned generation. Because regulators would want to assure that no windfall profits will occur, that phase in would likely involve contractual commitments to have the lowest cost generation be dedicated to the new T&D-only utility at cost for conceivably the life of the units. However, the higher cost units could be released relatively soon to compete with NUG power.

Regulators would continue to set rates for the T&D-only utility but would likely move to setting a mark-up based on the T&D costs over the competitive electricity price. That shift occurred when gas users were allowed to buy natural gas directly from a producer. The local utility was allowed by regulators to charge a fee to transport the gas to the user, which allowed recovery of costs. Thus, the gas utility became indifferent to transporting gas or supplying its own gas to users. The mark-up or margin was to be the same for both.

Another source of pressure prompting utilities spin off their T&D operations will be the complaints of energy services companies (ESCos). These ESCos usually offer to significantly reduce an electricity user's consumption with the future cost savings being split between the user and the ESCo. Frequently, the ESCo will make any necessary investments to achieve the conservation.

Could the U.K. Model Work in the U.S.?

It is possible that, once enough utilities have spun off their T&D operations into separate companies, that this new industry structure could last. It would be patterned on the United Kingdom model, with unregulated electricity generators competing to supply regulated T&D companies.

A generating company would be a cross between a commodity producing firm and an industrial company. The price of electricity would fluctuate based on demand and innovations in electricity production. Earnings would be highly volatile and the generators' common stock prices would show far more variation than the stocks of the T&D companies. The T&D companies would have many characteristics that used to apply to all utilities: a monopoly on supply (unless, of course, retail wheeling is allowed as it is in the United Kingdom), a regulated mark-up based on cost recovery including capital costs and growth depending on its service territory economics. This structure would not require retail wheeling as allowed in the United Kingdom. The T&D could still engage in planning and even some social ratemaking under the supervision of state regulators.

It is also likely that widespread mergers and recombination could occur among generating companies and T&D companies. It is possible that the prediction of fifty companies may become reality. Comparing the number of electric utilities west of the Mississippi River with those on the east, one could conclude that fewer utilities could serve America's needs. Mergers among competing companies would require anti-trust approvals as well as some kind of state acceptance. It seems possible that 20 to 30 generating companies would end up serving 40 to 60 T&D companies through competitive bidding by late in the 21st Century—a major change from today's integrated, rate-regulated industry structure.

At some point in the 21st Century, that vision of the future of the U.S. electric utility industry may occur. It is only one possibility based on the factors that are driving change now in the industry. Forecasting the future is fraught with uncertainty and most predictions turn out to be incorrect. We however must work with the knowledge we have and project on the basis of what seems reasonably possible. Industry participants resonding to changing busines risks—and new business opportunities—will shape the utlimate outcome.

All Good ... And Other ... Things End

In our opening chapter, we referenced the tale of the six blind villagers describing an elephant. We see a similarity with experts forecasting the future of the U.S electric utility industry. Those who do not seek to assess the prospects for change will be unprepared for coping with change. Thus, failing to consider, even in a clearly imprecise and imperfect manner, what the future will be like is also like being blind—that is, not being able to see. In that spirit, we close with the observation that there are none so blind as those who will not see—while a blind person has no choice on being able to see, those individuals who do not use their sight productively have the same limitation.

Appendix

Barbara R. Barkovich is a Principal at Barkovich & Yap, Inc. Barkovich & Yap provides strategic, economic, financial and regulatory consulting on a wide array of utility matters, including operations, cost analysis, industry structure, pricing, and regulation. Dr. Barkovich regularly represents large industrial electric customers in discussions with utilities and before state regulatory bodies on matters related to cost, service options, pricing, and demand side management. She was previously Director of Policy and Planning at the California Public Utilities Commission. She holds a BA degree in Physics from the University of California, San Diego, an MS in Urban and Policy Sciences from the State University of New York at Stony Brook, and a PhD in Energy and Resources from the University of California, Berkeley.

Terrence L. Barnich is a member of the Illinois Commerce Commission. Mr. Barnich was appointed Chairman of the Commission on October 10, 1989 and served as Chairman until February 14, 1992, since which time he serves as a Commissioner. Previously, Mr. Barnich served as General Counsel to Governor James R. Thompson, from 1984 until his appointment to the Commission. Prior to that he practiced law in Chicago. He holds a BA in History from Georgetown University, Washington, D.C. and a law degree from Fordham University, New York.

William H. Booth is a partner in the San Francisco law firm of Jackson, Tufts, Cole and Black. He represents large industrial customers of electric utilities in proceedings before the California Public Utilities Commission (CPUC). His practice also involves work for shippers of natural gas, both end users and producers, and work for a variety of telecommunications clients at the CPUC. Mr. Booth was employed by the CPUC in the mid 1970s as an attorney specializing in federal natural gas matters. He holds a BA in Political Science and an LLB from the University of California, Berkeley.

329

Stephen G. Brick co-founded MSB Energy Associates, Inc. in 1988. The firm specializes in utility planning and regulatory analysis, serving a wide range of clients. Mr. Brick leads the firm's environmental practice, and has recently focused on Clean Air Act implementation, market based approaches to emissions clean-up, and the interaction between energy efficiency programs and pollution prevention. Prior to forming MSB, he was employed in the planning division of the Wisconsin Public Service Commission and served as a staff aide to the Wisconsin Senate Committee on Energy and Natural Resources. Mr. Brick holds both BA and MS degrees from the University of Wisconsin.

Maurice Brubaker is Chief Operating Officer of Brazen-Brubaker & Associates, Inc., regulatory and economic consultants. He has been involved in the utility industry for over 20 years and represented numerous clients in regulatory proceedings and in contract negotiations. He holds a BS degree in Electrical Engineering from the University of Missouri at Rolla, an MBA (with a major in finance) and an MS in Engineering from Washington University in St. Louis, Missouri.

Julie M. Cannell is a securities analyst with Lord, Abbett & Co., a New York-based investment management company with over $16 billion of assets under management. She specializes in the electric utilities and telecommunications industries, and is the portfolio manager of America's Utility Fund. Prior to joining Lord, Abbett in 1978, she was a member of the faculties of the University of Colorado and Cameron College. Mrs. Cannell received a BA degree in English from Mary Baldwin College, an MLn from Emory University, and an MBA from Columbia University. A Chartered Financial Analyst, she is a member of the New York Society of Security Analysts and the Wall Street Utility Group.

John H. Chamberlin is Executive Vice President of Barakat and Chamberlin, Inc. Barakat and Chamberlin provides economic and management consulting services to the utility industry, and is one of the leading firms in the nation in the development of effective demand side management (DSM) strategies. Prior to co-founding the firm in 1985, Dr. Chamberlin was Senior Project Manager for DSM activities at the Electric Power Research Institute, and previously held positions at ICF Incorporated, and the Hanford Engineering Development Laboratory. He has a BA in Economics from California State University at Chico, and an MA and PhD from Washington State University.

Craig M. Clausen serves as Senior Policy Advisor to Commissioner Barnich of the Illinois Commerce Commission. Mr. Clausen joined the Commission in 1987 and has served as both the Executive Assistant and Senior Policy Advisor to the Chairman. Previously, Mr. Clausen served on the Policy Analysis Staff of the U.S. Department of Agriculture in Washington, D.C., analyzing cost allocation methodologies for specific programs. Mr. Clausen received his bachelors degree from Michigan State University in 1981, masters degree from the State University of New York at Syracuse in 1983 and is a PhD candidate in Resource Economics at Michigan State University.

Erroll B. Davis, Jr. is President and CEO of WPL Holdings, Inc. and Wisconsin Power and Light Company, and Chairman of the Board of Heartland Development Corporation. Headquartered in Madison, Wisconsin, WPL Holdings is the parent holding company of Wisconsin Power and Light (the company's regulated utility subsidiary) and Heartland Development Corporation, composed of 17 nonutility businesses that focus on energy, environmental services and affordable housing opportunities. Prior to joining WPL, Mr. Davis was on the corporate financial staffs of Ford Motor Company and Xerox Corporation. He currently serves on the Board of Directors of the American Gas Association and the Electric Power Research Institute as well as Sentry Insurance Company and Amoco Corporation. Mr. Davis is a member of the University of Wisconsin System Board of Regents and Wisconsin Association of Manufacturers and Commerce. Mr. Davis received his BS in Electrical Engineering from Carnegie Mellon University and his MBA from the University of Chicago.

Gregory B. Enholm is President of Electric Utility Research, Inc., based in Oakland, CA, a firm he founded in July 1992. Electric Utility Research offers commentary and data on U.S. electric utilities. Previously, Mr. Enholm was the senior electric utility common stock analyst for Salomon Brothers, Inc. which he joined in 1985. He was a securities analyst for Merrill Lynch & Co. from 1984-85. He has also served as a financial economist at the Public Service Commission of Wisconsin. He holds a BS degree in Business Administration and an MA degree in Economics from the University of Florida.

Thomas Fanning is the Chief Financial Officer of Mississippi Power Company. Mr. Fanning joined Mississippi Power Company in April, 1992. Between October 1991, and March 1992, he lived in Melbourne, Australia, heading up a team for Southern Electric International seeking to acquire ownership in generating units then owned by the State Electricity Commission of Victoria. Prior to that assignment, he held the positions of Director, Corporate Finance of Southern Company Services, Inc. and Treasurer of Southern Electric International in Atlanta, Georgia. Mr. Fanning holds a bachelor's degree in Industrial Management and a master's degree in Finance from the Georgia Institute of Technology.

Thomas H. Fehring is Manager of System Engineering for Wisconsin Electric Power Company, where he has been employed since 1970. He has held numerous positions at the utility, including the Director of the Financial Management Department, Manager of Pleasant Prairie Power Plant (a 1,200 MW coal-fired plant), and senior project engineer responsible for the licensing, engineering and construction of the Germantown Power Plant. In addition to his assignment in System Engineering, he is also currently serving as the acting department head of the Engineering and Construction Department. Mr. Fehring holds a BS in Mechanical Engineering and a master's degree in Engineering, both from Marquette University. He is a registered professional engineer in the state of Wisconsin.

Roger W. Gale is President of the Washington International Energy Group, a private consulting firm based in Washington, D.C., founded in 1987. The Washington International Energy Group offers analysis and interpretation of emerging trends in the electric utility industry, and environmental and trade issues. Mr. Gale has held senior level positions at the U.S. Department of Energy, the Environmental Protection Agency and the Federal Energy Regulatory Commission. Mr. Gale received his PhD in Political Science from the University of California at Berkeley.

John E. Hayes, Jr. is Chairman of the Board, President, and Chief Executive Officer of Western Resources, Inc. based in Topeka, Kansas. Western Resources serves over 1.6 million gas and electric customers. Previously, Mr. Hayes served as Chairman, President, and Chief Executive Officer of the Southwestern Bell Telephone Company and subsequently was Chairman of the Board of Triad Capital Partners, a St. Louis venture capital firm. Mr. Hayes is active in business and community service, serving as a board member of Boatmen's Bancshares, Inc.; Cellular, Inc.; Security Benefit Group; Edison Electric Institute; American Gas Association; Topeka Community Foundation; Boys Hope; the American Royal Association; Kansas Wildscape; and the National Association of Manufacturers. Mr. Hayes is also a member of the Board of Trustees of the Menninger Foundation, Midwest Research Institute, and Rockhurst College, where he serves as Vice Chairman of the Board. He is a graduate of Rockhurst College in Kansas City.

John L. Jurewitz is Manager of Energy Policy and Regulation for the Southern California Edison Company. Dr. Jurewitz joined Edison in 1978. He has testified extensively on a wide range of electric utility regulatory policy issues before the California Public Utilities Commission, the California Energy Commission, the California State Legislature, and the Federal Energy Regulatory Commission. Prior to joining the company, Dr. Jurewitz was an assistant professor of Economics at Williams College and Pomona College. Today, he continues to teach courses in Energy Policy, and Environmental and Natural Resources Economics at Pomona College and the Claremont Graduate School. He holds a PhD in Economics from the University of Wisconsin.

Mark D. Luftig is Senior Vice President of Kemper Securities, Inc., one of the largest full service investment banking and brokerage companies in the United States. He is in charge of electric utility equity research. Prior to joining Kemper Securities, Mr. Luftig was a Vice President of National Economic Research Associates, Inc., an economic and financial consulting firm specializing in micro-economics and litigation support. Previously, he was a Director of Salomon Brothers, Inc., in charge of utility equity research; General Attorney of New York Telephone Company, where he directed a group of regulatory attorneys; and a lawyer in private practice in New York City. He holds a bachelor's degree in Economics from Columbia College, a master's degree in Accounting from Columbia Graduate School of Business and a juris doctor degree from Columbia Law School.

J. Robert Malko is Professor of Finance in the College of Business at Utah State University. He serves as a Senior Consultant on a part-time basis for AUS Consultants. He also serves as a Director of the National Society of Rate of Return Analysts and as Chair of the Transportation and Public Utilities of the American Economic Association. He is a Fellow on the Council on Economic Regulation in Washington, D.C. Dr. Malko has served as Chief Economist at the Public Service Commission of Wisconsin (1975-77 and 1981-86) and has served as Chairman and Vice-Chairman of the Staff Subcommittee on Econmics and Finance of the National Association of Regulaotry Utility Commissioners. In 1978-80, he served as Program Manager of the Electric Utility Rate Design Study at the Electric Power Research Institute. Dr. Malko received a BS degree in Mathematics and Economics from Loyola College and the MS and PhD degrees in Economics from the Krannert Graduate School of Management at Purdue University.

Kenneth Nowotny is Professor of Economics and Acting Department Head of the Department of Economics and Associate Director of the Center for Public Utilities, New Mexico State University. He has been with New Mexico State since leaving the University of Texas where he received his PhD in Economics in 1977. He assisted in founding the Center for Public Utilities at New Mexico

State in 1986. With associates Dr. Nowotny has been offering training programs for commissions and utilities since 1978. He has consulted with a variety of utilities and commissions over the last fifteen years.

Philip R. O'Connor is Managing Director of Palmer Bellevue and of Demand-Side Resources, divisions of Coopers & Lybrand specializing in strategic utility consulting and the implementation of performance based demand side management. Prior to founding Palmer Bellevue in 1986, Dr. O'Connor was Chairman of the Illinois Commerce Commission. As the state's chief utility regulator, he advanced proposals for competition in natural gas, electricity and telecommunications. Dr. O'Connor also served as the Illinois Director of Insurance, political director for Governor James R. Thompson's successful third term election campaign in 1982 and was administrative assistant to U.S. Representative George Miller of California and former Illinois Governor Richard B. Ogilvie. Dr. O'Connor earned his AB from Loyola University of Chicago and his MA and PhD in Political Science from Northwestern University.

Judith B. Sack is an Advisor to Morgan Stanley and President of GLE, Incorporated. She is also a Director of Dominion Energy, Inc. Ms. Sack began her career at Girard Bank. In May 1977, she joined Morgan Stanley, specializing in the analysis of electric utilities. After a brief stint at Dean Witter, she returned to Morgan Stanley in 1984 as a Vice President and became a Principal in 1986. In addition to her analytical responsibilities, Ms. Sack worked with Morgan Stanley's Investment Banking Division and its Syndicate and Mergers and Acquisitions Departments. In March 1988, Ms. Sack left Morgan Stanley to form GLE, Incorporated, which provides financial advisory services to the electric industry. In July 1993, Ms. Sack rejoined Morgan Stanley as an Advisor to co-ordinate Morgan's global utility research. She is the firm's global electric utility strategist and is involved in Morgan's efforts in international utility privatizations. Ms. Sack served as Vice Chairman of the Advisory Council of the Electric Power Research Institute from July 1989 through June 1993, and as Chairman of EPRI's Strategic Issues Committee during that time. She is a Chartered Financial

Analyst, a member of the New York Society of Security Analysts, and past president of the Wall Street Utility Group. Ms. Sack holds a BS in Business Administration from Drexel University.

Michael E. Shames is Executive Director and Lead Counsel for Utility Consumers' Action Network (UCAN) a San Diego-based nonprofit utility watchdog group which he co-founded in 1983. UCAN is a frequent intervenor in Public Utilities Commission proceedings. He also teaches Corporate Responsibility and Business Ethics classes as an adjunct professor at the University of San Diego School of Business. Mr. Shames currently serves on numerous local and state Boards and Commissions as a consumer representative. He holds a BA in Public Administration from the University of California at Los Angeles and a JD from University of San Diego.

Gregory A. Wagener is a Partner and Senior Investment Analyst with Brinson Partners, Inc., a global investment management firm. Mr Wagener is responsible for the analysis of electric utilities and firms operating in the following industries: telecommunications services; telecommunication equipment; transportation services; natural gas transmission and distribution; and lodging and restaurants. In this capacity, he must judge the investment appeal of the common stock of assigned companies. Prior to joining Brinson Partners, Inc. in 1987, Mr. Wagener served as Chief Financial Analyst in the Public Utilities Division of the Illinois Commerce Commission. Previous to joining the Illinois Commerce Commission, Mr. Wagener held the position of Research Economist with the Illinois Department of Energy and Natural Resources. He also served as staff to Governor Thompson's Sunset Task Force on Utility Regulatory Reform. Mr. Wagener is a Chartered Financial Analyst and holds BS and MA degrees from the University of Missouri in St. Louis. He is a member of the Investment Analyst Society of Chicago and currently serves as President of the Utility and Telecommunications Securities Club of Chicago.